DECORATIVE LETTERING IN THE DIGITAL AGE

STEVEN
Heller
&
GAIL
Anderson
Thames & Hudson

NEW ORNAMENTAL TYPE
DECORATIVE LETTERING IN THE DIGITAL AGE

For Nicolas Heller – S. H.

For Cindy Cope – G. A.

ACKNOWLEDGMENTS

THE AUTHORS' ENDLESS GRATITUDE is extended to the staff at Thames & Hudson, whom we seldom saw, but always heard.

This book would not have been possible without the crackerjack research, constant support and many e-mails we received from Christine Thompson Maichin, whom we actually did see occasionally thanks to GPS technology.

And our thanks are extended to Mia Song, who, like Christine, researched her way through morning sickness – making New Ornamental Type *filled with even more surprises than* New Vintage Type.

Special thanks to Jeff Rogers for designing his way through too many Sundays of Domino's pizzas and Chinese food. And much appreciation goes to Lynn Staley, Céline Bouchez, Toan Vu-Huu, Dan Savage and everyone else who suggested contributors, answered our questions or just listened to our problems. We owe you one (book, that is).

– S. H. & G. A.

First published in 2010 in hardcover in the United States of America by Thames & Hudson Inc., 500 Fifth Avenue, New York, New York 10110

thamesandhudsonusa.com

Library of Congress Catalog Card Number 2009933802

ISBN 978-0-500-51502-0

Printed and bound in China by 1010 Printing International Ltd

DESIGN
Gail Anderson
Jeff Rogers

RESEARCH
Christine Thompson Maichin
Mia Song

12 GOTHIC
18 VICTORIAN
34 MODERN
40 HIPSTER
44 POP
50 PSYCHEDELIC
58 HIP-HOP
62 TECH
66 NON-ROMAN

BRANCHES 80
FLOWERS 86
HAIR 94
ELECTRIC 98
LIQUID 100
SMOKE 106
GREEN 110
HANDMADE 116
FELLA 126

130 OBJECT AS LETTER
140 LETTER AS OBJECT
144 CHAOTIC
148 PUZZLE
152 EMBELLISHED
160 OOH LA LA
164 STITCHED
170 ANTHROPOMORPHIC
180 MONUMENTAL
184 RIBBON
190 New Ornamental Fonts
190 Further Reading
191 Index of Designers and Illustrators

ISIS This topsy-turvy lettering for the Los Angeles band Isis was influenced by what Justin Kay calls their "doomy" and dark, epic sound. ART DIRECTOR/DESIGNER: Justin Thomas Kay CLIENT: Isis PRIMARY FONT: Custom made by Alex Trochut

ORNAMENT IS NOT A CRIME

When Austrian architect Adolf Loos mounted the barricades in 1908 with his essay "Ornament and Crime," proclaiming, "The evolution of culture marches with the elimination of ornament from useful objects," design was in an ornamental quagmire. Twelve years after the advent of Art Nouveau (*Jugendstil*, Vienna Secession) in 1896, forests of vines and tendrils – what critics have called "floriated madness" – covered everything from posters and typefaces to furniture and buildings. Loos's preference for "smooth and precious surfaces" derived from his fervent belief that functional objects swathed in ornament were guaranteed instantaneous obsolescence. For Loos, superfluous decoration was not merely a waste of a designer's time, it was downright immoral. Obsolescence was, therefore, on a par with venal sin. Yet barely twenty years later, just prior to the Great Depression, the strategy known as "forced obsolescence," or what the innovative American adman Earnest Elmo Calkins called "styling the goods," was celebrated for having brought the United States economy back to vitality from stagnation.

Loos's critique, published in Europe when Art Nouveau was at its most eccentric, made some philosophical and practical sense. The time was right to throw off the shackles of stultifying style and move forward to a more advanced stage of aesthetic evolution. Yet arguably, no matter how excessive the ornamentation, labeling it immoral may have been hyperbole. Not all decorative impulses are sinful. In fact, visual austerity could be seen as the denial of aesthetic pleasure, a puritanical notion practiced, among others, by the Shakers, who denied themselves all earthly pleasures. After all, who could argue that a Persian miniature, with its complex graphic layering, or the Book of Kells, with the interlocking patterns and serpentine filigree that fill its pages, are not among the most beautiful (and, in a sense, most functional) of graphic artifacts? How could Baroque and Rococo motifs be pilloried for crimes against the eye, or society in general, despite what they came to symbolize?

What better advocate for ornament than William Morris, the late-nineteenth-century artist, designer, printer, author, social critic, and founder of the Arts and Crafts movement? He exalted ornamentation as a high form of spiritual expression. The Kelmscott Chaucer, the pinnacle of his career as a book designer, reintroduced the Medieval or Gothic approach from its lavish ornamental borders to its decorative capitals and frames. But the Kelmscott Chaucer did more than simply revive an antique style. It was the realization of Morris's belief that a combination of modern printing techniques and traditional arts and crafts could counteract the corrosive impact of industrialization. Ornament was not merely a veil to hide ugly industrial machines and wares, it was an antidote to the perceived poisons spewing from factory chimneys – a prescient concept at that time.

Ornament is not inherently evil, nor does it pander to the base nature of man or woman. As with any graphic manner or style, its symbolic or literal meanings derive from the reality of the thing or idea that is represented. Nonetheless, passions are ignited when ornamentation is injected into high-minded matters of design.

The Bauhaus masters rejected the idea of a Bauhaus style. Yet even this progressive German design institution proffered and maintained an overriding ethos, expressed largely through its distinctive graphic persona, rooted in the New Typography. Though it rejected excessive ornamentation as the relic of an older bourgeois order, Bauhaus design was not entirely ornament-free. It replaced unnecessary flourishes with minimal functional ornament (black and red rules and bars), which was by any other name still decoration, albeit with a structural underpinning. Even to this day, followers of the Bauhaus and adherents of Modernism maintain the belief that minimalism enables the clearest communication. They deride what advertisers in the 1920s and 1930s called frou-frou decoration. Yet there has long

LOVE LOUD The style of lettering in this logo for Revolve Clothing means exactly what is says, reports Paul Sych: "Let your love be loud and resonating."
DESIGN FIRM: Faith ART DIRECTOR/ DESIGNER: Paul Sych CLIENT: Revolve Clothing PRIMARY FONT: Hand lettering

been a desire – indeed, a compulsion – among designers to introduce graphic complexity into design languages. This tendency emerged as a full-blown movement with the growth of Post-Modernism in the late 1970s, which incorporated passé decorative elements onto otherwise austere modern structures.

From that point on, ornament has made a spectacular comeback. Since the late 1990s, it has been as widespread as it was in the Victorian and Arts and Crafts eras at the turn of the twentieth century. But the rationale – the desire for aesthetic delight – is not unfamiliar; even in Modernist times the decorative instinct was minimized but never totally dissipated, and its popularity has swung like a pendulum. During the mid-to-late 1960s, for instance, eclectic designers – notably New York's Push Pin Studios, founded by Seymour Chwast and Milton Glaser – responded to the dominance of the Swiss International Style's typographic economy (or, for some, sterility). They reclaimed outmoded approaches – Victorian, Art Nouveau, and Art Moderne (also known as Deco, for "decoration") – and inspired others with their decorative playfulness. The Push Pin style fell out of favor in the early 1980s, but with the advent of the computer things changed yet again. In the late 1980s and early 1990s, graphic designers initially leaned toward gridlocked austerity, precisely the style that the computer produced so well. Yet that preference quickly "devolved" into the more cluttered, anarchic, indeed flaw-inspired typographic designs typified by David Carson and his kindred graphic "grunge-mongers." This was not ornamental as such, but it was "unclean."

Sometime during the early 2000s, well over a decade after the computer became the state-of-the-art design tool, neo-Art Nouveau – serpentine, floral ornamentation – returned with a vengeance. Perhaps the impetus was rebellion against template-driven, computer-generated design; or, more likely, the realization that difficult drafting processes were made simpler through digital applications. No less significant was the fact that the traditional boundaries of design and illustration had once again become blurred, as they had at the turn of the previous century, when the *Sachplakat* (object poster) holistically brought type and image together. The introduction in the 1990s of font-creation software enabled illustrators to become more engaged in letterform and type design. The grunge and DIY movements of the mid-1990s contributed to the growth of digital foundries that offered scores of "novelty" faces made from an array of non-traditional type materials, including such vernacular items as cans, razor blades, and toy soldiers, and such naturalistic ones as twigs, flowers, and trees. From these hothouse experiments a new era of floriated madness blossomed.

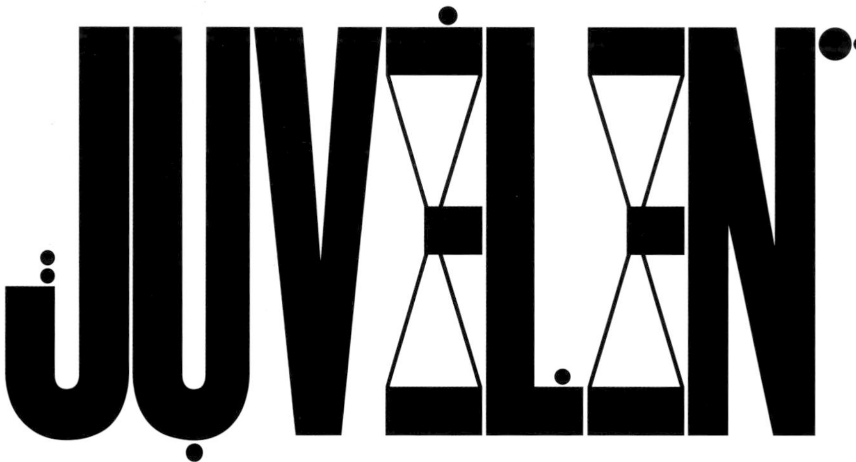

JUVELEN This custom lettering for a record sleeve is a slightly deconstructed form of a somewhat traditional condensed font. The band's music uses a lot of clichés, but still manages to come across as contemporary. The type attempts to accomplish the same.
DESIGN FIRM/ART DIRECTOR/DESIGNER: Grandpeople CLIENT: Hybris/Juvelen PRIMARY FONT: Custom made

1234 This treatment was inspired by Chinese New Year prints (*nianhua*) and grafted onto a punk-rock aesthetic.
DESIGN FIRM: Q2 Design ART DIRECTOR/ DESIGNER/ILLUSTRATOR: Qian Qian CLIENT: Self PRIMARY FONT: Custom made

In addition, a groundswell of interest in historical (or retro) ornament took hold during the early 2000s. Advertisements and package designs inspired a new wave of ornamentation, including patterns of countless formats and descriptions. These were largely born out of the Hip-Hop or street culture aesthetic rising in various media, from textiles to the Web and print. Typography became the principal vehicle for ornamentation. Illustrated letterforms – not calligraphy in the classical sense, nor illumination in the biblical context – became the most common approach to "the new lettering." Handwritten lettering in variegated forms – stitching, collaging, scrawling, scraping, carving, and more – added yet further ornament to design in the twenty-first century.

Ornamentation is now sought after for print, screen, motion, and various other tactile forms of design. Whether neo-Art Nouveau, pseudo-Art Deco, crypto-Victorian, or any combination or hybrid of these historical and contemporary, vintage and futuristic patterns, type wrapped in decorative veneers is ubiquitous. This tendency might seem to be a rejection of the coldness of computers. But new ornamental type is largely enabled by the computer; a comparatively small number of the examples shown here are generated by hand. This book is a survey of the most popular manners and methods in current use. From faux-naturalism (what we call Green), to the integration of graffiti (what we call Hip-Hop), and more, this is a raucously esoteric time for letterforms, and, we might say, for the decriminalization of ornament.

HIST

ASK INSIDE This sparkly logo for Revolve Clothing was designed for a clothing line that uses typography as its main visual element. DESIGN FIRM: Faith ART DIRECTOR/ DESIGNER: Paul Sych CLIENT: Revolve Clothing PRIMARY FONT: Custom made

DESIGNERS DERIVE ALMOST as much joy from debating the merits and demerits of appropriating history as they do actually designing. Injecting passé design conceits into contemporary work – a method also known as retro, as in "retrograde," a word inherently negative in tone and meaning – has long been part of the design process. So much owes its existence to precedents established decades or centuries before that the entire debate should be moot. Nonetheless, some critics argue that living in the present demands a design language that reflects the here and now. Retro is, they insist, essentially nostalgia, and nostalgia, like neuralgia or aphasia, is in the strictest definition a disorder. Others who are less judgmental or dogmatic refuse to believe that history should either be ignored or pickled in brine. As Tom Wolfe once said, design history is a "big closet" from which to draw inspiration. Design builds on a variety of styles and methods, either as a measured response or a violent reaction to the distant or recent past.

Ornament is one of the metrics of design history. Like the rings of a tree trunk, it can often be used to accurately date a work, or at least signify its aesthetic pedigree. The various styles of ornament developed during specific periods mirror the concerns, economies, technologies, and cultures of those times. Usually the designer's proficiency in using said ornament reveals where and when the work was created. Some styles were short-lived, while others, including Baroque, Rococo, or Art Nouveau, lasted for a generation or more. Certain designers, like today, rejected a particular ornament if they felt it represented an aesthetic or concept that had outlived its

STINGRAYS:
PART SHARK
And, we Suspect,
PART UFO

STINGRAYS This logo was designed for a poster promoting Toronto Zoo. It plays on the Victorian fascination with nature, which at times could approach hysteria. The tone was meant to be light-hearted in a way that was evocative of circus posters.
DESIGN FIRM: Lowe Roche Advertising ART DIRECTOR: Adam Thur DESIGNERS: Adam Thur, Ian Brignell LETTERER: Ian Brignell CLIENT: Toronto Zoo PRIMARY FONTS: Hand lettering

usefulness. Others clung to timeworn styles because they were comfortably familiar and their audience still comprised a viable market. For yet others, ornament was much more than a superficial veneer that could be put on and taken off at will; it symbolized an aesthetic viewpoint with relevance far beyond the mere object of design.

Most contemporary design employing historical ornamentation is not entirely slavish to the source. When pastiche (the deliberate copying of a style) is not the foremost concern, the aim is more reference than exact copy. For instance, the sub-genres of type and lettering in this section may be liberally influenced by such vintage mannerisms as Gothic, Victorian, or Modern, but in only rare instances can they be mistaken for being what they are not – that is, created when the styles were current. Historical ornamentation is the underpinning for hybrids that are mixtures of various styles, not the styles themselves. Categories such as Hipster, Pop, Psychedelic, Hip-Hop, Tech, and Non-Roman are not (with the exception of Psychedelic) academic styles, but they build on historical reference points to produce a present-day typographic lexicon. While all of the typography in this section refers to bygone eras, the overall aim, and result, is to create type and lettering that signals "now." What makes effective letterforms varies greatly, depending on context and purpose. The goal of some is to evoke a particular context, while for others it is to play with form, to exact a pleasing image using all the vintage or contemporary conceits available.

Gothic

BLACK LETTER dates back to Gutenberg's fifteenth-century invention of the printing press and moveable type. The spiky graphic forms, which came from the pen and brush strokes of medieval scribes, turned from ecclesiastical into nationalist lettering when the Nazis adopted it as "Volks" type ("the people's" type). In its benign form, it has been used for newspaper mastheads as well as in other contexts that demand an official look or an enduring style. In recent years, variations on Gothic lettering – and there are many – have been adopted by street and Hip-Hop culture, as well as being used in heavy metal and Goth aesthetics. Gothic is also the favorite of tattooists.

15.05

130 TIM KRING FOR *HEROES*
134 HENRY LOUIS GATES JR.
135 J. K. ROWLING
136 THE ALLEN BRAIN ATLAS
138 BRIAN K. VAUGHAN
139 CLIFF BLESZINSKI & TIM SWEENEY
140 ALFONSO CUARÓN
142 ARIANNA HUFFINGTON
143 GREGG GILLIS
144 WALTER DE'SILVA
146 JEN CHUNG
147 WORLDVISTA
148 MICHAEL WESCH
149 MARK SHUTTLEWORTH
150 ARNOLD SCHWARZENEGGER

WIRED

the 2007 RAVE AWARDS

To find the 22 innovators, instigators, and inventors to honor with a Rave Award this year, we started by looking for the most intriguing breakthroughs in the world today—then tracked down the individuals who made them happen. Each honoree told a unique story, but they tended to have one thing in common: Before changing the game in technology, business, or culture, they first changed themselves. There's the actor who became a politician (Arnold Schwarzenegger) and the politician who became an entrepreneur (Arianna Huffington), not to mention an entrepreneur turned philanthropist (Paul Allen) and a philanthropist turned open source warrior (Mark Shuttleworth).
The lesson seems obvious: Reinvent yourself, reinvent the world.

LETTERING BY MARIAN BANTJES

131

15.05 This splash page lettering for *Wired* magazine combines geometric, techno and Art Nouveau sensibilities. It is structured around circles, with the zero as the centerpoint and everything leading into or flowing around it. "The type is like sci-fi armadillos. Why? Absolutely no logical reason," says Marian Bantjes.
CREATIVE DIRECTOR: Scott Dadich ART DIRECTOR/DESIGNER: Maili Holiman ILLUSTRATOR: Marian Bantjes CLIENT: *Wired* magazine PUBLISHER: Condé Nast PRIMARY FONT: Hand lettering

BLIK DREZ NIKON Daniel Blik's self-promotional piece is influenced by vintage Gothic or Medieval lettering, but the color gives it a more contemporary sensibility.
DESIGN FIRM: Blikdsgn ART DIRECTOR/DESIGNER: Daniel Blik CLIENT: Self PRIMARY FONT: Custom made

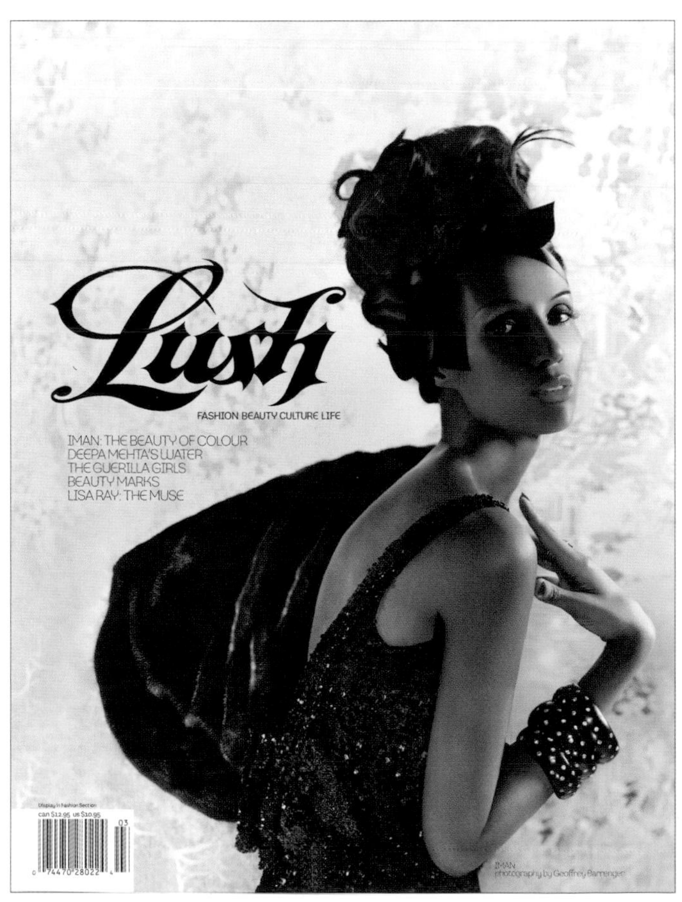

LUSH MAGAZINE The hand-drawn lettering for "Lush" was constructed by mixing various Gothic and traditional scripts. Haute couture is made to order for a specific customer with hand stitching and a detailed finish, so Paul Sych mimicked this in the construction of the type, as *Lush* contains many haute couture collections. A heart is also an integral part of this mark. Can you find it?
DESIGN FIRM: Faith ART DIRECTOR/ DESIGNER: Paul Sych PHOTOGRAPHER: Geoffrey Barrenger CLIENT: *Lush* magazine PUBLISHER: Bassett Publishing PRIMARY FONT: Hand lettering

GOTHIC

BACK IN BLACK The idea behind Kay's approach was to create an edgy, Gothic aesthetic for Express Clothing's tagline, while retaining an overall sense of style in keeping with the clothing and dark, Victorian brand image.
ART DIRECTOR/DESIGNER: Justin Thomas Kay CLIENT: Express Clothing PRIMARY FONTS: Fette Fraktur, Trade Gothic, Carousel

CALARTS Every year, CalArts has a T-shirt show and sale as a fund-raiser for the student chapter of the American Institute of Graphic Arts (AIGA). All the shirts are designed by the faculty and students; the only requirement is that they be one color and say "CalArts." For 2007, Mr. Keedy "decided to do Disney meets heavy metal," he says.
DESIGNER: Mr. Keedy CLIENT: California Institute of the Arts (CalArts) PRIMARY FONT: Custom made

LETTERING Influenced by the richness and texture of sixteenth-century flourished Swiss Gothic lettering, Ian Brignell wanted to create a mark that, he says, expressed the wonder "I felt when I first saw this type of lettering." DESIGN FIRM: Ian Brignell Lettering Design ART DIRECTOR/DESIGNER: Ian Brignell CLIENT: Self PRIMARY FONT: Hand lettering

TATTOO TEARDROP The style for this logo, for a film about gangs in Los Angeles, was influenced by graffiti and Latin gang tattoos. DESIGN FIRM: Chase Design Group ART DIRECTOR/DESIGNER: Margo Chase CLIENTS: David Schmier, Michael Wilson PUBLISHER: M.A.D. Pictures PRIMARY FONT: Kruella

GOTHIC

BEAUTIFUL WORLD This lettering for a poster about the future of the world was inspired by the Psychedelic style of the late 1960s Fillmore West rock palace posters, and "ambigrams" (lettering that reads in both directions).
DESIGN FIRM: Chase Design Group ART DIRECTOR/ DESIGNER: Margo Chase PRIMARY FONTS: Custom made

NORA KEYES The singer Nora Keyes uses fairy-tale imagery in both her performances and comics to evoke a hidden, dark, gothic narrative world. She dresses in a cute costume and sings in different voices, sweet and evil. The style for this poster was inspired, says Zeloot, by the Renaissance portraits "I loved so much when I studied painting."
DESIGN FIRM: Zeloot DESIGNER/ILLUSTRATOR: Zeloot CLIENT: De Garage PRIMARY FONT: Hand lettering

THE CHURCH OF THE NON-BELIEVERS Gothic derivation is fitting for this headline that takes up the issue of religion in contemporary life. The lettering evokes ecclesiastical traditions. ART DIRECTOR: Maili Holiman ILLUSTRATOR: Marian Bantjes PHOTOGRAPHER: Steve Peixotto CLIENT: *Wired* magazine PUBLISHER: Condé Nast PRIMARY FONT: Hand lettering

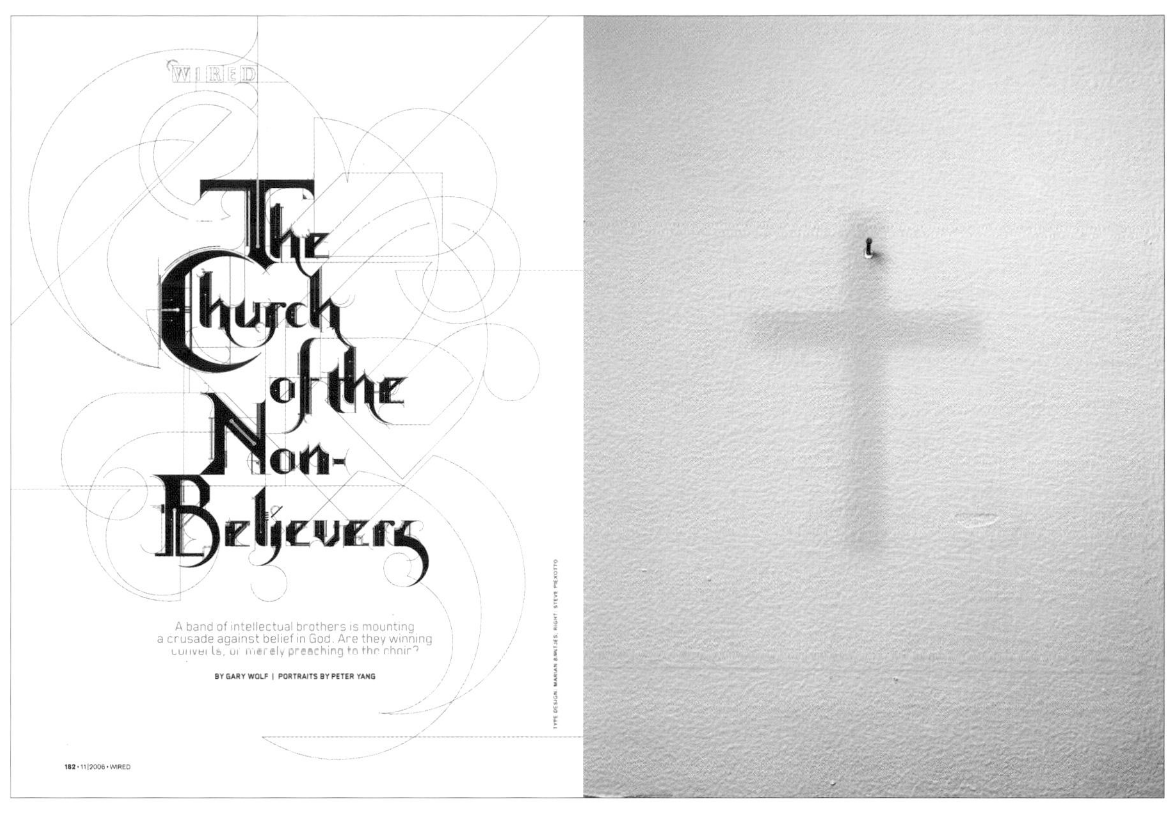
WIRED

The Church of the Non-Believers

A band of intellectual brothers is mounting a crusade against belief in God. Are they winning converts, or merely preaching to the choir?

BY GARY WOLF | PORTRAITS BY PETER YANG

182 • 11|2006 • WIRED

CALL OF THE WILD The master of the macabre, Edgar Allan Poe, inspired this story. The styling of the highly surreal black-and-white image is laden with darkness and mystery. And the black bird cried out: "Quoth the Raven, 'Nevermore.'" ART DIRECTOR/DESIGNER: Edward Leida PHOTOGRAPHER: Mert Alas, Marcus Piggott CLIENT: *W* magazine PUBLISHER: Condé Nast PRIMARY FONT: Fette Fraktur

VICTORIAN

THE VICTORIAN ERA – the period broadly covering the second half of the nineteenth century – was named for the reign of Queen Victoria (1837–1901), whose husband, Prince Albert, launched many of the great British design initiatives of his day. The Victorian sensibility is noted for extreme ornamentation, despite the lack of it in Victoria's own austere life. The typographic forms most associated with the style are slab serifs, bifurcated Latins, and excessive decoration as found on buildings of the period. This was a time of increased commercialization, and the lettering reflected the look-at-me exhibitionist demands of advertising. Today, Victorian styling bears little relation to its original context, and most users probably don't even know the name Queen Victoria. But its look is well suited to an era in which exhibitionism is yet again on the rise.

HI Inspired by bifurcated wood type that features faux embroidered decoration on its face, this type "is making something ordinary lavish," says Ray Fenwick. ILLUSTRATOR: Ray Fenwick CLIENT: Self PRIMARY FONT: Hand lettering

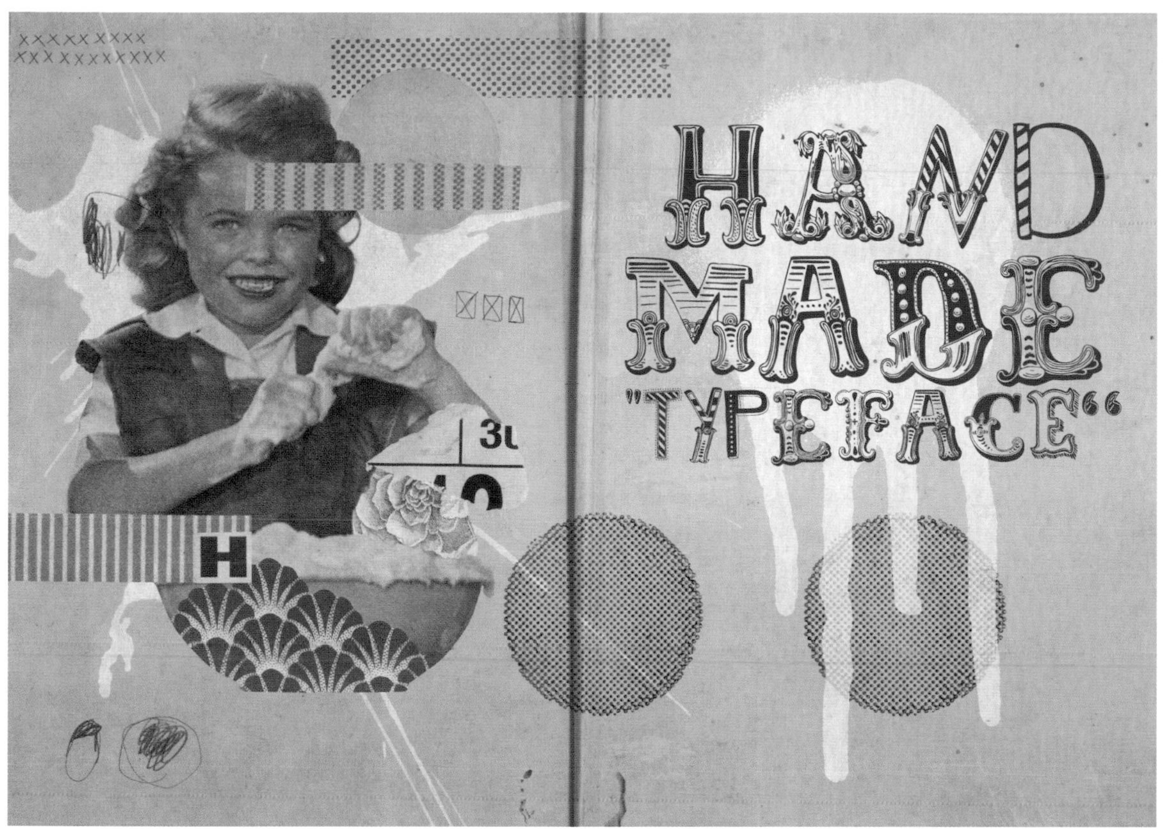

HANDMADE This elaborate font is a poster typeface appropriately called HandMade, created using various versions of bifurcated nineteenth-century Tuscans.
DESIGN FIRM: Misprinted Type ART DIRECTOR: Eduardo Recife CLIENT: Self PRIMARY FONT: HandMade

GREAT CIRCUS A poster for a font called Great Circus draws upon the clichéd circus poster typefaces that were common in the US during the late nineteenth century.
DESIGN FIRM: Misprinted Type ART DIRECTOR: Eduardo Recife CLIENT: Self PRIMARY FONT: Great Circus

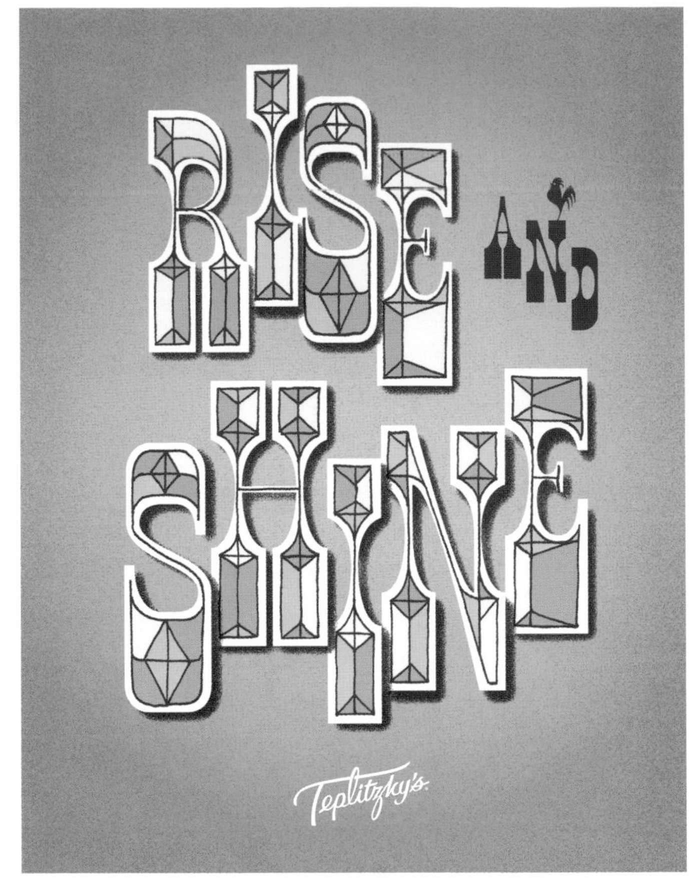

TEPLITZKY'S MENU Teplitzky's is a 1960s-style diner and café named after a kosher hotel that once occupied the same space. The restaurant is meant to feel as though it was once owned by someone's grandparents and has since been passed down through generations with little change. The lettering is quirky, colorful, and slightly mismatched, and is arranged in varying compositions. The shadowing and textures are intentionally grainy to mimic the commercial art of the turn of the twentieth century.

DESIGN FIRM: Mucca Design ART DIRECTOR: Matteo Bologna DESIGNER/ILLUSTRATOR: Steven Jockisch CLIENT: Cape Advisors PRIMARY FONT: Teplitzky's Regular by Steven Jockisch and Matteo Bologna

ABRAMESQUE This is one of Fiodor Sumkin's first experiences of hand-drawing typography. "I always try to use a hard mix of 'brutal' or filthy language and very gentle, beautiful fonts," he says. The bulbous alphabet was inspired by the typographer T. J. Lyons's book *A Biography and Critical Essay*, and *The Solotype Catalog*, a wellspring of vintage wood type.
DESIGNER/ILLUSTRATOR: Fiodor Sumkin CLIENT: Self PRIMARY FONT: Hand lettering

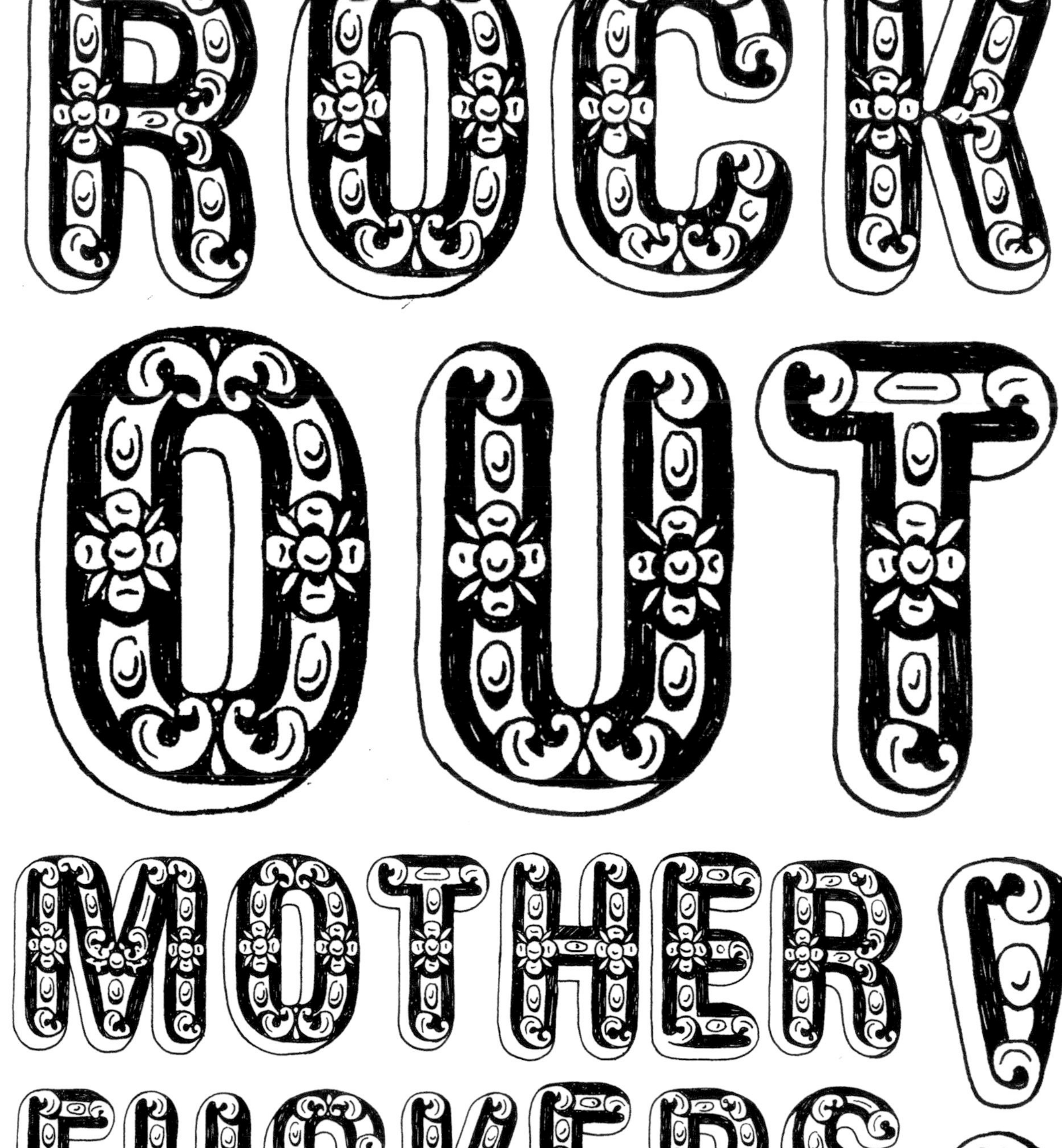

VICTORIAN

RESTRAINT This is an ornamental font that happens to contain vintage letterforms. "I designed it initially as an amusement, and Ross Mills convinced me to partner with him in turning it into a typeface," says Marian Bantjes.
DESIGNERS: Marian Bantjes, Ross Mills PRIMARY FONT: Restraint

BIGELOW CAMPAIGN The various components of this venerable drugstore logo were based on material from the historical graphic archives of the C. O. Bigelow Company. Ian Brignell wanted to bring as much authenticity as possible to a modern treatment of the packaging line. DESIGN FIRM: White Dot ART DIRECTOR: Amanda Lawrence LETTERER: Ian Brignell CLIENT: C. O. Bigelow PRIMARY FONT: Hand lettering

ESTABLISHED 1838.

Clarence O. Bigelow,
Apothecary.

SIXTH AVENUE BELOW NINTH STREET, NEW YORK.

Acetone is trip hop.
Aether is a
dingbat for
writing
Sighlence

ACETONE Acetone, a font, and Aether, a dingbat, are inspired by music known as trip-hop, which is comprised of classical elements, breaks, and samples. "Aether is based on the odd fact that, typographically, breaks and silences are always portrayed as blank space – emptiness," says Kenn Munk. DESIGN FIRM: Kenn Munk ART DIRECTOR/DESIGNER/PUBLISHER: Kenn Munk PRIMARY FONT: Acetone

ALA KAZAM This composition was designed to be printed on a child's T-shirt. The theme was "magic," so the letters were hand-made in the style of vintage magic posters.
DESIGN FIRM: Maki ART DIRECTOR: Chris Coleman
DESIGNERS/ILLUSTRATORS: Kim Smits, Matthijs Maat
CLIENT: WGSN PRIMARY FONT: Hand lettering

TAKIN' IT This was a collage of various lettering styles that have been popular throughout history. Rather than recreating one specific period, says Jon Contino, "this composition feels more like something that might be graffiti on a wall done by several different people over the course of time."
DESIGN FIRM: Onetwentysix ART DIRECTORS: Jon Contino, Matt Gorton DESIGNER/ILLUSTRATOR: Jon Contino CLIENT: The Brooklyn Circus PRIMARY FONT: Hand lettering

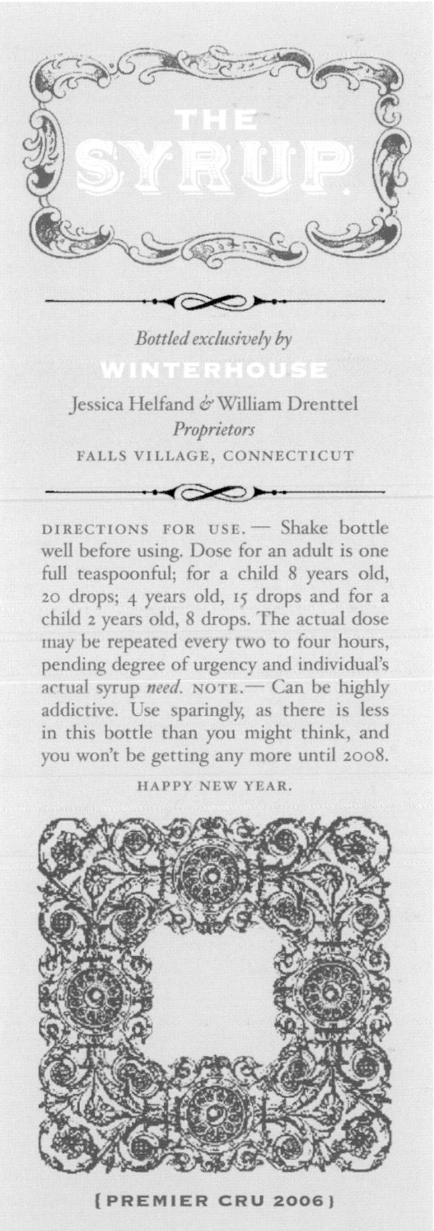

THE SYRUP, 2006 The elegant label for this bottle of home-made maple syrup was designed to have the aesthetic of a finely printed piece of letterpress ephemera.
DESIGN FIRM: Winterhouse ART DIRECTORS: Jessica Helfand, William Drenttel CLIENT: Winterhouse PRIMARY FONTS: Angelface, Copperplate, Hoeflertext

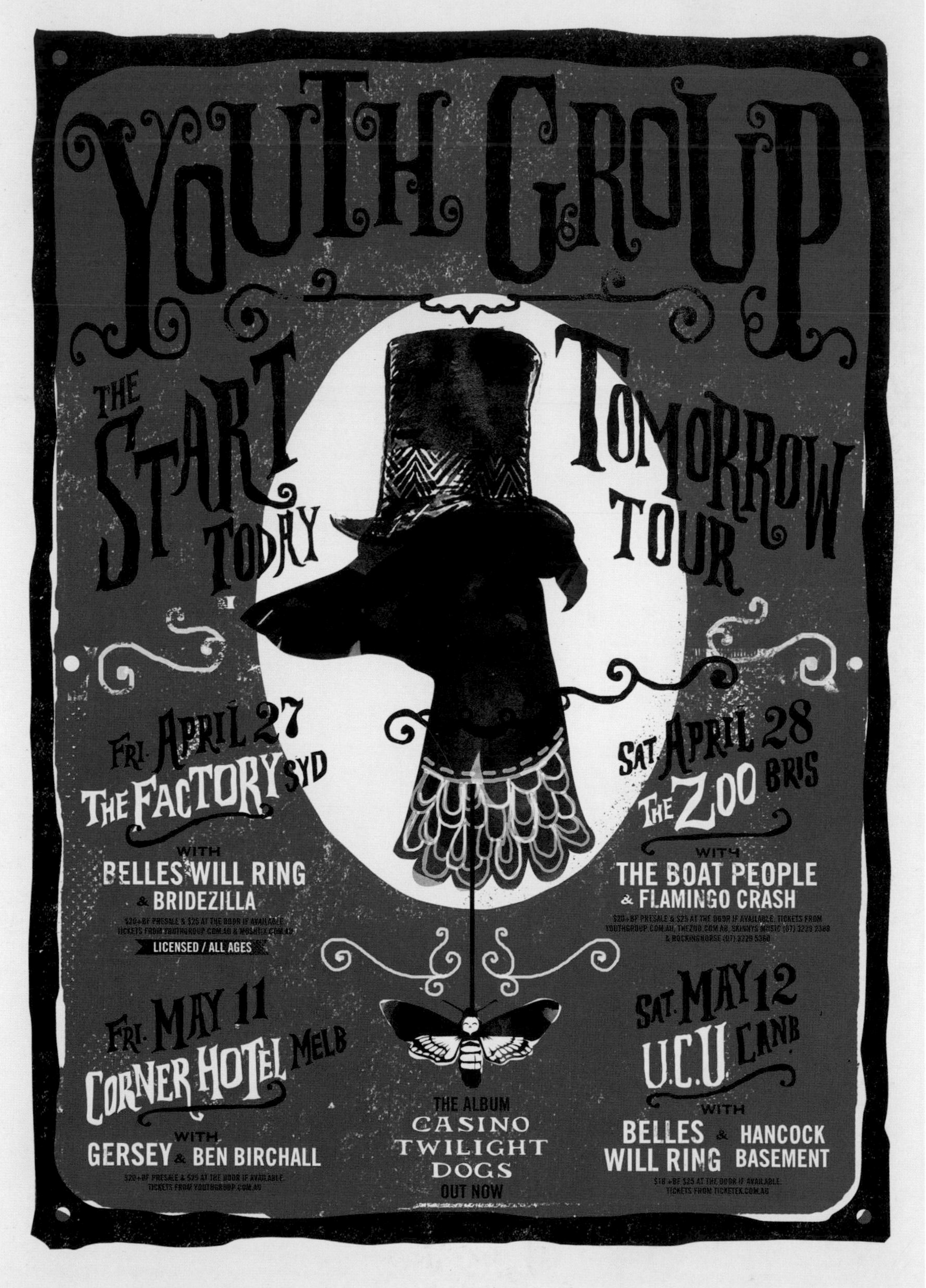

YOUTH GROUP The gig poster for Youth Group's "Start Today Tomorrow" tour was based on the album artwork, which in turn was inspired by the chap book illustrations and hand-drawn type of José Guadalupe Posada. "The type was drawn to curl around the poster, and distorted as though printed a little off-register," says Biddy Maroney. DESIGN FIRM: Webuyyourkids ART DIRECTORS/DESIGNERS: Biddy Maroney, Sonny Day ILLUSTRATOR: Biddy Maroney CLIENT: Winterman & Goldstein Management PRIMARY FONTS: Mostly hand lettering, Trade Gothic Bold Condensed No. 20, Grotesque MT Bold Extended

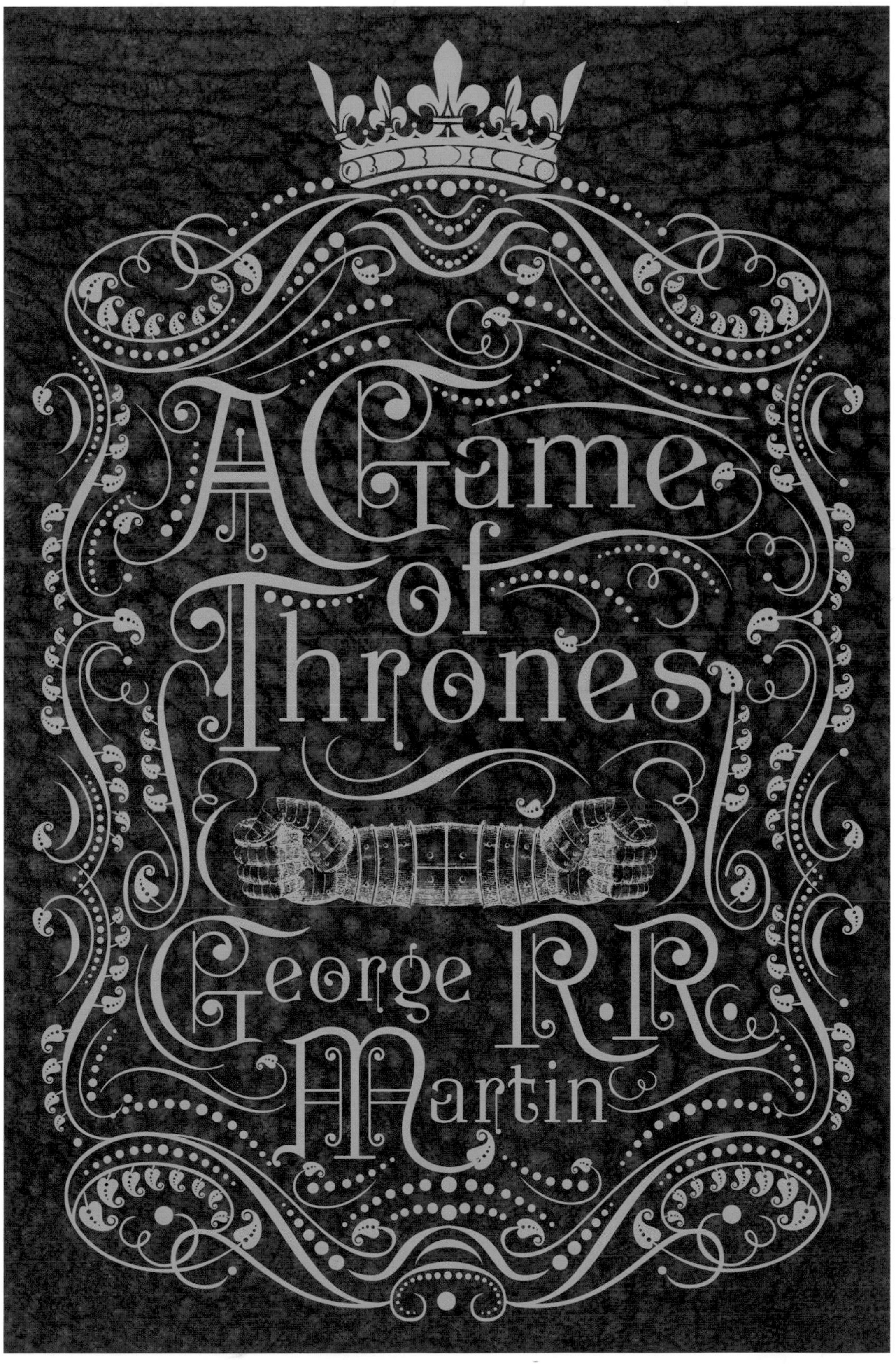

A GAME OF THRONES This Victorian fairy-tale book cover has Her Royal Majesty Queen Victoria and Prince Albert written all over it; the motif is a pitch-perfect pastiche of the era. DESIGN FIRM: de Vicq design ART DIRECTOR: Paolo Pepe DESIGNER: Roberto de Vicq de Cumptich CLIENT: Ballantine PUBLISHER: Random House PRIMARY FONT: P22 Kilkenny

VICTORIAN

SAVOIR FARE LONDON
ELAINE LOUIE
THE LITTLE BOOKROOM
DINING AFFORDABLY AND WELL—VERY WELL—IN LONDON IS QUITE POSSIBLE, IT TURNS OUT, IF YOU FIND THE PLACES Londoners themselves have discovered and love best. Author Elaine Louie has followed the leads of some of the city's most fashionable epicures—architects, curators, designers, and others with discriminating taste and exacting palates—and selected 50 venues that would be great finds at any price and where a meal (not including tip and beverage) can be enjoyed for $25 or less. Without exception, the food is superb and always perfectly complemented by an atmosphere of British cool and charm.
Elaine Louie is on the staff of The New York Times, where she contributes to the Home, Dining, and Sunday Styles sections
The Little Bookroom
NEW YORK
Design by Louise Fili Ltd.

SAVOIR FARE A chalkboard restaurant menu is the conceit for this book cover, created using the Art Nouveau swash lettering style of the late nineteenth and early twentieth centuries. DESIGN FIRM: Louise Fili Ltd ART DIRECTOR: Louise Fili DESIGNERS: Louise Fili, Jessica Hische ILLUSTRATOR: Jessica Hische PUBLISHER: The Little Bookroom PRIMARY FONT: Hand lettering

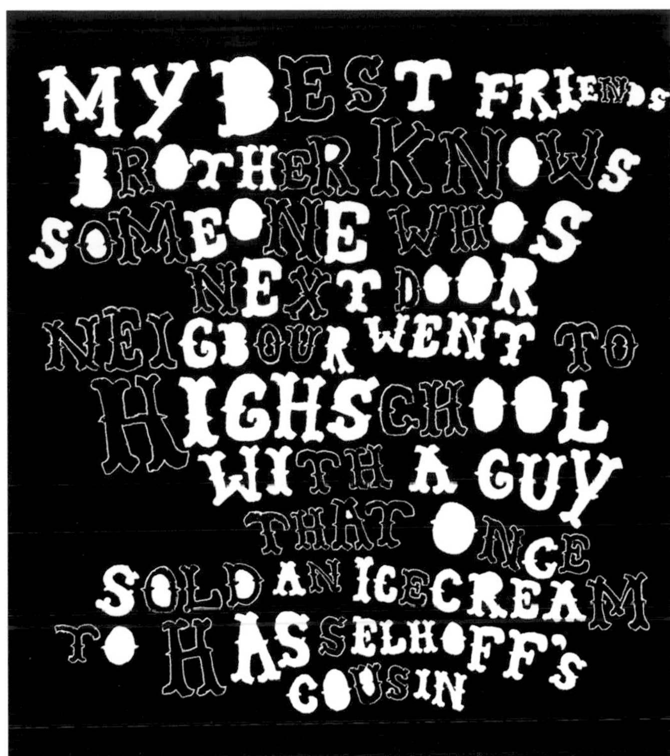

HASSELHOFF This is a type and lettering experiment, based on the curious notion that we are all connected: that everyone knows someone who knows someone who knows someone famous.
DESIGN FIRM: Maki DESIGNERS/ ILLUSTRATORS: Kim Smits, Matthijs Maat CLIENT: Self
PRIMARY FONT: Hand lettering

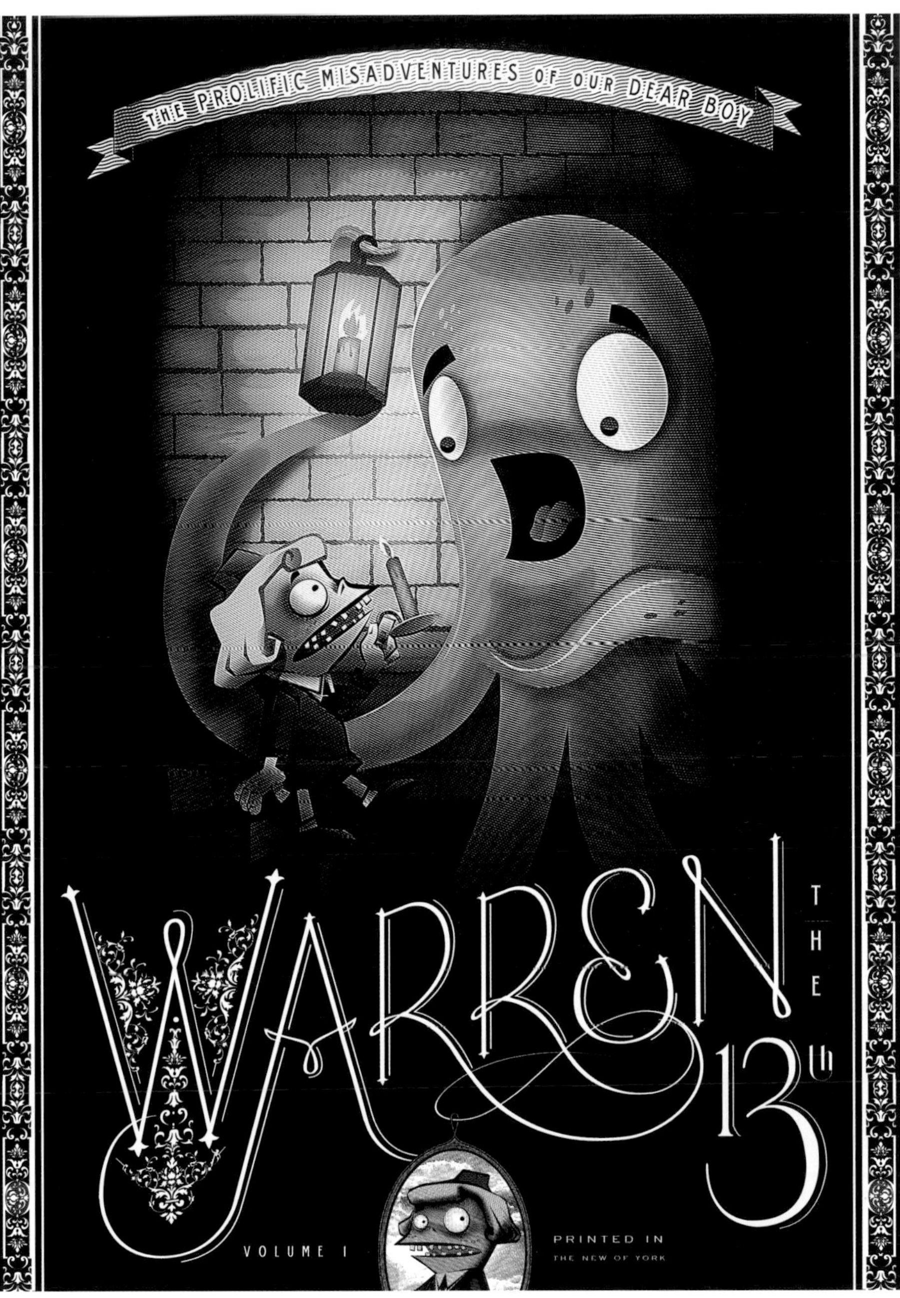

WARREN THE 13TH Warren the 13th is a cursed Victorian bell-hop who lives in an old hotel, says Will Staehle, his creator. This poster draws from various influences, including vintage magic posters of the day. Part of Staehle's infatuation with Victorian art and design stems from his over-flowing collection of antiques. "Growing up, I was surrounded by turn-of-the-century grandfather clocks, vintage woodcuts, music boxes and gas lamps," he says. "I now attempt to find space in crowded drawers and closets for all the odd goods and ephemera that I can't help but buy at flea markets."
DESIGN FIRM: Lonewolfblacksheep ART DIRECTOR/DESIGNER/ILLUSTRATOR: Will Staehle PRIMARY FONTS: Hand lettering, LHF Billhead

VICTORIAN

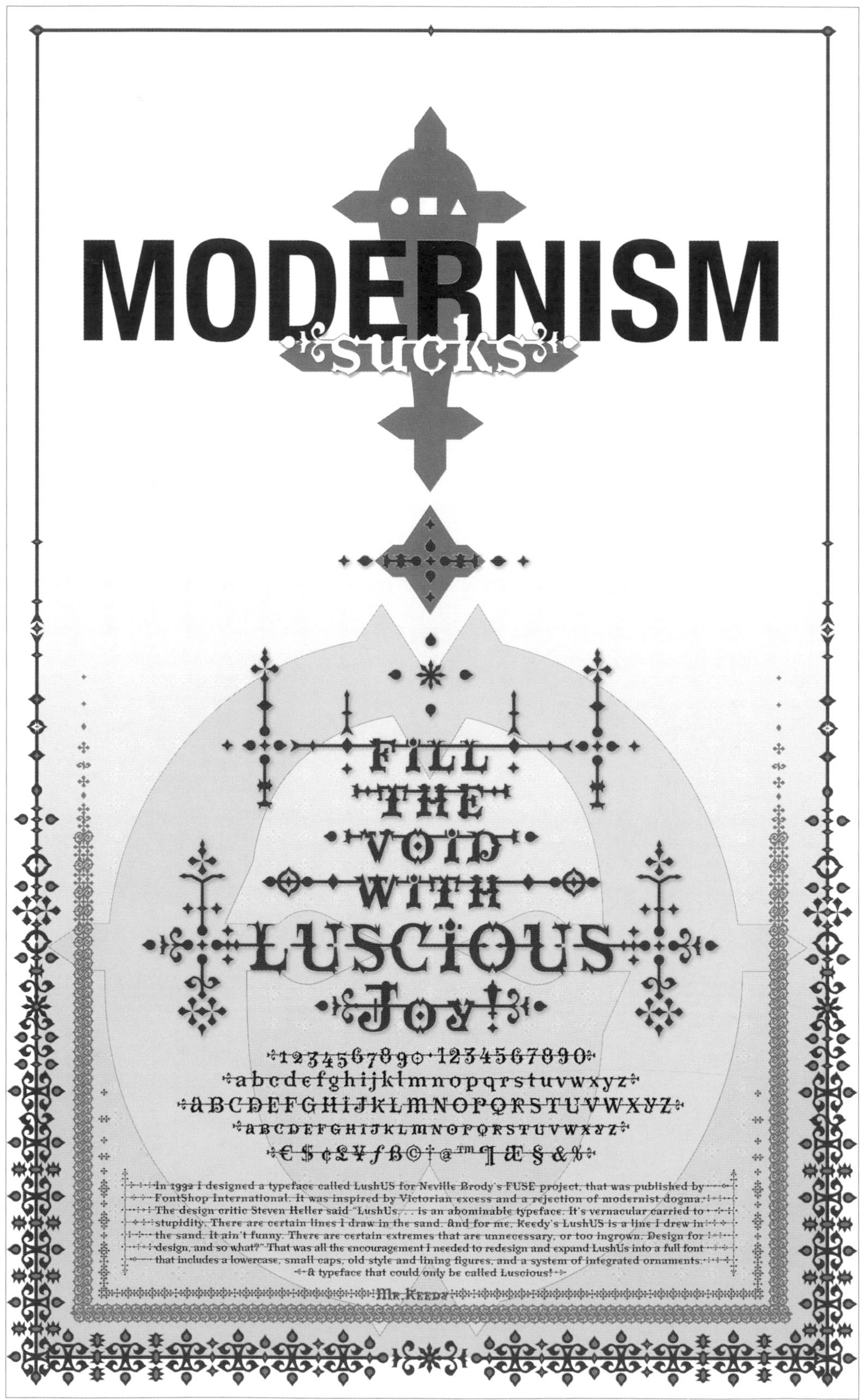

LUSCIOUS POSTER The typeface Luscious was designed in 1992 for Neville Brody's Fuse Font project, a magazine in a box, which included a poster and disk containing the font. Mr. Keedy expanded the typeface to include lower case, small caps, figures, and ornaments. It is a Victorian-inspired display font.
DESIGNER: Mr. Keedy CLIENT: Ciphertype PRIMARY FONT: Luscious

EST. THE 1827

DOLLAR DREADFUL FAMILY LIBRARY

PRINTED IN THE NEW OF YORK

HIGH-QUALITY BOOKLETS

HERE AT THE DOLLAR DREADFUL FAMILY LIBRARY, WE believe in publishing only the cheapest and most disposable escapism to be found here in these united states. Kindly make yourself familiar with our current spectacular roster which is presented below with the intention of intriguing and impressing you, and thereby inspiring you to then purchase your own copies of our titles to read, enjoy, and pass on!

STAPLES ADDED FOR YOUR LEISURE & PLEASURE

INVESTIGATOR OF THE MACABRE

ARCHIBALD GREY

ARCHIBALD GREY is the owner of the Skeleton Key, which, in addition to opening any lock, also allows him to enter the Ether, land of the dead!.

VOL. ONE........................$ 2.00

DR. OCTAVIOUS WATT AND HIS PNEUMATIC BRIDE

DR. OCTAVIOUS WATT, HIMSELF

OR: SCIENTIFIC ADVENTURES IN MATRIMONY

DR. OCTAVIOUS WATT is an inventor of many marvelous things, including his own wife, who is a pneumatic woman. He is quite protective of his creations, fearful of those who would steal his secrets. Enjoy his domestic adventures as he avoids the spies who would betray him!

VOL. ONE........................$ 2.00

WE PRESENT THIS TERM 4 NEW TITLES FOR YOUR PERUSAL

EST. DD 1827

THE DOLLAR DREADFUL FAMILY LIBRARY

3W'S DOT DOLLARDREADFUL DOT COM

JONAH OAKTREE

THE APPALACHIAN SENSATION

JONAH OAKTREE is a mountain man born of two giants. Regular in size, but large of heart and bravery, he is a man of the land who sets out to seek his own fortune!

VOL. ONE........................$ 2.00

THE DRESS MAKER'S DETECTIVE JOURNAL

A PERFECT COMPANION FOR YOUR LADY

THE DRESSMAKERS are a group of women who gather each Tuesday to work on their sewing and knitting together. But what few realize is that these women are also detectives who meet to discuss their latest cases!

VOL. ONE........................$ 2.00

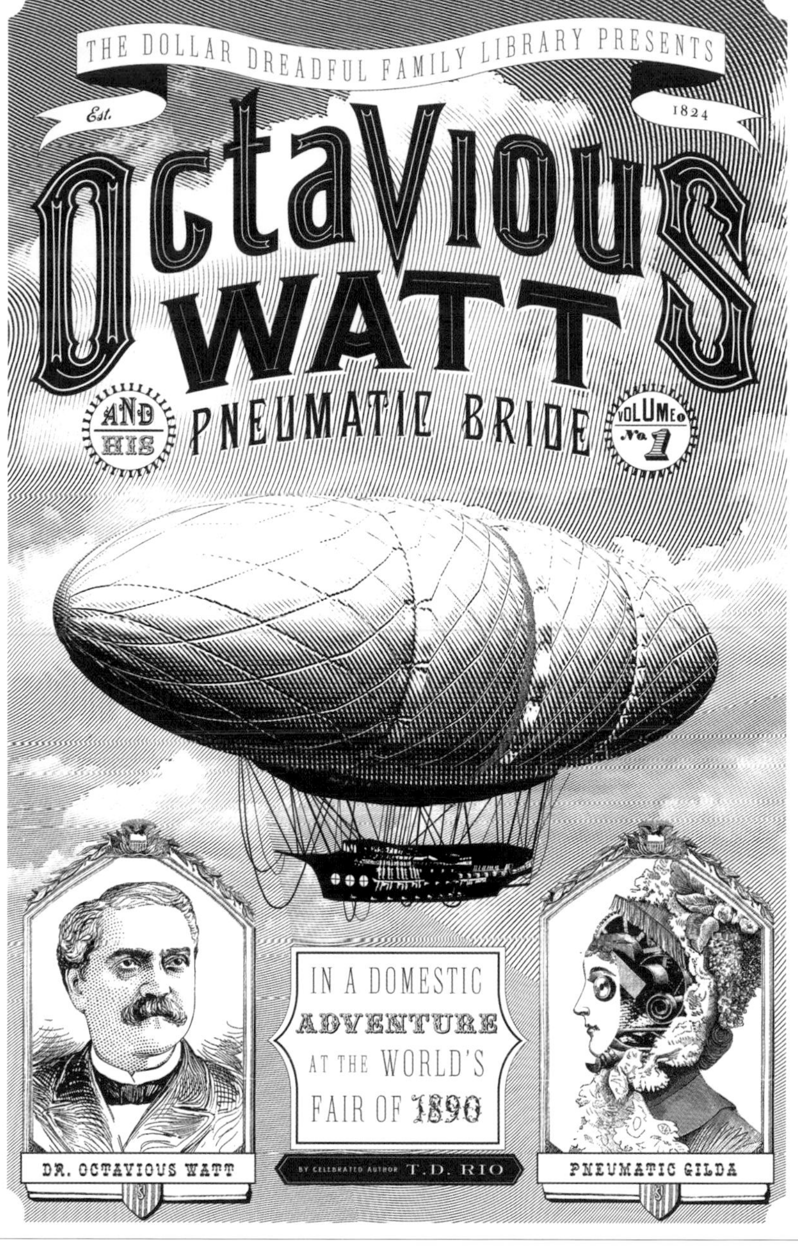

THE DOLLAR DREADFUL FAMILY LIBRARY PRESENTS
Est.
1824
Octavious
WATT
AND HIS
PNEUMATIC BRIDE
VOLUME No. 1
IN A DOMESTIC
ADVENTURE
AT THE WORLD'S
FAIR OF 1890
DR. OCTAVIOUS WATT
BY CELEBRATED AUTHOR T. D. RIO
PNEUMATIC GILDA

OCTAVIOUS WATT AND HIS PNEUMATIC BRIDE The Dollar Dreadful Family Library is a series of short escapist stories that are based on Victorian publications such as the old penny dreadfuls or dime novels. The packaging for the series draws on the engravings and ornate, hand-drawn titles that were popular at that time. "The covers are a mix of modified type," Will Staehle explains, "hand-drawn lettering, collage, original art, and even some 3-D models, wrapped in engraved texture maps."

DESIGN FIRM: Lonewolfblacksheep ART DIRECTOR/DESIGNER/ILLUSTRATOR: Will Staehle CLIENT: The Dollar Dreadful Family Library PUBLISHER: The Dollar Dreadful Family Library PRIMARY FONTS: LHF Argentine Solid (modified), LHF Naylorville (modified), Elongated Roman, Ringmaster

VICTORIAN

MUCCA FIVE-LINE PICA Five-Line Pica Italian, a typeface originally created in the mid-to-late nineteenth century by the Bruce Type Foundry in New York, inspired Mucca Five-Line Pica. This is a cleaner, more modern version that has even greater contrast between thick and thin, but still maintains much of the wonderful weirdness of the original design.
DESIGN FIRM: Mucca Design ART DIRECTOR: Matteo Bologna
DESIGNERS/ILLUSTRATORS: Matteo Bologna, Steven Jockisch
CLIENT: Mucca Design PRIMARY FONT: Custom made

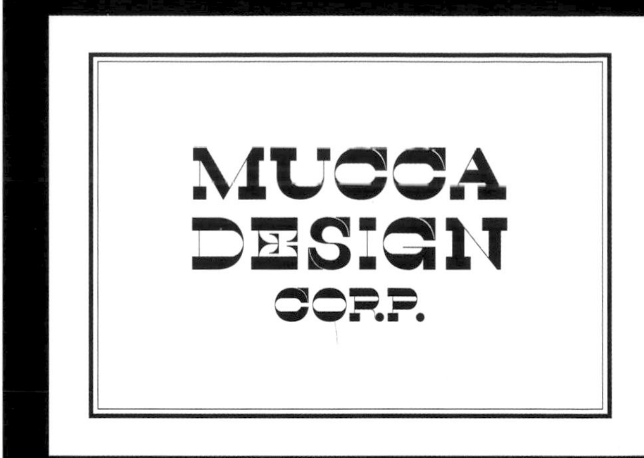

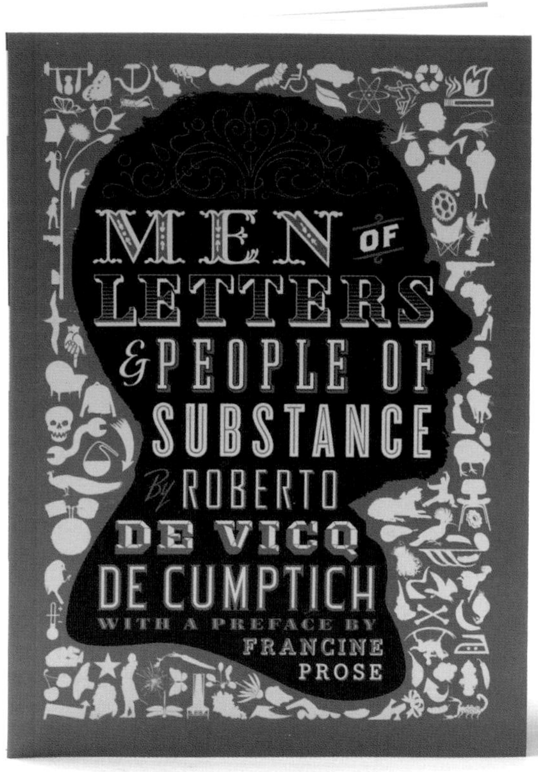

MEN OF LETTERS & PEOPLE OF SUBSTANCE These are literary portraits made from typographic letters and ornaments, inspired by the Italian Giuseppe Arcimboldo, who was famous for painting portraits using compositions of fruits, vegetables, and other objects. Roberto de Vicq de Cumptich identified just the right alphabets to show likenesses.
DESIGN FIRM: de Vicq design ART DIRECTOR/DESIGNER/ILLUSTRATOR: Roberto de Vicq de Cumptich PUBLISHER: David R. Godine PRIMARY FONTS: "Too many to count…."

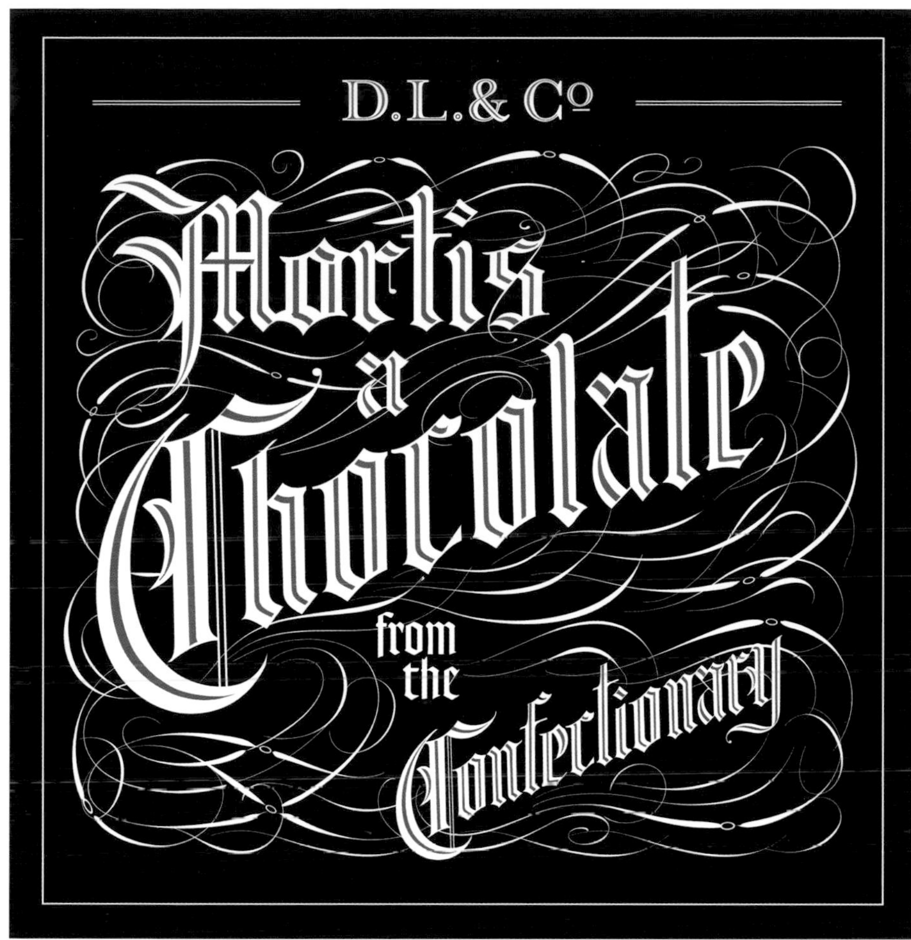

DEATH BY CHOCOLATE So many influences, so little space: included are Dutch chocolate packaging, nineteenth-century gravestone rubbings, and Norwegian black metal music, to name but a few.
DESIGN FIRM: Dustin Edward Arnold CREATIVE DIRECTOR: Douglas Little DESIGNER: Douglas Little LETTERER: Dustin E. Arnold PHOTOGRAPHER: Dana Maione CLIENT: D. L. & Co FONTS: Adobe Garamond, custom made

CALEA The label for this wine derives from an Italian poster design from the 1920s, which was part of the Novecento style.
DESIGN FIRM: Louise Fili Ltd ART DIRECTOR: Louise Fili DESIGNERS: Louise Fili, Jessica Hische CLIENT: Polaner Selections PRIMARY FONT: Hand lettering

MODERN

THE MODERN ERA in art and design begins shortly after the turn of the twentieth century and reaches its apex during the interwar years. Avant-garde movements in Holland, Italy, Germany, Eastern Europe, and the Soviet Union introduce a "New Typography" that challenges the archaic practices of previous styles. Modernism begins in a raucous manner with Futurism before settling down to a regulated and regimented rationality with the Bauhaus, and ultimately the clean economy of the Swiss Style. Today, designers still revere the heroes of Modernism and use it as a starting point for contemporary typographic work. While the Bauhaus still reigns, Art Moderne, or Art Deco – the Modernistic style – is also the source of much typographic playfulness.

FACELESS From the era of supergraphics comes this modern, heavily shadowed letterform. It speaks loud, if not exactly clear, in a dynamic manner.
DESIGN FIRM: Blikdsgn ART DIRECTOR/DESIGNER: Daniel Blik ILLUSTRATOR: Blikdsgn CLIENT: Self PRIMARY FONT: Hand lettering

BLACK Lodma was commissioned to illustrate a concept for the word "black" for *Revista Colectiva*, and chose to portray it by using a variant of Bifurk, an Italian Futurist typeface. DESIGN FIRM: Lodma. Location Doesn't Matter Anymore™ ART DIRECTOR/DESIGNER/ILLUSTRATOR: Paulo Garcia CLIENT/PUBLISHER: *Revista Colectiva* magazine PRIMARY FONT: Bifurk

ALMOST FAMOUS As a means of showing transparency and monumentality, another variation on the Futurist typeface Bifurk becomes more than a mere headline; it is a sculptural design. ART DIRECTOR/DESIGNER: Carl De Torres CLIENT: *Wired* magazine PUBLISHER: Condé Nast PRIMARY FONT: Bifurk

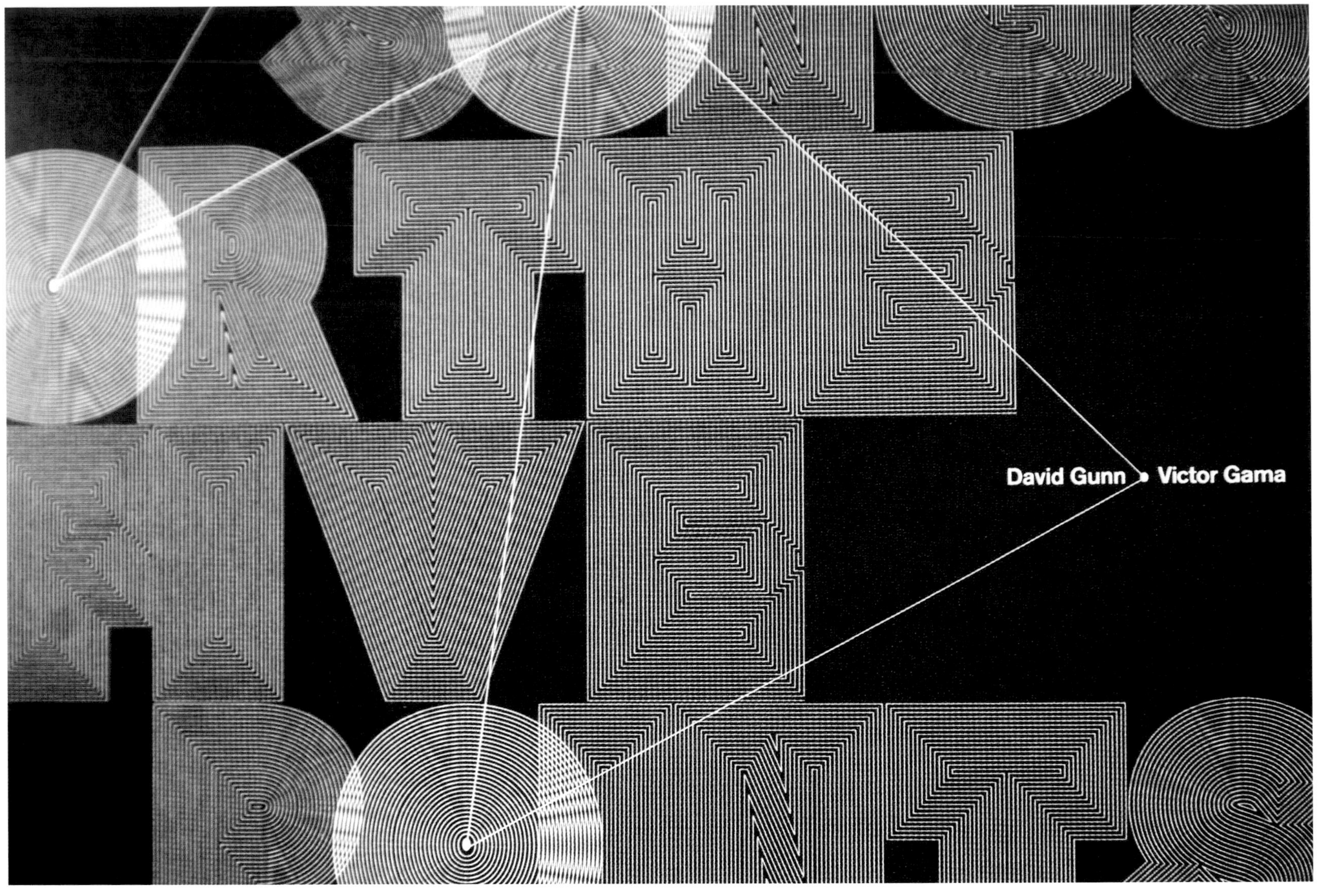

FOLK SONGS FOR THE FIVE POINTS ALBUM This CD is the audio artifact of a project commissioned by the Tenement Museum, responding to contemporary immigrant experiences in New York City. The artist, David Gunn, a British immigrant, collected found sound from the Five Points area in Lower Manhattan, where many cultures and clashing socio-economic groups still cross paths. The music is an abstract layering and interweaving of multiple voices and soundscapes, which are at times unsettling; it is matched visually by a mix of disorienting concentric lines, mazes, and moiré patterns. A direct inspiration was the Mexico Olympics identity by Lance Wyman (1968), which uses concentric lines as a device.

DESIGN FIRM: Joe Marianek DESIGNER: Joe Marianek CLIENTS: Victor Gama, David Gunn PUBLISHER: The Lower East Side Tenement Museum PRIMARY FONTS: Akzidenz Grotesk, custom lettering

FRIDA & DIEGO This poster was produced for the curator of an exhibition celebrating the 100th anniversary of Diego Rivera and Frida Kahlo in Mexico. The lettering derives from Modernist sensibilities.
DESIGNER/LETTERER: Carin Goldberg PRIMARY FONT: Custom made

STRANGE RESTING PLACES Lettering by playful Futurist Fortunato Depero and traditional Maori tattoos influenced this poster for a play about a Maori battalion in Italy in World War II.
DESIGN FIRM: The Letterheads Ltd. ART DIRECTOR/ DESIGNER: Kris Sowersby CLIENT: Taki Rua Productions
PRIMARY FONT: Hand lettering

FRI. MAR 16, 2007 | DOUBLE DOOR | CHICAGO, IL | W/ BRIGHTON MA AND GRINGO STAR

THE SLIP For this concert poster, Nate Duval wanted to make the text part of the geometric style. He says, "This was the best solution I found to incorporating text into a textured, colorful, geometric image while keeping its legibility." It reflects the layering and Cubist mannerisms of the 1920s and 1930s. DESIGN FIRM: NateDuval.com ART DIRECTOR/DESIGNER/ ILLUSTRATOR: Nate Duval CLIENT/PUBLISHER: The Slip PRIMARY FONT: Hand lettering

FUNKY TYPEFACE EXPERIMENT Building on the concept of A. M. Cassandre's quirky Bifur and other funky Art Deco typefaces, this piece combines Modern (Bauhausian) and Modernistic (Art Deco) ideas. DESIGN FIRM: Acme Industries DESIGNER: Andrei Robu PRIMARY FONT: Funky Typeface

BARCENOVA This was a logo designed for *Barcelona* magazine, which was then made into a full-blown typeface. Its influences derive from modular Art Deco type such as Novel Gothic. DESIGN FIRM: Andreu Balius ART DIRECTOR/DESIGNER: Andreu Balius CLIENT: Revistas Exclusivas S. L. PRIMARY FONT: Barcelona

HIPSTER

STYLES, LIKE PLANETS, take time to complete their orbits in the retro universe. Usually, it takes a generation or two to appreciate that what has become passé still retains some value for a new wave of artists or designers. Often when the styles do come around again they are not exactly the same as before. The Hipster style is a hybrid: a mix of 1950s, 1960s, and a bit of early 1970s mainstream Pop culture, with a contemporary – in this case digital – edge. Hipster type and lettering is often hand-drawn, usually comic, if not also goofy, and suggests a thrift-store or flea-market aesthetic, mixed with the look of classic UPA animated cartoons from the 1950s and 1960s.

FUCKED UP SHIT "The form for this T-shirt design," explains Ray Fenwick, "needed to be a bit zany to offset the vulgarity of the language, and this is the zaniest lettering I could come up with."
ILLUSTRATOR: Ray Fenwick CLIENT: Gama-Go PRIMARY FONT: Hand lettering

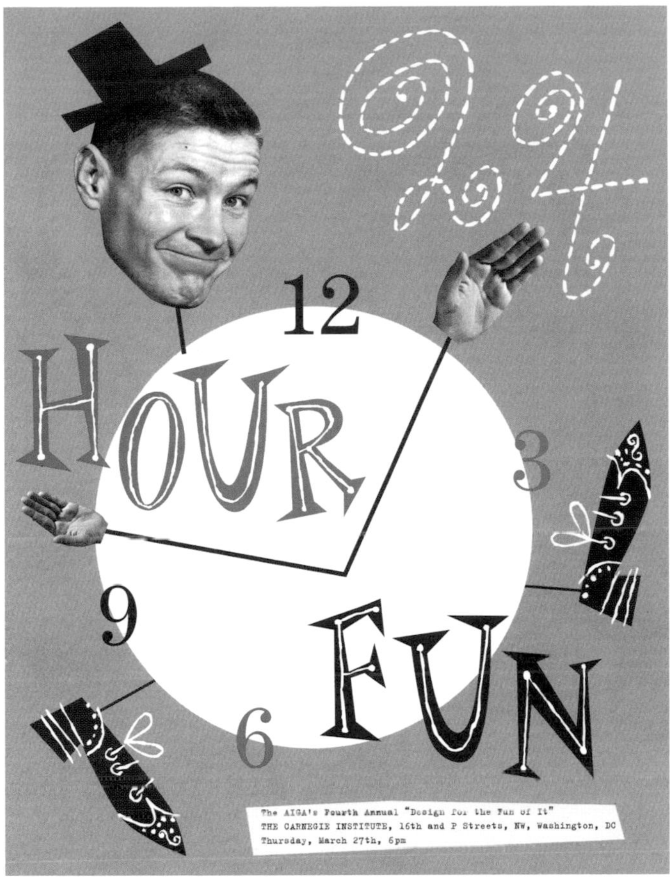

24 HOUR FUN The influences for this AIGA conference brochure included Paul Rand and John Heartfield, adapted to look "hipsteresque." Working as both the illustrator and designer on this project, Melinda Beck mixed the typography with the illustration and created, she says, "a fun, whimsical look, communicating the feeling of the event." DESIGNER/ILLUSTRATOR: Melinda Beck CLIENT: AIGA PRIMARY FONTS: Hand lettering, Caslon, Courier

Realise
all your
Dreams*
WITH OUR HELP
FOR A SHORT TIME

REALISE This design from the book *Secret Weapon: 30 Hand-Painted Spam Postcards* was inspired by traditional carnival and circus signage, folk art, and 1950s promotional and advertising ephemera.
ILLUSTRATOR: Linzie Hunter CLIENT: Chronicle Books EDITOR: Christina Amini PRIMARY FONT: Hand lettering

HIPSTER

VIRTUE This painting was included in an exhibition called "Virtue" (2005, Jonathan LeVine Gallery, New York). The show was an attempt to explore the virtues of craft and decorative art within the realm of a decidedly intellectual, concept-heavy contemporary art world. ILLUSTRATOR: Tim Biskup CLIENT: Self PRIMARY FONT: Custom hand-painted text

DESTROY This six-color serigraph print was folded in half and included in a set of mutilated prints titled "The Wrecker Portfolio." The style of the font is inspired by the "Fancy" period in American design (1790–1840), according to Tim Biskup.
ILLUSTRATOR: Tim Biskup CLIENT: Self PRIMARY FONT: Custom hand-painted text

WATER MIST SPRAY ON YOUR FACE SALON "The general inspiration," says Ray Fenwick, "are those hyper-eclectic and often trashy 1950s signs, the ones that seem to exist only in Vegas and outside old motels."
ILLUSTRATOR: Ray Fenwick CLIENT: Self PRIMARY FONT: Hand lettering

WHAT IS THE difference between Hipster and Pop? The primary distinction is simple: Pop is closer to the disco aesthetic, often forming a hybrid of post-Psychedelic type and ornament combined with slick, mid-1970s style. The typefaces are more raucous than Hipster, and more colorful. Pop finds its form in the advertising of the period, but also in Op-Art and supergraphics, with their primary, clashing colors.

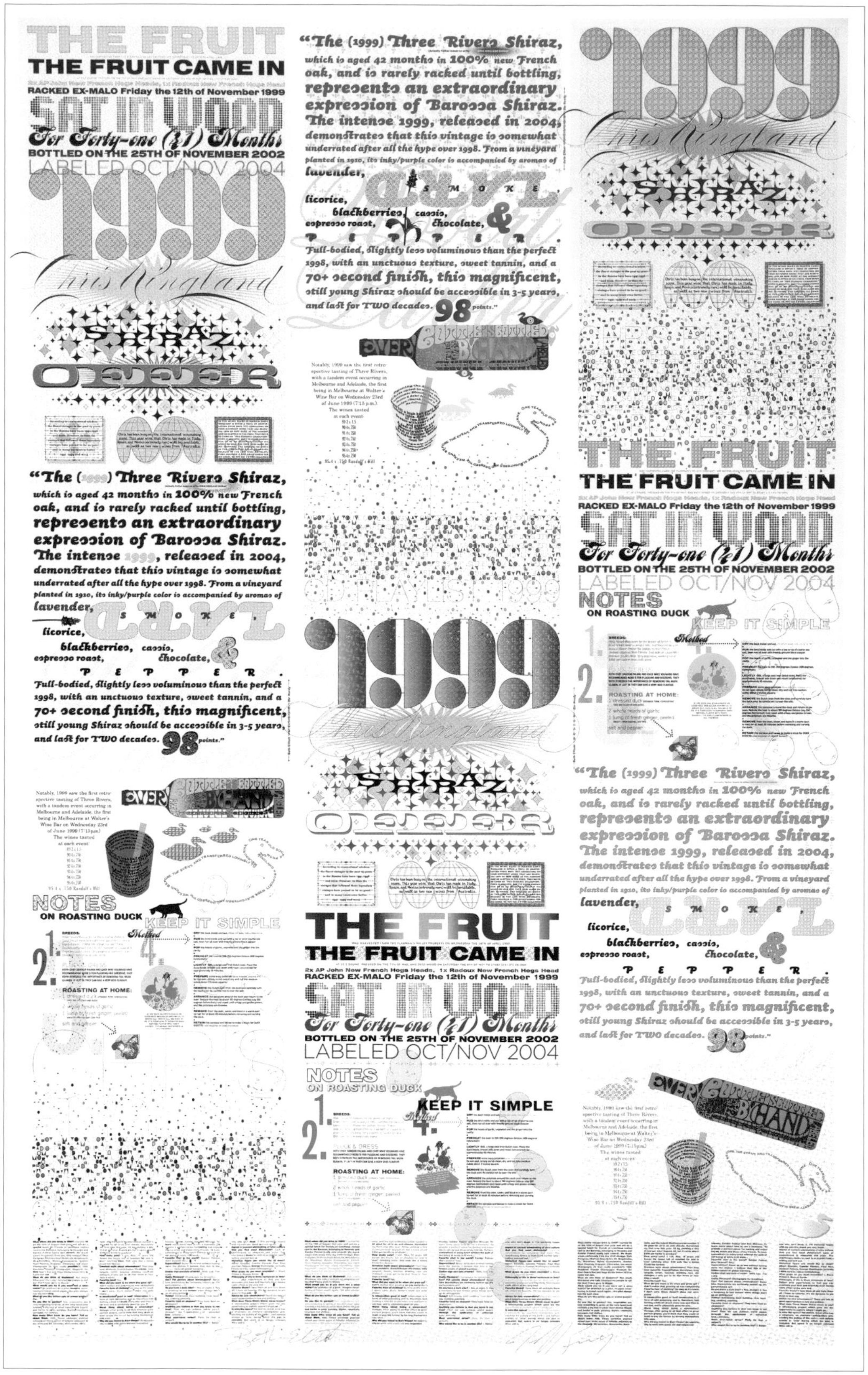

CHRIS RINGLAND SHIRAZ OFFER

A contemporary take on the nineteenth-century broadsheet or playbill is here given Pop exuberance using custom patterns and lettering. The poster was printed three on a sheet and the three different versions were accordion-folded and mailed out. Some were left untrimmed and unfolded for this large commemorative poster.

DESIGNERS: Beth Elliott, Mr. Keedy
CLIENT: Ringland Vintners PRIMARY FONTS: Sauna, lettering by Mr. Keedy

10 WAYS TO GET A JOB This type treatment was based on the face CG Barnum Block. After building a solid composition, white lines were used to define the letter shapes. A major inspiration was the amazing black-and-white work of Charles Burns, which used geometric white lines, and the work of Non-Format.
DESIGNER: Alex Trochut CLIENT: *Computer Arts* magazine PUBLISHER: Future Publishing Ltd. PRIMARY FONT: Type treatment on CG Barnum Block

12.10.06

ON LANGUAGE BY WILLIAM SAFIRE

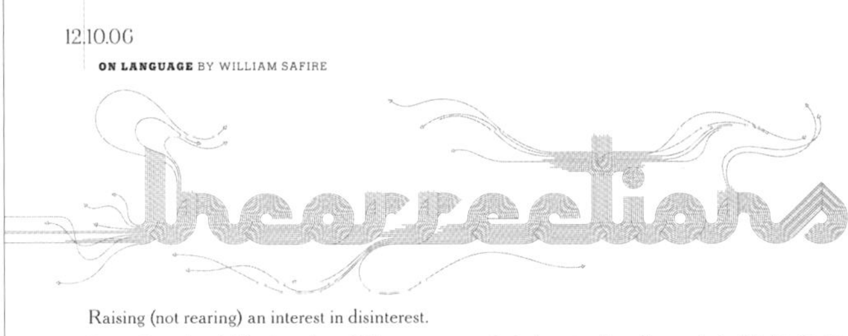

Raising (not rearing) an interest in disinterest.

You got to know when to hold 'em, know when to fold 'em.

As a young language maven, whenever I heard someone say, "That's how I raise my kids," I would pass along the rule "You *raise* cattle but you *rear* children."

That's the correct usage that I was brought up (or *reared*, never *raised*) to say. The "rule" was easy enough to remember: *Raise* animals or crops, rear little human beings. As the years smoothed the sharp corners of my irascibility, whenever I heard a friend slip into that solecism, I zipped my lip; still, a little gong went off in Wernicke's area of my brain, where word meanings are recognized.

With the increased coverage of the same-sex marriage issue, the constant gonging keeps me awake nights. "Growing numbers of couples," reports The Boston Globe, "are choosing to *raise* children, buy homes and build family lives without religious or civil approval of their partnerships." The gay New York Blade notes, "We go to work, *raise* children, pay taxes and live in the boring 'burbs." And on the cover of The New York Times Magazine last month was the headline: "An Extended Nuclear Family? Gay men, lesbians and the kids they are making and *raising*, sort of together."

Other reports on nontraditional marriage adhere to traditional usage: The Washington Post writes of "new possibilities for lesbians and heterosexual women to *rear* children successfully." The Richmond Times-Dispatch quotes a former lawmaker describing marriage as the best way "in which to *rear* children."

So which is it to be? (So I offend good usage by beginning a sentence with *so*. So what? Idioms is idioms.) Etymology is no help; both *raise* and *rear* as verbs come from the same Scandinavian root, the earliest meaning being "to set upright, to stand on its end," the way a horse rears, or raises, itself on its hind legs. Over a millennium, *raise* covered more meanings than *rear*; no poker player says, "I'll see you and rear you." *Rear* has become a loser verb, used only in clichés like "*rears* its ugly head."

Although I'm usually a prescriptive usagist, I'll now argue that to tut-tut at "I'm *raising* my kid to be a billionaire" is to commit an incorrection. (That relatively new noun means "a correction that is itself incorrect.") My advice to the stalwart *rear/raise* differentiators, drawing to an inside straight: fold 'em. *Raise* takes the pot.

Disinterest (Yawn)

"I don't have a dog in that fight" has long been a favorite Texas saying of former Secretary of State James Baker (now cuttingly called "acting secretary of state"). Now that he is back in the news as co-chairman of the Iraq Study Group, we can anticipate such a description of non-canine involvement — along with a more benign Bakerism, "singing from the same hymn book" — as a way of declaring his impartiality in striking a compromise between "cut and run" and "stay the course," between dovish "timetable" and hawkish "benchmark." His search for common ground will be determinedly disinterested.

That word *disinterested* presents a problem. It means "impartial; free of bias; without any ethical conflict or selfish motive or financial interest." It does not mean *uninterested*; the word with the *un-* prefix, less frequently used, means "lacking interest; indifferent; disengaged to the point of terminal boredom."

A big difference in meaning, right? The *dis-* word deals with ethical purity, while the *un-* word deals with the lack of attention. No argument; no semantic overlap; everything clear in everyone's mind.

And yet, and yet. In 1954, the literary critic I.A. Richards dared to say, "More people seem to be saying *disinterested* when they mean *uninterested*" and worried "that would only mean that a noble distinction, hard to replace, would be lost." Like a clockwork orange, in 1985 the British linguist-novelist Anthony Burgess agreed, calling the use of *disinterested* to mean *uninterested* "one of the worst of all American solecisms."

Hmph! snorted E. Ward Gilman of Merriam-Webster, the most influential usagist in America. In a lengthy entry in his magisterial 1989 Webster's Dictionary of English Usage, he reported that nearly three-quarters of the citations of *disinterested* in their files used the ethical sense and that "reports of its demise have been shamefully exaggerated." His conclusion, meekly followed by his army of acolytes ever since: "The alleged confusion between *disinterested* and *uninterested* does not exist."

As M-W's previous paragon of permissivism, Philip Gove, might say: Ain't so. It may well be that most published citations still preserve the distinction, but to my ear the breaking down is under way, especially in the spoken word and the blogosphere.

Recent examples from the newspaper with the most eagle-eyed copy editors in the U.S.: a cultural critic noted "Bush's *disinterest* in serious policy analysis"; an anonymous letter alliteratively attacked a prelate for "dishonesty, deception, *disinterest* and disregard"; one sportswriter described a Mets player as having "waved at the television in *disinterest* and ignored the Phillies game"; while another described a Redskins football coach's "*disinterest* in controlling the ball and the clock."

The alarmists of a generation ago were right to warn of barbarians at the gate. To paraphrase a poet: Rear up and rage, rage against the dying of an enlightening distinction.

P.S. to the Phrasedick Legion: The source of "You got to know when to hold 'em, know when to fold 'em" was the song "The Gambler," by Don Schlitz, recorded in 1978 by Kenny Rogers. The aphorism was probably used earlier and was reflected in the card game of a couple of generations before named Texas Hold 'Em. ■

Send comments and suggestions to: safireonlanguage@nytimes.com.

24

Lettering by Mario Hugo

INCORRECTIONS Every week, William Safire writes about a word or phrase that is relevant to the moment. For the past three years *The New York Times Magazine* has invited artists, designers and illustrators to interpret the words in their own unique way.
ART DIRECTOR: Arem Duplessis DESIGNER: Gail Bichler LETTERING: Mario Hugo CLIENT: *The New York Times Magazine* PUBLISHER: *The New York Times* PRIMARY FONTS: Stymie NYT, Cheltenham NYT

Medicine Show
Alphabet Lounge
Sat. 2-25-06 8PM

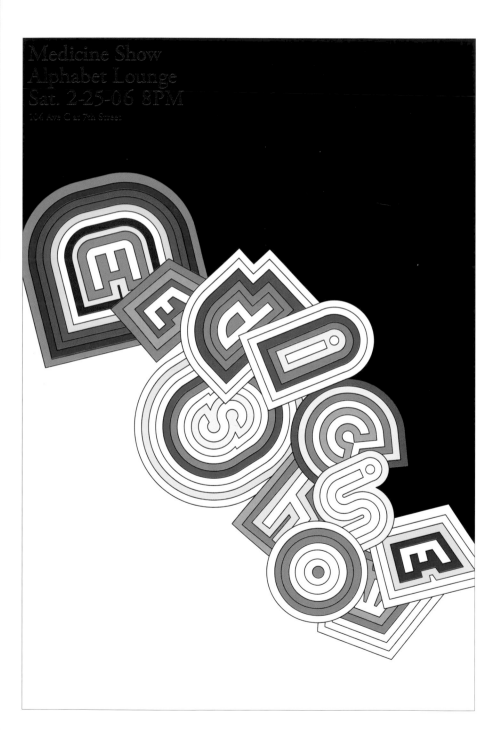

MEDICINE SHOW The Medicine Show's "space-ambient-noise" music uses a stark mix of electronic found sound with a more folksy, eclectic blend of banjo, guitar, and tuba. For the poster, "it seemed like a good idea to mix diametrically opposed 'found' visual references, and somehow incorporate varying levels of clarity and distortion," says Joe Marianek. The inspiration was Milton Glaser's *Dylan* poster from 1966 and the associative Zeitgeist that surrounds it. In the end, the goal became to appropriate the recognizable elements in Glaser's poster as economically as possible without parodying it.
DESIGN FIRM: Joe Marianek ART DIRECTOR/DESIGNER: Joe Marianek CLIENT: The Medicine Show PRIMARY FONTS: Bayer Fonetik, ITC Garamond

PLAYOUT Playout is a record label and event builder in Antwerp. They wanted something simple, elegant, and fun. Here, each letter is composed of thirteen different and geometrical forms. The aim was to illustrate the variety and playfulness of the label. The letters are like toys.
DESIGNER: Merci Bernard CLIENT: Playout PRIMARY FONT: Hand lettering

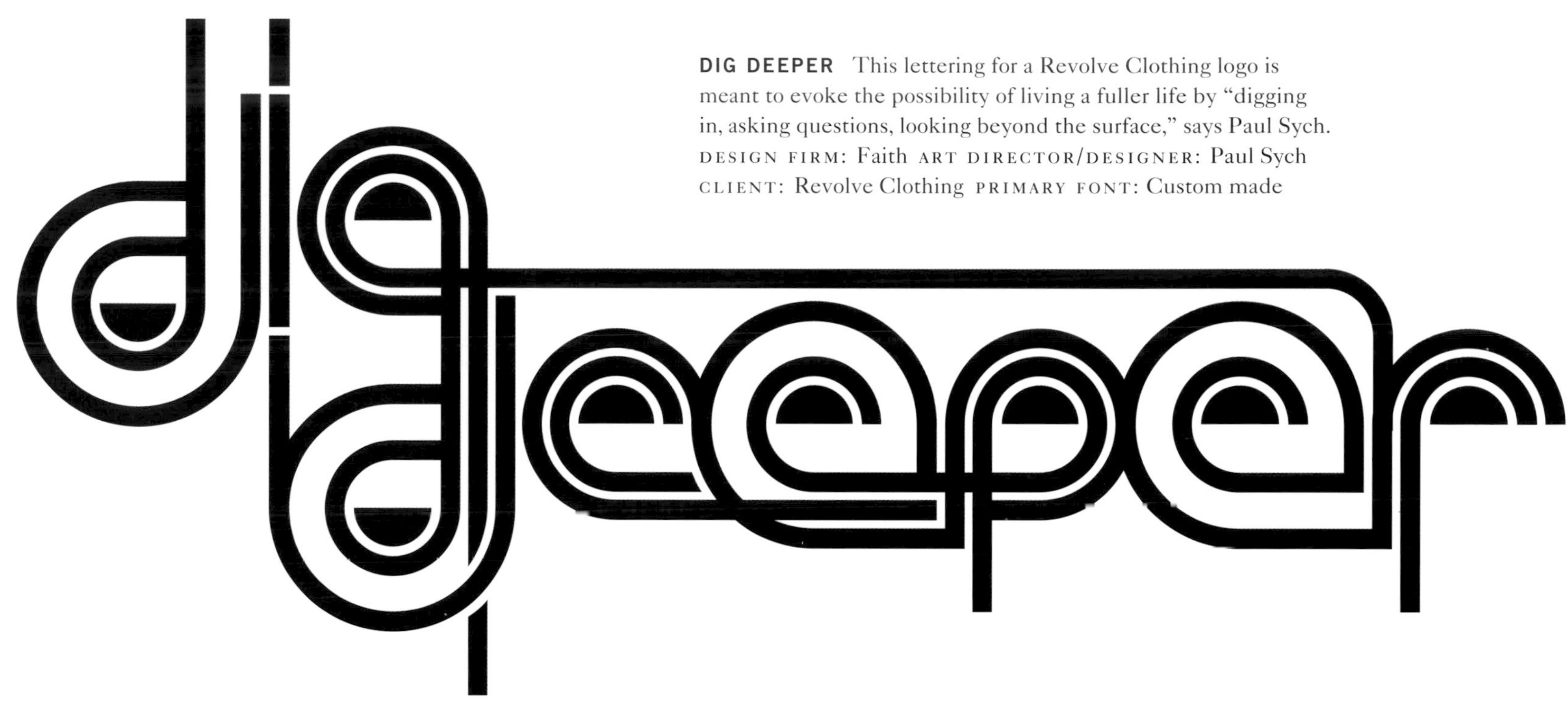

DIG DEEPER This lettering for a Revolve Clothing logo is meant to evoke the possibility of living a fuller life by "digging in, asking questions, looking beyond the surface," says Paul Sych. DESIGN FIRM: Faith ART DIRECTOR/DESIGNER: Paul Sych CLIENT: Revolve Clothing PRIMARY FONT: Custom made

SALUTE THE SOUND This typeface was custom designed for a music production company event. "I attempted to create a typeface by using various line weights that would emit vibrations when it was viewed," says Paul Sych. DESIGN FIRM: Faith ART DIRECTOR: Paul Sych DESIGNER: Paul Sych CLIENT: Bass the Beat Productions PRIMARY FONT: Custom made

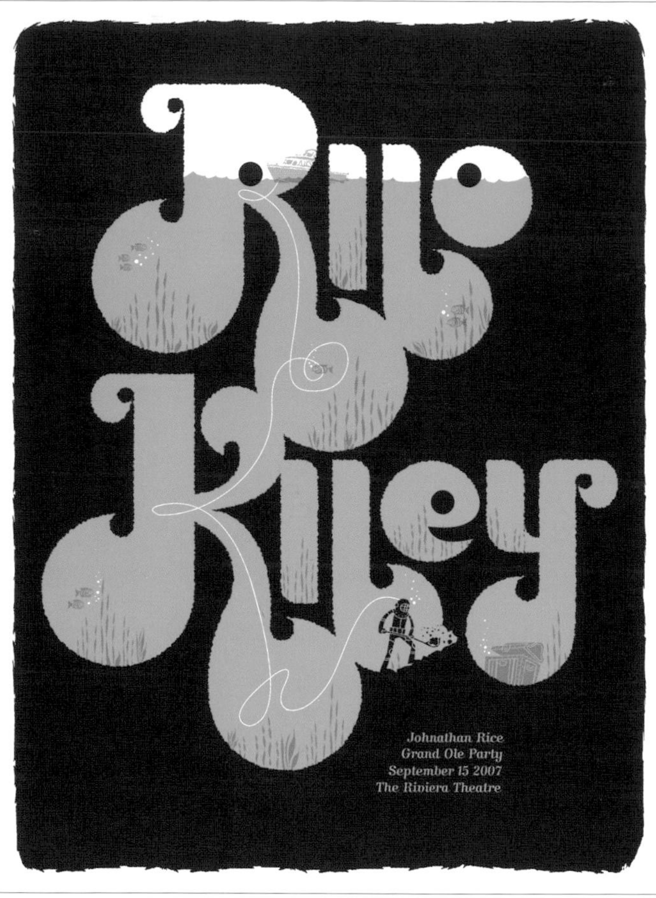

RILO KILEY There is a kids' Pop influence in this concert poster, which John Solimine suggests is derived from "watching too many *Jonny Quest* reruns." DESIGN FIRM: Spike Press ART DIRECTOR/DESIGNER/ILLUSTRATOR: John Solimine CLIENT: Metro Chicago PUBLISHER: Spike Press PRIMARY FONT: Hand lettering

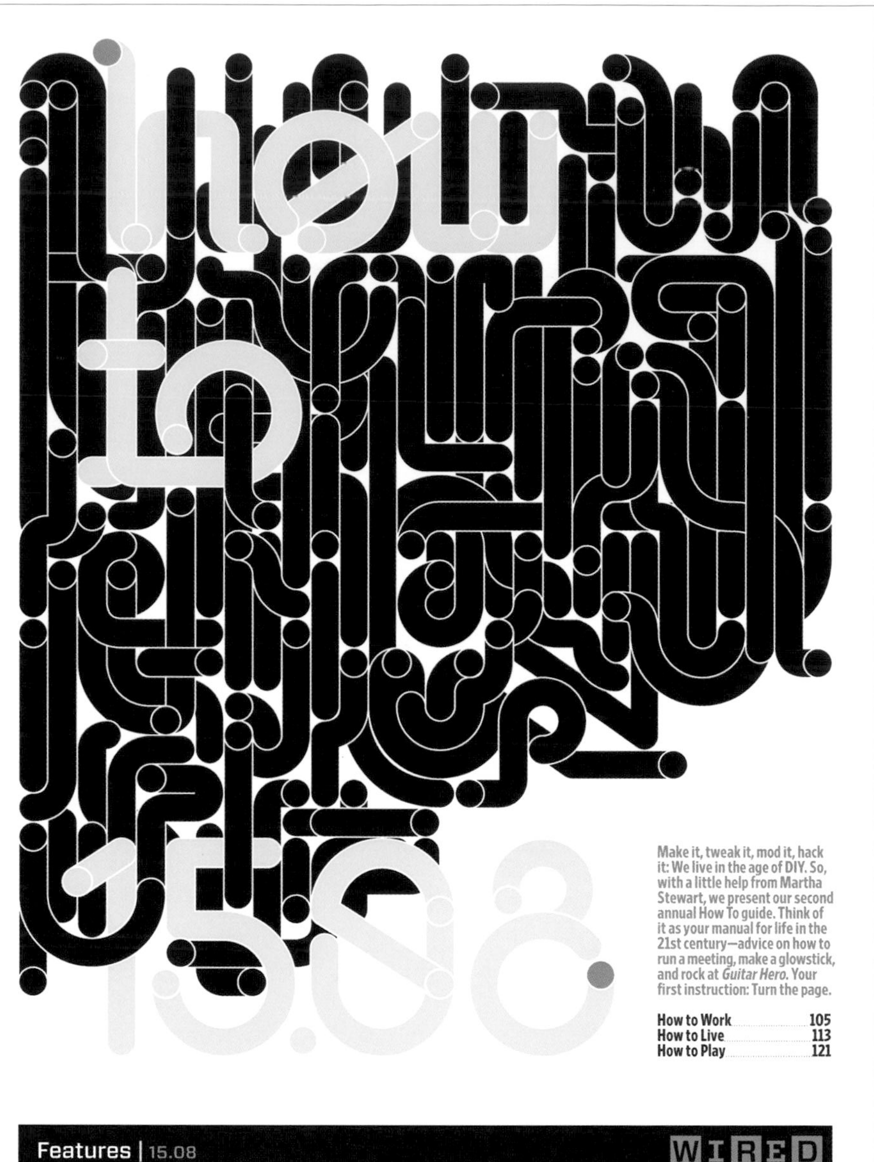

15.08 HOW TO This splash page for *Wired* magazine looks like a mess of circuit wires but, if examined closely, is actually composed of letters. It recalls the supergraphics of the 1970s. CREATIVE DIRECTOR: Scott Dadich ART DIRECTOR/DESIGNER: Maili Holiman ILLUSTRATOR: Seth Ferris CLIENT: *Wired* magazine PUBLISHER: Condé Nast FONT: Custom made

DOUBLE DAGGER This logo featured on *Luxury*, a cassette released by the post-punk band Double Dagger, which was recorded on a boombox with one microphone. "The visual effect of the repeating lines matches the intense volume of the band, while the shaky lines and overlapping letters could be influenced by the lo-fi recording," says Bruce Willen, "or it could just look cool." DESIGN FIRM: Post Typography ART DIRECTOR/DESIGNER: Bruce Willen CLIENT: Double Dagger PRIMARY FONT: Hand lettering

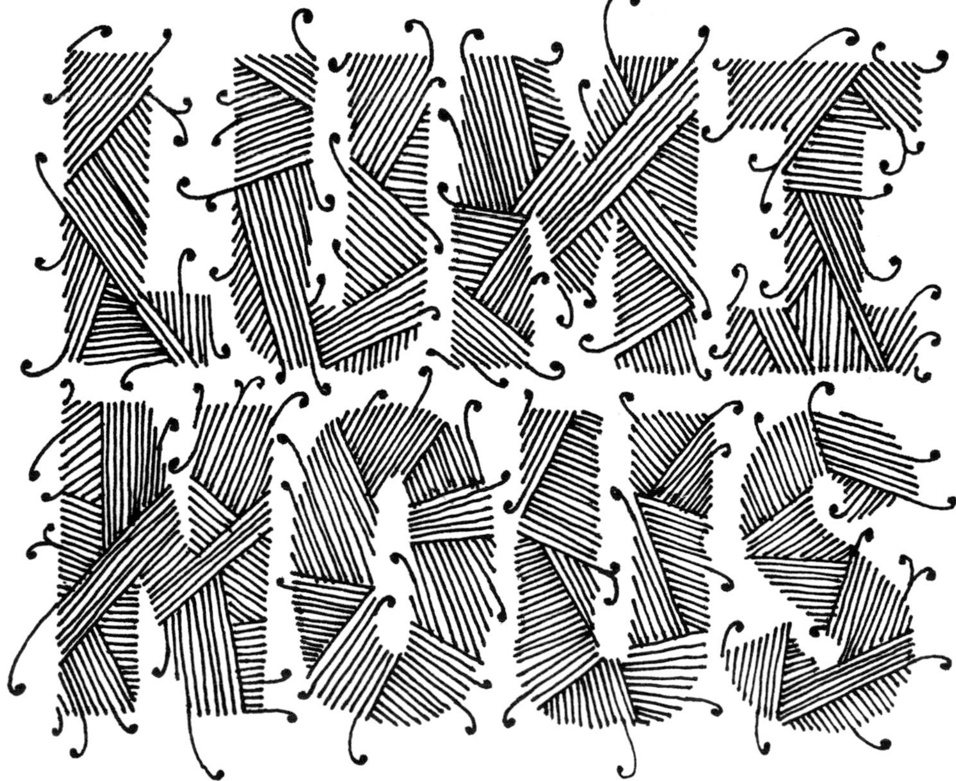

LUMINOUS Kris Sowersby did not reference anything in particular for this book-jacket type (which was not used in the final design). "It just grew out of a session of sketching!" he says. Yet it nonetheless is apt for the Zeitgeist. DESIGN FIRM: The Letterheads Ltd. ART DIRECTOR/DESIGNER: Kris Sowersby CLIENT/PUBLISHER: Huia PRIMARY FONT: Hand lettering, based on National Compressed Extrabold

PSYCHEDELIC

FOR SOME, PSYCHEDELIC design symbolized misspent, addled youth. For others, it encapsulated the very best of times (or, on a bad trip, the worst). Now, it is the graphic style that represents the sex, drugs, and rock 'n' roll era of the late 1960s, when visual language was an important cultural form, and lettering and typography (borrowed in part from the Victorian and Art Nouveau periods) was a code for an alternative generation. Psychedelic styles faded by the early 1970s, but in the 1990s the vibrating colors and pulsating, curvilinear letterforms returned as a way of signaling a new, hip culture. Today's Psychedelic is less drug-influenced, more pastiche, but nonetheless joyously evokes a period when the rules of type were thrown out the window.

PLEASE The combination of hand lettering and digitally created decorative elements in this self-promotional piece recalls the halcyon days of the 1960s, when virtually all the ambient design was done by hand.
DESIGN FIRM: Yulia Brodskaya ART DIRECTOR/DESIGNER/ ILLUSTRATOR: Yulia Brodskaya CLIENT: Self PRIMARY FONT: Hand lettering

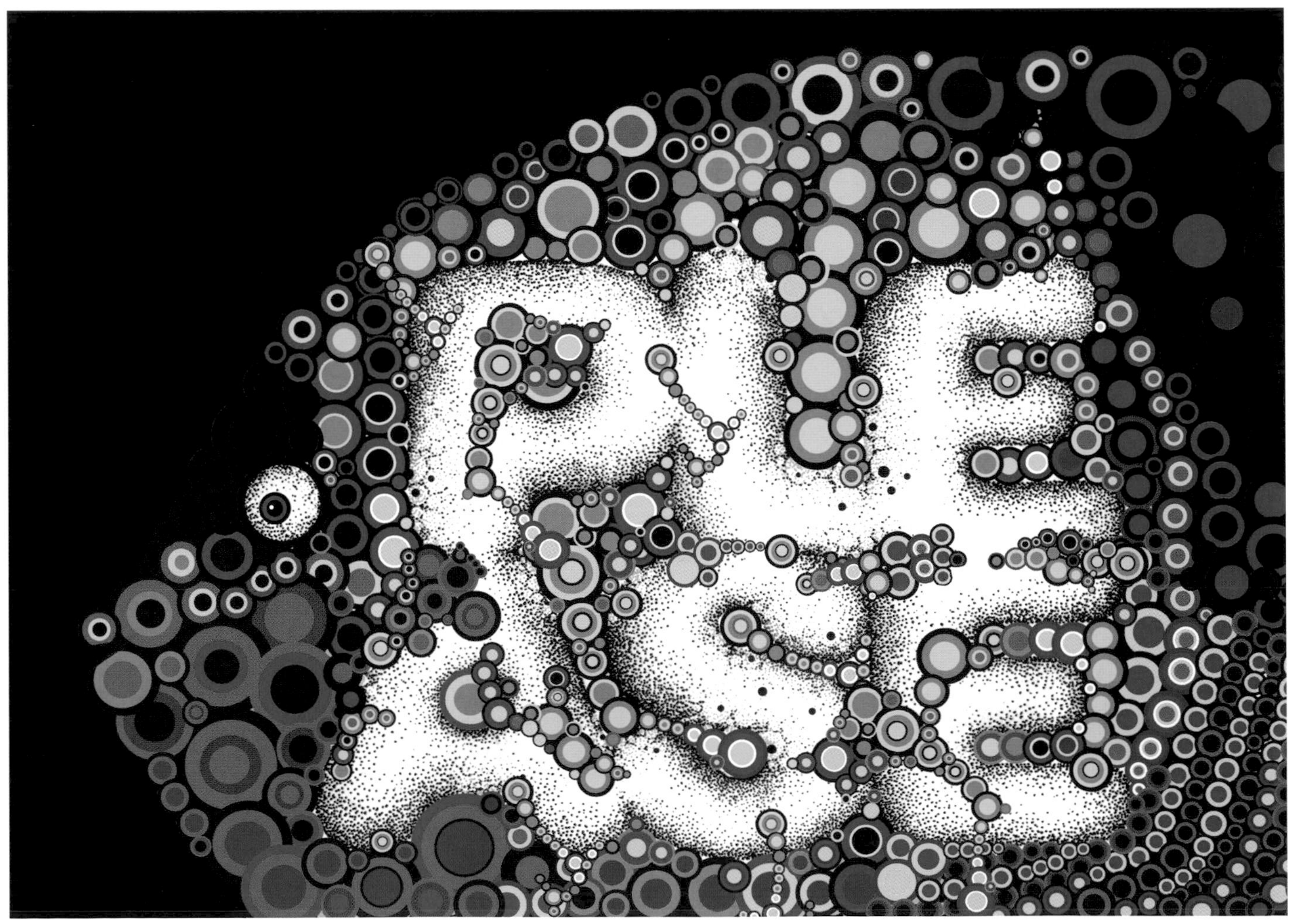

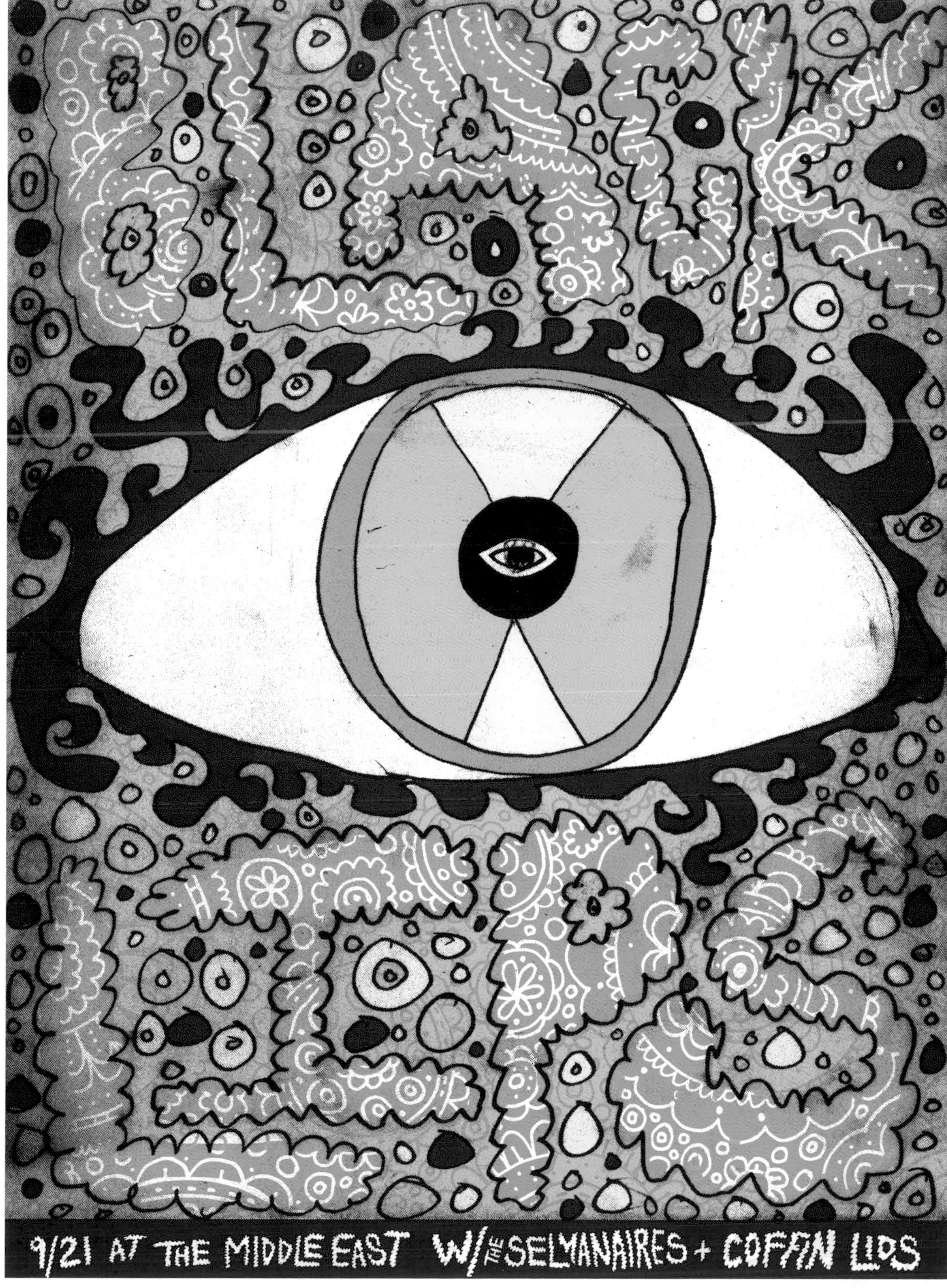

BLACK LIPS It seems like only yesterday it was current, yet the Psychedelic poster style is now over forty years old. Today it is being channeled through designs such as this concert poster.
DESIGN FIRM: NateDuval.com
ART DIRECTOR/DESIGNER/ ILLUSTRATOR: Nate Duval CLIENT: The Middle East Club PUBLISHER: Self PRIMARY FONT: Hand lettering

FLAMING LIPS This poster was inspired by old sci-fi posters and book covers, and was heavily influenced by listening to the Flaming Lips's music during the design.
DESIGN FIRM: Modern Dog Design Co. ART DIRECTOR/DESIGNER/ILLUSTRATOR: Michael Strassburger CLIENT: Sasquatch Music Festival, Live Nation, Adam Zacks PRIMARY FONT: Hand lettering

MUDCRUTCH FILLMORE POSTER
Mudcrutch was Tom Petty's first band, originally formed thirty-five years ago, "so we wanted the revival poster to be in a style inspired by some of the classic Fillmore posters," says Marq Spusta. "I've always admired the freehand liquid lettering and illustrations of those early Fillmore poster artists like Rick Griffin and Greg Irons, and that is coming through on this one."
ART DIRECTORS: Arlene Owseichik and the Man Behind the Curtain DESIGNER/ ILLUSTRATOR: Marq Spusta CLIENT: Bill Graham Presents PRIMARY FONT: Hand lettering

PSYCHEDELIC

NOISECAPE 2 Zeloot based this poster design on an image of planets from a Chinese science textbook. "The images for Noisecape needed to arouse some sort of uneasy physical sensation as it is a noise and performance festival," she explains. Noise-music is a very raw, often improvised kind of music in which the body of the musician is an important part of the performance.
DESIGN FIRM: Zeloot DESIGNER/ ILLUSTRATOR: Zeloot CLIENT: De Garage PRIMARY FONT: Hand lettering

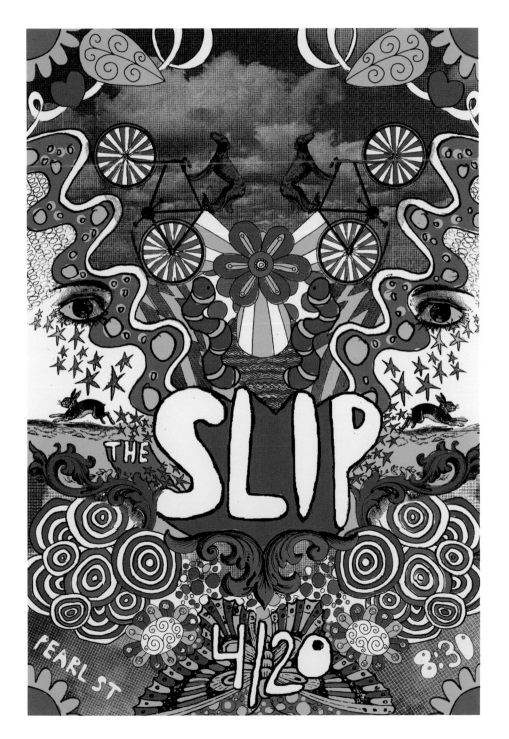

LET LEONARD IN The most obvious references for this poster for Seattle Aquarium derive from 1960s rock imagery, specifically from posters for the Fillmore West, San Francisco.
DESIGN FIRM: Modern Dog Design Co. ART DIRECTORS: Michael Strassburger, Robynne Raye DESIGNER/ ILLUSTRATOR: Shogo Ota CLIENT: Seattle Aquarium PRIMARY FONT: Hand lettering

THE SLIP The Slip is a three-piece rock band, heavily based on the blues/rock format, so Nate Duval decided to reference Cream's *Disraeli Gears* album cover (another, classic, three-piece blues-based band) as inspiration for this poster. He used song lyrics and titles to inspire the visual content. To enhance the Psychedelic concept, he hand-printed the poster, using black light-sensitive inks that glow brightly under UV light.
DESIGN FIRM: NateDuval.com ART DIRECTOR/DESIGNER: Nate Duval ILLUSTRATORS: Nate Duval, Jen Skelley CLIENT: Iron Horse Entertainment Group PUBLISHER: Nate Duval PRIMARY FONT: Hand lettering

PSYCHEDELIC

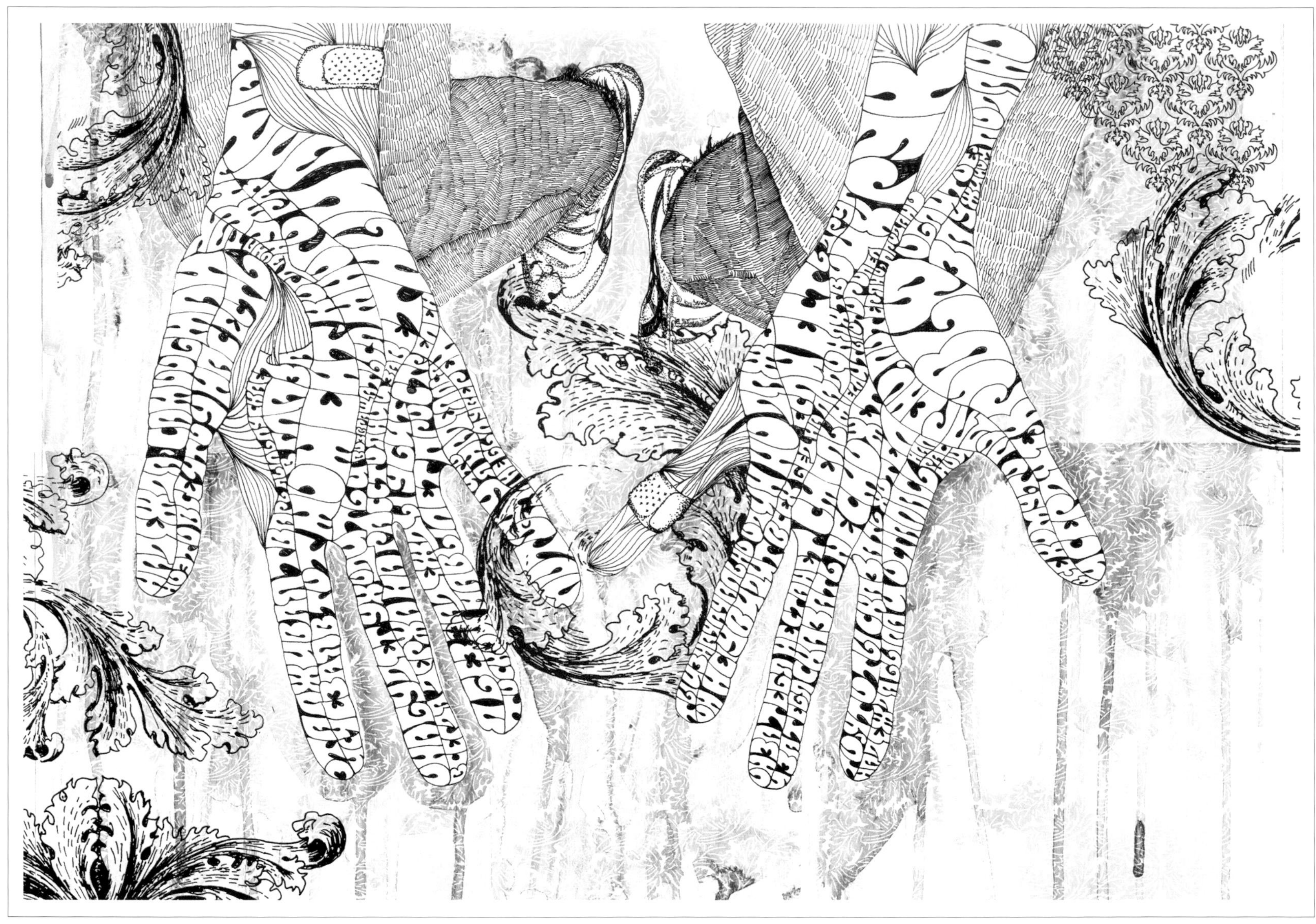

SPERANZA Explaining his influences, or lack thereof, Fiodor Sumkin says of this self-promotion piece: "There are no wild, flowing flourishes or [Victor] Moscoso letters in this restrained piece; it's still my own style."
ART DIRECTOR/DESIGNER/ILLUSTRATOR: Fiodor Sumkin
CLIENT: Self PRIMARY FONT: Hand lettering

AIGA This bag, produced for an AIGA lecture, was inspired by 1960s patterns and typography; an old style, but definitely not forgotten.
DESIGN FIRM: Urban Inks ART DIRECTORS/DESIGNERS/ILLUSTRATORS: Reed Burgoyne, Sarah Mead CLIENT: Self-initiated for AIGA lecture giveaway bags PUBLISHER: Urban Inks PRIMARY FONT: Hand lettering

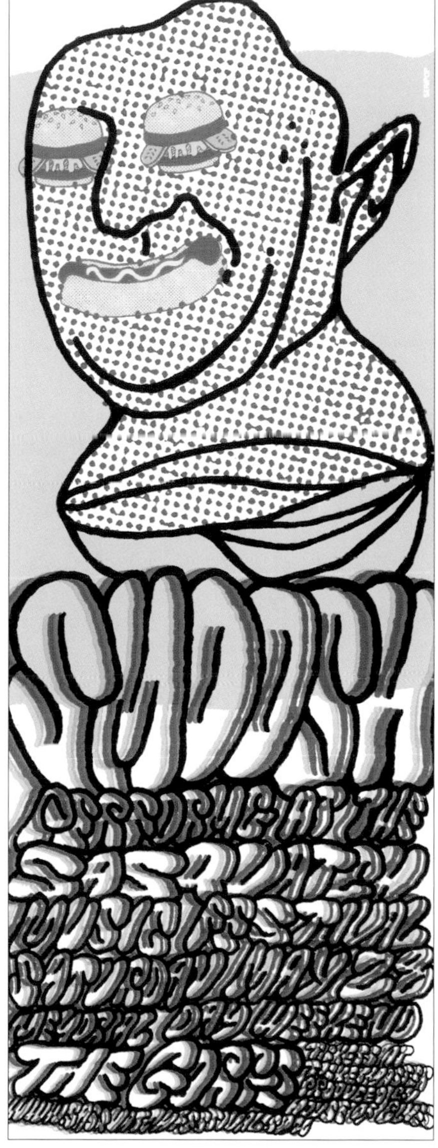

SMOOSH The face drawing shown here was something that Seripop had created previously; the lettering was produced to replicate the face in letterforms, trying to stay close to the idea of child drawings and sugary pop music. The fast-food items are puns for the weird pop flavor of the teenage band, but, says Chloe Lum, "I can't stop having afterthoughts of a vague reference to the lures used for child kidnapping…I guess it ended up being a very dark pun on the age of the band members. I swear it was unconscious."
DESIGN FIRM: Seripop ART DIRECTORS/DESIGNERS/ILLUSTRATORS: Yannick Desranleau, Chloe Lum CLIENT: Sasquatch Festival PRIMARY FONT: Hand lettering

HIP-HOP

FOR MOST PEOPLE, Hip-Hop conjures up waves of graffiti, the scrawled, bulbous letters that evoke the inner city and were once found mostly on tagged subway trains. Graffiti has always existed, but when tagging became a virtual movement in the late 1970s and early 1980s, the style changed from artless to artful. All of a sudden monumentally shadowed letters and combinations of script and block came to characterize the form. Now that Hip-Hop is a bona fide fashion style, the graphics are decidedly more self-conscious and mannered, but the bravado remains.

BADROOM The "Badroom" was a two-man art exhibition in a Carhartt shop in Budapest, which featured the work of Blik and Drez, two street-influenced designers. The "Bad" is an amalgamation of the two names.
DESIGN FIRM: Blikdsgn ART DIRECTOR/DESIGNER/ILLUSTRATOR: Daniel Blik CLIENT: Self PRIMARY FONT: Hand lettering

STRANGE For this self-promotional piece, quintessential graffiti lettering is combined with neo-Art Nouveau graphic ornamentation in a marriage of street art and mannered mélange.
DESIGN FIRM: Blikdsgn ART DIRECTOR/DESIGNER/ILLUSTRATOR: Daniel Blik CLIENT: Self PRIMARY FONT: Hand lettering

FREAK The type treatment for this *GQ* spread is inspired by rapper Lil Wayne's many tattoos.
DESIGN DIRECTOR: Fred Woodward DESIGNER/ILLUSTRATOR: Chelsea Cardinal PHOTOGRAPHER: Terry Richardson CLIENT: *GQ* magazine PUBLISHER: Condé Nast
PRIMARY FONT: Hand lettering

HIP-HOP

GRAFFITI These abstracted computer-generated letterforms are drawn directly from a graffiti tag: "Trick," Andrei Robu's nickname as a street artist. In general, graffiti artists paint only their names, using different shapes and styles. These were hand drawn and then vectorized in Adobe Illustrator.
DESIGN FIRM: Acme Industries ART DIRECTOR/DESIGNER: Andrei Robu PRIMARY FONT: Custom made

CULTURAL URBANA This orgy of black-and-white letters was influenced by the 1970s, Letraset press-down type, and Alex Trochut's favorite source: *Phil's Photo*, a type catalog from the 1980s. DESIGN FIRM: Alex Trochut and Inocuo The Sign ART DIRECTOR: Inocuo The Sign DESIGNER: Alex Trochut CLIENT: Inocuo The Sign PRIMARY FONTS: 1970s hard-shadowed treatment for various fonts and modular systems

BY ITS NATURE, Tech should not be ornamental; it should be spare and mechanical. Yet it has evolved into a new form of ornament by borrowing from historical and vernacular sources. On the one hand, Tech type is bitmapped and computer-esque; on the other, it manipulates lettering to give it a high-technology aesthetic. Tech makes the old look new, and the new look even newer.

SWIM Edward Leida says, "The severe minimalist black swimsuit along with the graphic nature of this photograph immediately reminded me of the bar code. Being true to the style, varying widths of rules are used in order to create contrast. To finish the piece, the headline and credits are generated from a combination of inverted and flipped numerals and letters."
ART DIRECTOR/DESIGNER: Edward Leida PHOTOGRAPHER: Paolo Roversi CLIENT: *W* magazine PUBLISHER: Condé Nast
PRIMARY FONTS: Libris, Italian Garamond

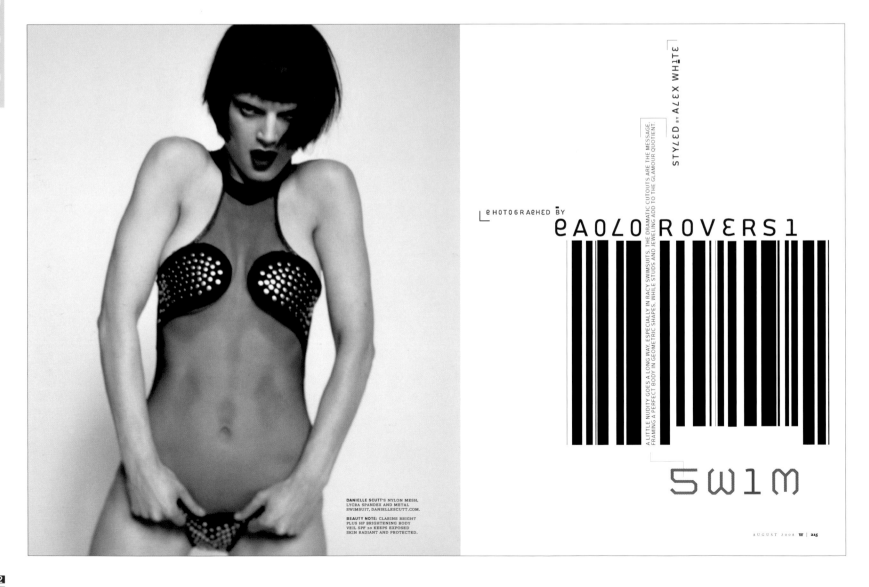

DANIELLE SCUTT'S NYLON MESH, LYCRA SPANDEX AND METAL SWIMSUIT, DANIELLESCUTT.COM.

BEAUTY NOTE: CLARINS BRIGHT PLUS HP BRIGHTENING BODY VEIL SPF 20 KEEPS EXPOSED SKIN RADIANT AND PROTECTED.

STYLED BY ALEX WHITE

A LITTLE NUDITY GOES A LONG WAY, ESPECIALLY IN RACY SWIMSUITS. THE DRAMATIC CUTOUTS ARE THE MESSAGE, FRAMING A PERFECT BODY IN GEOMETRIC SHAPES, WHILE STUDS AND JEWELING ADD TO THE GLAMOUR QUOTIENT.

PHOTOGRAPHED BY PAOLO ROVERSI

SWIM

AUGUST 2008 W | 215

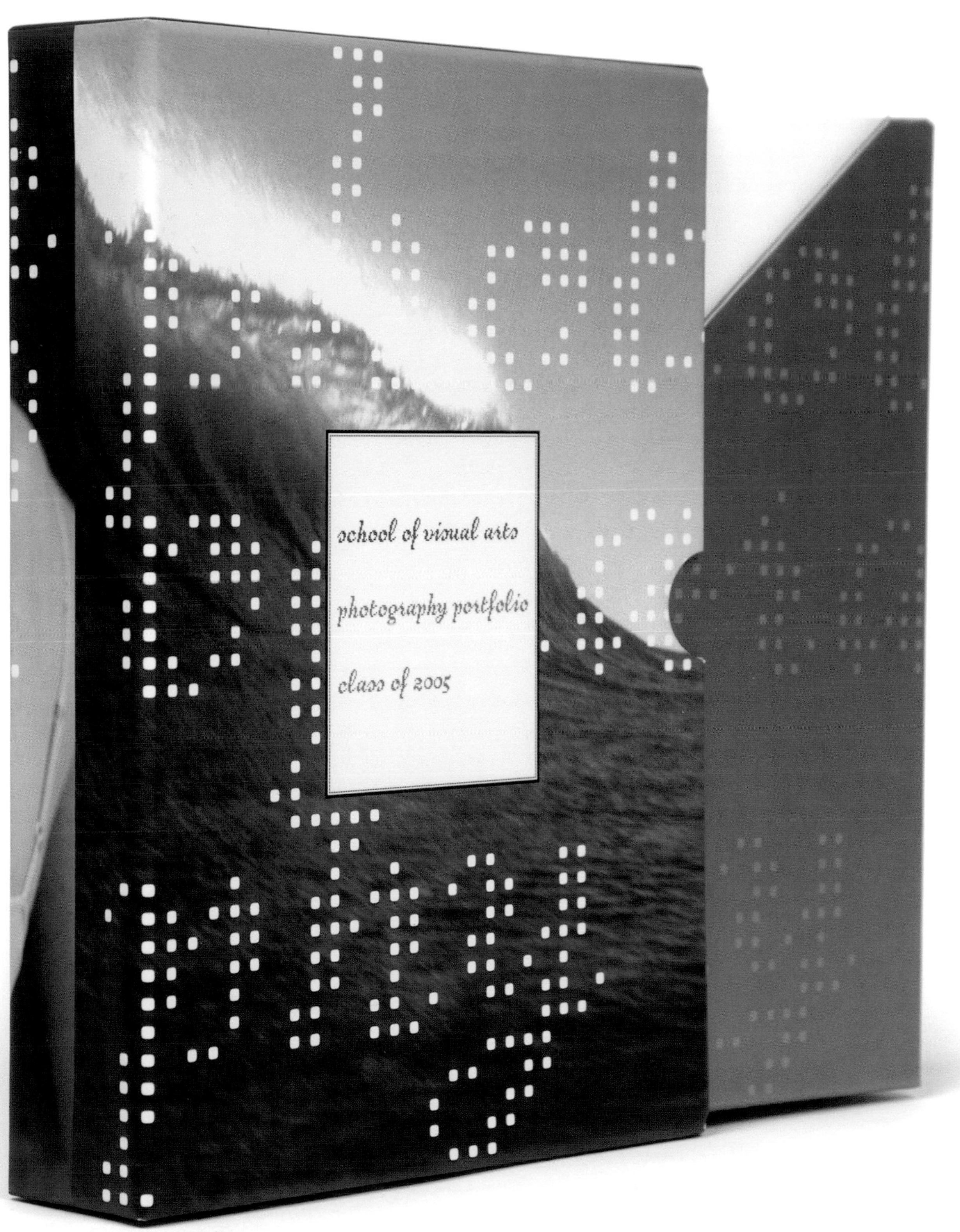

BFA PHOTOGRAPHY PORTFOLIO 2005 This typography was inspired partly by dot matrix patterns and partly by signage in industrial or transportation contexts, including train and LED signs. "These can be very decorative and ornamental when taken out of context, placed over an unexpected image or wrapped around a box of photographs," says Brankica Kovrlija.
DESIGN FIRM: Visual Arts Press
ART DIRECTOR: Michael J. Walsh
DESIGNER: Brankica Kovrlija
PHOTOGRAPHER: Loreto Caceres
CLIENT: The School of Visual Arts, BFA Photography Department
PRIMARY FONT: Custom made

STARTLE Each letter here is represented by simple 3-D cubes. Daniel Howe repeatedly applied a noise function in order to texture each cube face in a unique way. Since each cube is a 3-D object, when displayed digitally the different parts of each letter can move about or rotate independently. And, because the noise function is "probabilistic," each time a letter is rendered, it is unique – that is, no two "A"s will look exactly alike.
DESIGNER: Daniel C. Howe CLIENT: Self PRIMARY FONT: Startle

FindReplace

Show Available Discs Only

Find What:

InvalidObject %macro.end

REPLACE

Now Paste From Clipboard

Uninstall

SQL syntax error 0215.769

Encoding:

FINDREPLACE This family of faces is the result of experimentation with the FindReplace feature in the program FontLab 4.6 (renamed Find Outline in FontLab Studio 5). Just as in word-processing programs, the feature will find and replace elements with new components. Here, the thinnest weight was designed and refined and then simply replaced with progressively thicker elements to make the bolder weights. DESIGNER: Eric Olson PUBLISHER: Process Type Foundry PRIMARY FONTS: FindReplace Thin, Light, Regular, Medium, Bold and Black

FIG

Lens cleaner
Now free with manufacturers coupon
New Specials
have been added to increase speed
LONG PLAYING
Audio source connection
Connection Speed
FINISH AUDIO
systematically structured
Golden Oldies

FIG FIG is named after and inspired by the collaboration of Frank Sheeran, Ian Chai, and Glenn Chappell that produced the FIGlet computer application, which is used for making large letters out of ordinary text. DESIGNER: Eric Olson PUBLISHER: Process Type Foundry PRIMARY FONTS: FIG Sans, FIG Serif, FIG Script

NON-ROMAN

THE PRIMARY SOURCE of Western type is the Roman letter. But not every nation uses it. Chinese and Japanese pictograms are possibly a more efficient kind of lettering – certainly, a more sculptural kind. Cyrillic is also exotic to Western eyes, and through the influence of Russian Constructivism led the way in modern typography of the 1920s. Arabic lettering, while the least sophisticated in terms of typographic trends, is one of the most gorgeous of all calligraphic alphabets. Other non-Roman typographies provide a variety of unique perspectives on composition, some of them significant in the West. Transforming these alphabets into conceptual letterforms can be challenging, and sometimes beautiful.

SHADOW PLAY IS FUN These characters, featured in the "China Shadow" graphics exhibition (Shanghai, 2006), were devised from traditional Chinese paper cuts and shadow plays, with a hint of the Post-Modern primitive for good measure.
DESIGN FIRM: Q2 Design ART DIRECTOR/DESIGNER/ILLUSTRATOR: Qian Qian CLIENT: China Shadow Project PRIMARY FONT: Song (Heavy)

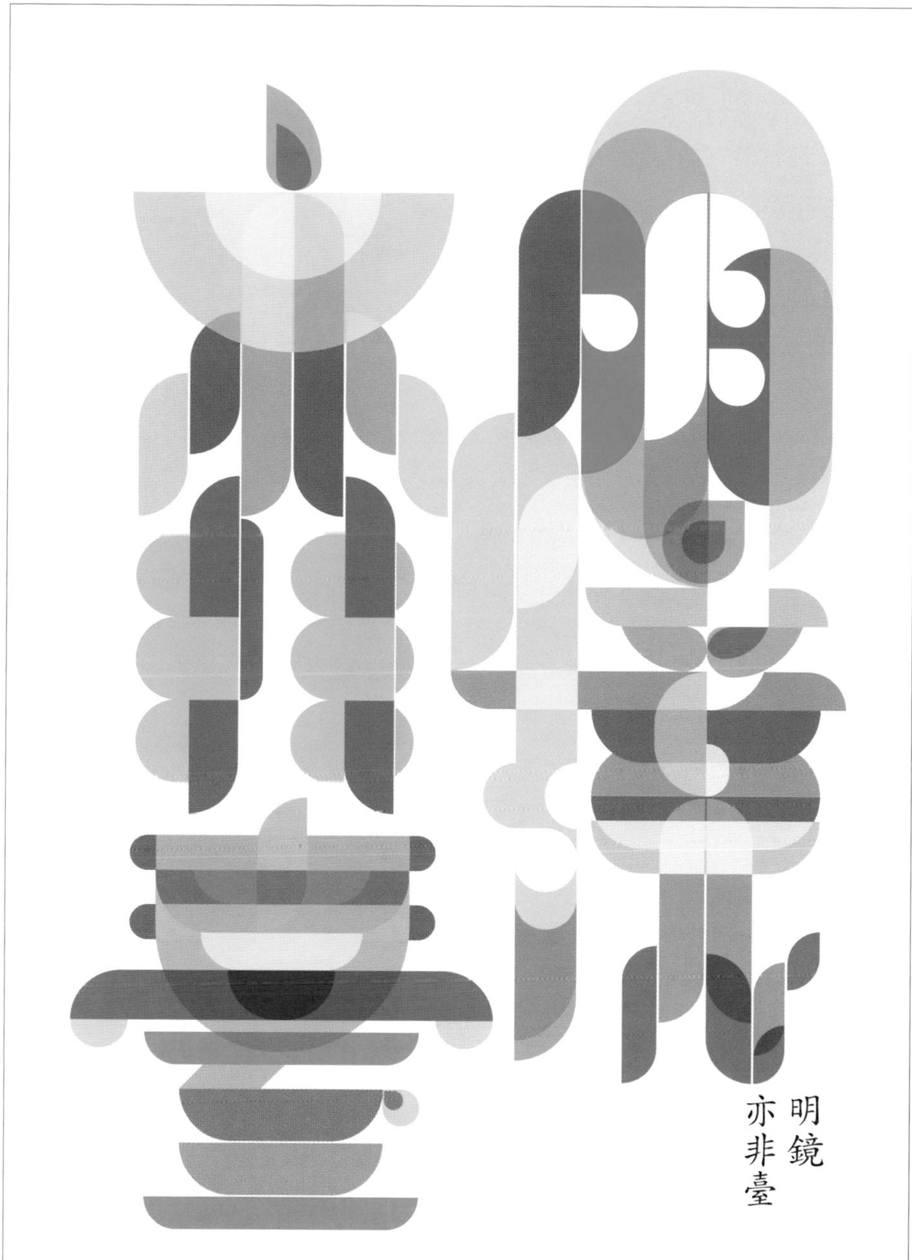

пол теру

Путешественник Гилстреп или тоска по родине

перевод-Светланы Силаковой. иллюстратор-Дилан Марторелл

В кронах рожковых деревьев стоял гвалт. Ясное дело, бабуины. Эти неугомонные твари любят восседать на ветках, скорчившись в три погибели, и щелкать стручки, радостно скаля свои острые собачьи зубы.

В радиусе пятидесяти футов от рожкового дерева ночевать нежелательно. Но Гилстреп ничуть не расстроился. – Ладно! – вскричал он с бодрым фатализмом, подкрутив усы. Им руководила высокая цель.

Он вознамерился отыскать племя, известное под именем «Толстопалые тамбо». Как всякий настоящий исследователь, Гилстреп знал: любое путешествие – лишь нескончаемая череда нежданных столкновений, и бабуины, роняющие вокруг с веток рожкового дерева, – это еще ерунда. Зато он на Зимбабе (так звалась местная река в нижнем ее течении).

Зато он не в Мадфорде: не в родном городе, покинутом так давно, что Гилстреп напрочь позабыл, что за деревья там растут и что за люди живут – в памяти застряли лишь те, кто изводил его в детстве, да женщина, тщетно ожидавшая его из странствий. Звали ее Эльвира Хауи. Мадфорд бесповоротно остался в прошлом. Как все, что помнится нам лишь смутно, он казался каким-то ненастоящим и слегка абсурдным, словно то был не реальный город, а детская игрушка, которую Гилстреп забросил, еще тогда, когда его называли «Фредди с Уэбстер-стрит».

Гилстреп охотно терпел лишения, но нестерпимо страдал, если ему досаждали. Потому-то он и бежал из Мадфорда. И с Эльвирой порвал: она ведь едва не связала его по рукам и ногам, поскольку ни за что не желала покинуть этот уродливый город.

Скоро Рождество. Отлично! Он там, где ему хочется быть, на другой стороне земного шара, в Центральной Африке, на берегах Зимбабы под сенью рожковых деревьев и винтерторнов. Гилстреп сознавал: если бы сейчас он находился в любой другой точке планеты, его неудержимо тянуло бы назад, на Зимбабу.

Иногда во время пеших переходов, шагая в одиночестве вдоль реки под жаркими лучами солнца, погрузившись в приятный транс полной удовлетворенности собой, Гилстреп вдруг вспоминал Мадфорд более отчетливо и морщился. [illegible] Эльвира Хауи, зарабатывающая на жизнь уроками музыки, и гостиная ее дома, где она занимается с учениками, и весь ее дом, стоящий у Крэддокского моста в двух шагах от федерального шоссе; и само шоссе, проходящее по эстакаде, которая днем отбрасывала на город зловещую тень, а ночью озаряла его ослепительным светом фар и прожекторов; и шум машин, заглушающий арфу Эльвиры. Даже в темное время суток Мадфорд не знал, что такое тишина.

Опоры эстакады были разрисованы граффити, а под ее сводами ютились в своеобразных вигвамах бомжи и алкаши. Тут Гилстреп начинал перебирать в памяти все, что было ему особенно омерзительно: мусор, грязные задние сиденья мадфордских такси, бессмысленные улыбки таксистов. Звуки закусочной: «хлюп-хлюп-хлюп» засасываемой кока-колы, громкий скрежет ледяных кубиков на зубах. Цирковые тигры и собачки, надетые задом наперед бейсболки, ликующая фальшь статей в «Мадфорд мессенджере». Грязные руки, холодные глаза, рекламные щиты, дурной запах изо ртов, почти все

118 *Esquire* ИЮЛЬ – АВГУСТ 2006

PAUL THEROUX'S STORY A story by the travel writer and novelist is set in Cyrillic lettering with accompanying ornamental illustration for Russian *Esquire* magazine.
ART DIRECTORS: Dmitry Barbanel, Maksim Nikanorov
ILLUSTRATOR: Dylan Martorell CLIENT: *Esquire* magazine
PUBLISHER: Independent Media Sanoma Magazines PRIMARY FONTS: Hand lettering

THE PUTI TREE "I am a follower of Buddhism and believe that creativity can be derived from its teachings," says Nod Young. "This work is a typographic interpretation of two poems quoted from the original Zen classic, *The Platform Sutra of the Sixth Patriarch*, which dates back almost 1,500 years." These poems teach us not to believe all that exists, not even the reflection of ourselves in a mirror. We must learn instead to overcome the rules and boundaries of our existence in order to reach a state of enlightenment, unfettered by the perceived limitations of life. "I have used basic visual elements and colors to create a typographical work that represents my interpretation of design and Buddhism," says Young.
DESIGN FIRM: Khaki Creative & Design ART DIRECTOR: Nod Young CLIENT: Self PRIMARY FONT: Not based on any fonts

NON-ROMAN

ЖИЗНЬ
ПРЕКРАСНА!

ST CLAIR "This is part of my early typographic research," says Fiodor Sumkin. "In my opinion, in Cyrillic, St Clair has not lost its Roman charm and looks like it is from tsarist Russia." In Russian the text says, "LIFE IS BEAUTIFUL!"
ART DIRECTOR/DESIGNER/ILLUSTRATOR: Fiodor Sumkin CLIENT: Self PRIMARY FONT: Hand lettering

قناة الغد

مباشر

خبر عاجل

الاخبار السياسية

و

خط عربي صُمم خصيصاً للشاشة

قناة الغد ATV Jordan

هل العالم كله يشاهد؟

العالم كله يشاهد

Regular الغد Ghad

Bold الغد Ghad

Regular الغد: الخط المعتمد للقناة الفضائية الأردنية

Bold الغد: الخط المعتمد للقناة الفضائية الاردنية

ATRISSI-GHAD Tarek Atrissi's website has been developed to promote Arabic typography and lettering. The font used here is from his ongoing series of contemporary Arabic typefaces.
DESIGN FIRM: Tarek Atrissi Design ART DIRECTOR/DESIGNER: Tarek Atrissi CLIENT: *Al Ghad* newspaper, Amman, Jordan PRIMARY FONT: Atrissi-Ghad Arabic Regular and Bold

NINE WORDS This font was specially designed for an organizer of onstage Kung Fu productions. Each character tells a story, and was based on traditional character motifs used in old Chinese scriptures and modern typefaces. DESIGN FIRM: Khaki Creative & Design ART DIRECTOR: Nod Young CLIENT: Poly Agency PRIMARY FONT: Custom made, based on standard Hei and Buddhist Scripture typefaces

DUBAI In this advertisement the shape of a plane is created from the forms of Arabic calligraphy. The word spelled out within the design is: "SOON."
ADVERTISING AGENCY: RKCR/Y&R ART DIRECTORS: Rob Messeter, Mike Crow DESIGNER: Rob Messeter ILLUSTRATOR/HAND LETTERER: Alison Carmichael CLIENT: Virgin Atlantic PRIMARY FONT: Hand lettering

ANKARA This typeface was inspired by the highly stylized Arabic characters that decorate the Emir Sultan Mosque in Bursa, Turkey. It is a cross between Arabic and modern Western faces, and was designed to promote an online resource for Turkish graphic design. ART DIRECTOR/DESIGNER: Serifcan Ozcan CLIENT: biyografik.com PRIMARY FONT: Ankara

NON-ROMAN

WELCOME TO BEIJING Top (from left): Guomao/Central Business District, Di'anmen Gate, Shatan. Middle (from left): Dashanzi 798 Art District, Summer Palace, Zhongguancun Technology District, Beijing Zoo. Bottom (from left): Yonghegong (Lama Temple), Panjiayuan Antique Market, "Ghost" Street Restaurant Row. Chinese words are constructed as pictographs, so every character can be seen as an image. For this series, Nod Young used the "locational" features of each landmark to express its characters graphically. For instance, Panjiayuan Antique Market is expressed as a traditional engraved chop (a chop is a stamp used to identify individual and organizational entities), and Yonghegong (the Lama Temple) is shaped like the temple itself. DESIGN FIRM: Khaki Creative & Design ART DIRECTOR: Nod Young CLIENT: Khaki Creative & Design PRIMARY FONTS: Traditional Chinese fonts and graffiti

حرية
The beauty of Rajae's art is complex. It is bathed in the love of a passionate soul, it shines with the hopes & dreams of an idealist, it bleeds from the wounds of an UNJUST WORLD, it marches forward with the courage of a revolutionary, it carries the infinite wisdom of a learned sage, it laughs with the innocence of a blissful child, it flies with the freedom of an enlightened spirit. It is rock, it is jazz, it is pop, it is drum 'n bass, it is Arab, it is European, it is native, it is foreign, it is poetry, it is philosophy, it is unique, it is beauty in every word, every chord and every beat. The spirit of Rajae now flows to the world through her art as her songwriting, composing, producing and singing have given birth to a form of music that is truly her own
رجاء

ARTIST PROMOTIONAL POSTER Classic Arabic calligraphy is the basis for the lettering on the singer Rajae El Mouhandiz's jacket, which says, "Freedom." The skirt, however, is Western. The words reflect Rajae's own life, as she has broken many of the norms and expectations surrounding the lives of Moroccan women.
DESIGN FIRM: Tarek Atrissi Design ART DIRECTOR/DESIGNER: Tarek Atrissi CLIENT: Rajae El Mouhandiz PRIMARY FONTS: Hand lettering and AXT Bassima

FASHION STORY Actors, directors and writers were invited to Mikhailovskoe, Pushkin's estate, by the editors of Russian *Esquire* to take part in making this special issue. The display text is a variant of Art Nouveau in Cyrillic and the fonts were taken from Pushkin's *The Tale of Tsar Saltan*, illustrated by Ivan Bilibin in 1913.
ART DIRECTOR/DESIGNER: Dmitry Barbanel PHOTOGRAPHER: Pavel Samokhvalov LETTERING: Yury Gordon CLIENT: *Esquire* magazine, Russia PUBLISHER: Independent Media Sanoma Magazines PRIMARY FONTS: Historic fonts

NON-ROMAN

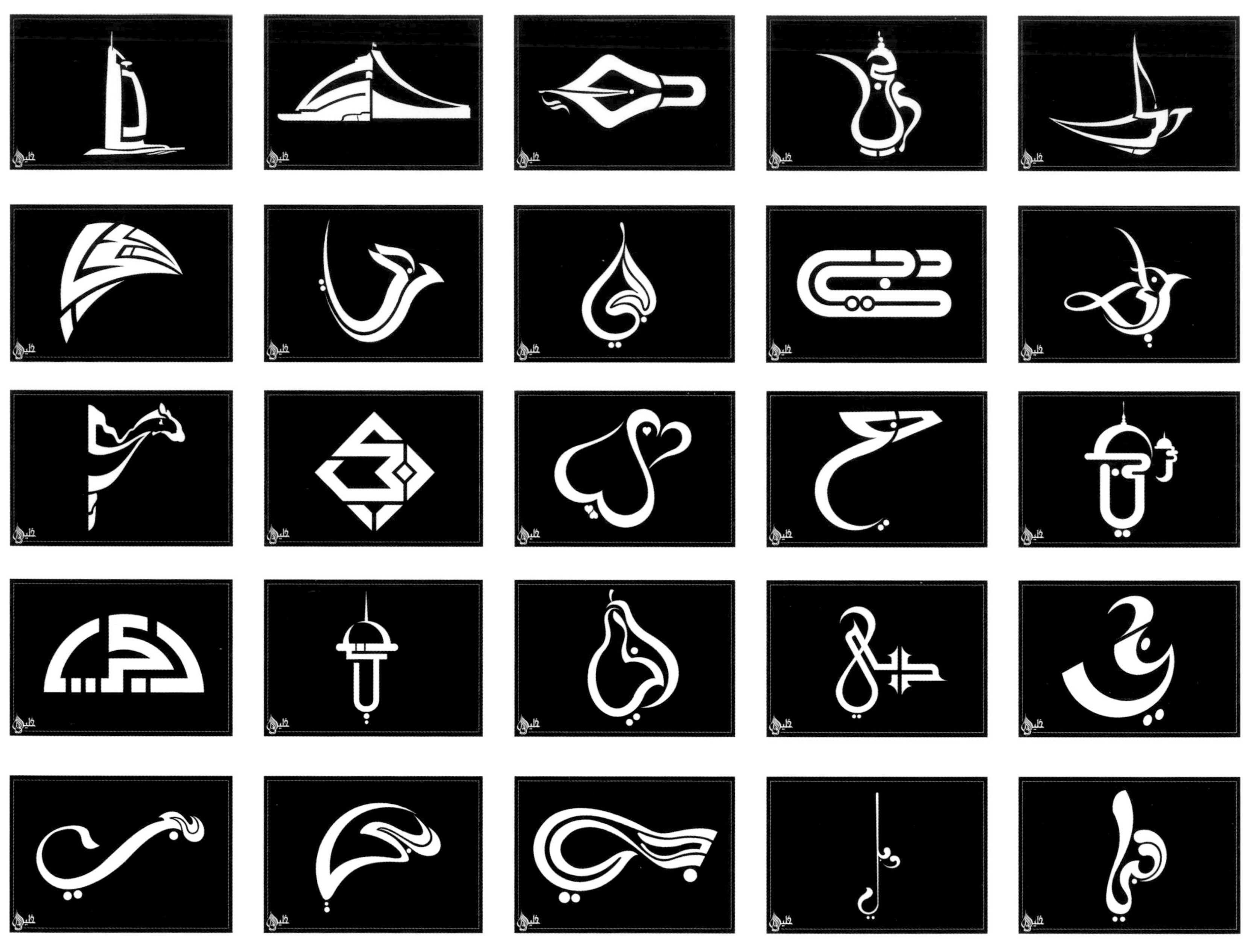

DUBAI – 25 TYPES "I am the only artist to have drawn calligraphy of the same word, 'DUBAI,' in 100 different shapes," explains Khaleelullah Chemnad, who calls himself "the only anatomic Arabic calligrapher." Only twenty-five are shown here. DESIGN FIRM: worldofcalligraphy.com CALLIGRAPHER: Khaleelullah Chemnad PRIMARY FONT: Custom made

Мастерская
Мастерская
Дети – учащиеся четырех московских студий дизайна показывают и рассказывают, чем они занимаются сейчас. Пройдет двадцать лет – и весь мир, в котором мы живем, будет делом их рук
Фотографии…Стас Тарнопольский, Владислав Кирпичев, Андрей Ягубский
Текст…Артем Дежурко

KIDS-DESIGNERS These constructed Cyrillic letters, which read "Kids-Designers" in Russian, are collages made by children. Each is perfectly legible – if one reads Cyrillic script, that is. ART DIRECTORS: Dmitry Barbanel, Dmitry Raspopov DESIGNERS: Evgeny Evgrafov, Evgeny Chulyuskin CLIENT: *Interni* magazine PUBLISHER: Independent Media Sanoma Magazines PRIMARY FONT: Kid-made

AHL EL RIYADAH This distinctive lettering, a logo for the sports TV programme *Ahl El Riyadah*, is based on Arabic forms finessed with a decidedly Modernist sensibility.
DESIGN FIRM: Tarek Atrissi ART DIRECTOR/DESIGNER: Tarek Atrissi CLIENT: Cup & League TV, Qatar PRIMARY FONT: Hand lettering

HORSE AND BIRD The horse calligraphy depicts selected lines from the poems of Sheikh Mohammed Bin Rashid Al Maktoum. The bird displays words from the Holy Qur'an: "Was I not even able to be as this raven?"
DESIGN FIRM: worldofcalligraphy.com CALLIGRAPHER: Khaleelullah Chemnad PRIMARY FONT: Hand lettering

ЕСЛИ БЫ МЕНЯ ПОПРОСИЛИ
В ОДНОМ СЛОВЕ ВЫРАЗИТЬ ВСЕ,
ЧТО НУЖНО ХОРОШЕМУ МЕНЕДЖЕРУ,
Я БЫ СКАЗАЛ „РЕШИТЕЛЬНОСТЬ“

Я БЕРУ НА РАБОТУ
Л·Ю·Д·Е·Й
УМНЕЕ СЕБЯ И НИКОГДА
не лезу В ИХ ДЕЛА

У НАС
в „КРАЙСЛЕРЕ“
СТАРОМОДНЫЙ
ПОДХОД
К ДОЛГАМ —
МЫ ИХ ВОВРЕМЯ
ВОЗВРАЩАЕМ

СКОРОСТЬ
БОССА
ОПРЕДЕЛЯЕТ
СКОРОСТЬ
ВСЕЙ КОМАНДЫ

Фишка
В ТОМ, ЧТОБЫ
не умереть,
поджидая, пока
УСПЕХ ПРИДЕТ
К ТЕБЕ САМ

МЫ
ПОСТОЯННО
СТАЛКИВАЕМСЯ
С ВЕЛИКИМИ ВОЗМОЖНОСТЯМИ,
ТЩАТЕЛЬНО
ЗАМАСКИРОВАНЫМИ
ПОД НЕРАЗРЕШИМЫЕ ПРОБЛЕМЫ

СУТЬ БИЗНЕСА
можно свести
К трем словам:
*ПЕРСОНАЛ
*ПРОДУКТ
*ПРИБЫЛЬ
ЕСЛИ
У ТЕБЯ
ПРОБЛЕМЫ
С ПЕРВЫМ
ПУНКТОМ,
О ДВУХ ДРУГИХ
МОЖЕШЬ ЗАБЫТЬ

CLASSIFIED ADS These faux classified ads are inspired by Russian nineteenth-century newspaper typography and decorative borders.
ART DIRECTOR/DESIGNER/ILLUSTRATOR: Fiodor Sumkin
CLIENT: *CEO* magazine PRIMARY FONTS: Unidentified old Russian fonts

WAKEFIELDS "W" CREST The history and aesthetic of wood type printing inspired this identity for an alt-country band from Seattle. The lettering connotes the rural traditions of country music, while the dramatic, natural forms create a slightly eerie tone. These two diverse aesthetics combine in a striking crest that stands out among other band logos and provides ample opportunities for merchandising.

DESIGN FIRM: agrayspace ART DIRECTORS: Robb Smigielski, Jamie Gray CLIENT: The Wakefields PRIMARY FONTS: American wood type, from wood impressions

DURING THE LATE NINETEENTH century, illustrators and designers (though the term "graphic designer" had not yet been coined) used nature as a primary inspiration for graphic frames, borders, fleurons, dingbats, and letterforms. It was fairly common to see headlines in periodicals and newspapers or logos on playbills and brochures that were diligently engraved to replicate all kinds of flora and fauna. Often these graphic devices directly illuminated the themes of the books or articles in which they appeared. A rustic novel might have a title page made from intertwining twigs, while a book on English gardening might have words made out of flowers. Typographic and printer's cut (or cliché) sample books were filled with pages of these popular graphic doodads. Although they were often seen as an affront to the finer standards of typography, they weren't even considered novelties, because they were so commonly, albeit deftly, used. They were part of the design vernacular of the day.

During the twentieth century this entire genre of fussy imagery went out of fashion as though it never existed, only reappearing in the contexts of humour or pastiche. And, as curios in vintage clip-art books, the decorations were offered to designers as quaint or silly artifacts.

Perhaps it is because the computer has made it easier, or possibly because doing such things is so rebelliously retrograde, but in recent years the tendency toward using natural tropes in contemporary lettering and type has increased dramatically (and it is no coincidence that it has grown in relation to awareness of global warming, too). Photoshop has certainly made it simple, if not also more fun, to create letters out of natural things such as trees, twigs, and blades of grass. Usually, they have a specific purpose in illustrating stories related to the environment, but they also evoke a sense of freshness that lends advertisements, packages, and logos a carefree and joyous aura.

Vines and tendrils are not the only naturalistic motifs to be used in contemporary typography. In this chapter we find that hair – human and animal – has oddly become a formidable, and not all that unusual, material from which designs are made. Another frequent trope is electricity – lightning bolts have historically been used as letters, but now we see a variety of uses for this concept. Liquid – puddles, drops, even ice flows – makes for, well, fluid alphabets. And then there is smoke.

In the 1960s a psychedelic letterform called Smoke was fairly common, yet it didn't really look like its name. Today letters are being made from smoke, and where there is smoke there is fire, as typography too. In the Green section we find a veritable compost of alphabets made from grass, weeds, and moss – and there are many.

But Au Naturel is not solely about physical materials. Hand lettering is as natural as it gets when making type, and this has been perhaps the most widespread new/old genre of the post-digital alphabetic experimentation. The hand is a simple, if sometimes contrived, way of making words, and while perilously close to commonplace, the results are still pleasurable to see.

MT MT commissioned Inksurge to illustrate the company name and they decided to use floral ornaments as embellishments for the type. DESIGN FIRM: Inksurge ART DIRECTORS: Rex Advincula, Joyce Tai DESIGNER: Joyce Tai ILLUSTRATOR: Rex Advincula CLIENT: Media Temple PRIMARY FONTS: Client supplied MT type/logo

BRANCHES

THE ANCIENT RUNIC ALPHABETS, used in Nordic and Germanic lands before the adoption of the Latin alphabet, were originally composed from branches and twigs. Branch lettering has a long history, as a sign system for rustic homes and campsites as well as in graphically illustrated lettering. One of the most popular nineteenth-century novelty faces was Figgins's Rustic (or Log Cabin), made from logs. Current use is not much different, albeit more witty in purpose. When done well, it can be surrealistically beautiful. When done poorly, it's better off as kindling.

BRANCHES This lettering, inspired by a Homer Hiccolm & the Rocketboys CD cover, was used in *O, The Oprah Magazine*. DESIGN FIRM: HandMadeFont ART DIRECTORS/DESIGNERS: Vladimir Loginov, Maksim Loginov PHOTOGRAPHER: Tanja Muravskaja CLIENT: *O, The Oprah Magazine* PUBLISHER: Hearst Corporation PRIMARY FONTS: Custom made

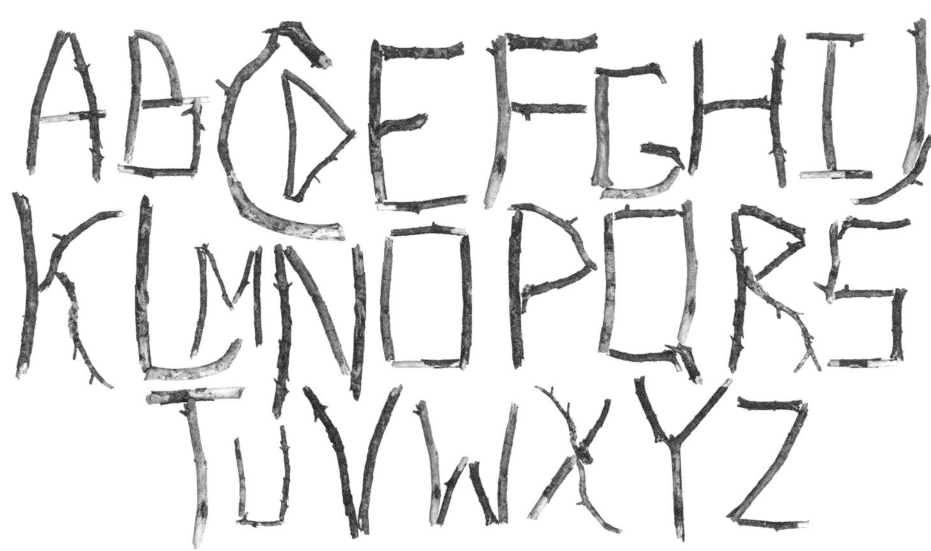

LANDMINE MARATHON Landmine Marathon is a hardcore metal band with roots in punk music and a foreboding political message. The typographic treatment for their debut album, *Wounded*, used the distressed and photocopied mannerisms of the punk era as a reference point. When that aesthetic was combined with natural plant forms, a strong message was expressed about nature's ability to thrive long after we have inevitably destroyed ourselves through war.
DESIGN FIRM: agrayspace creative ART DIRECTORS: Robb Smigielski, Jamie Gray CLIENT: Landmine Marathon PUBLISHER: Level Plane Records PRIMARY FONT: DIN EngSchrift

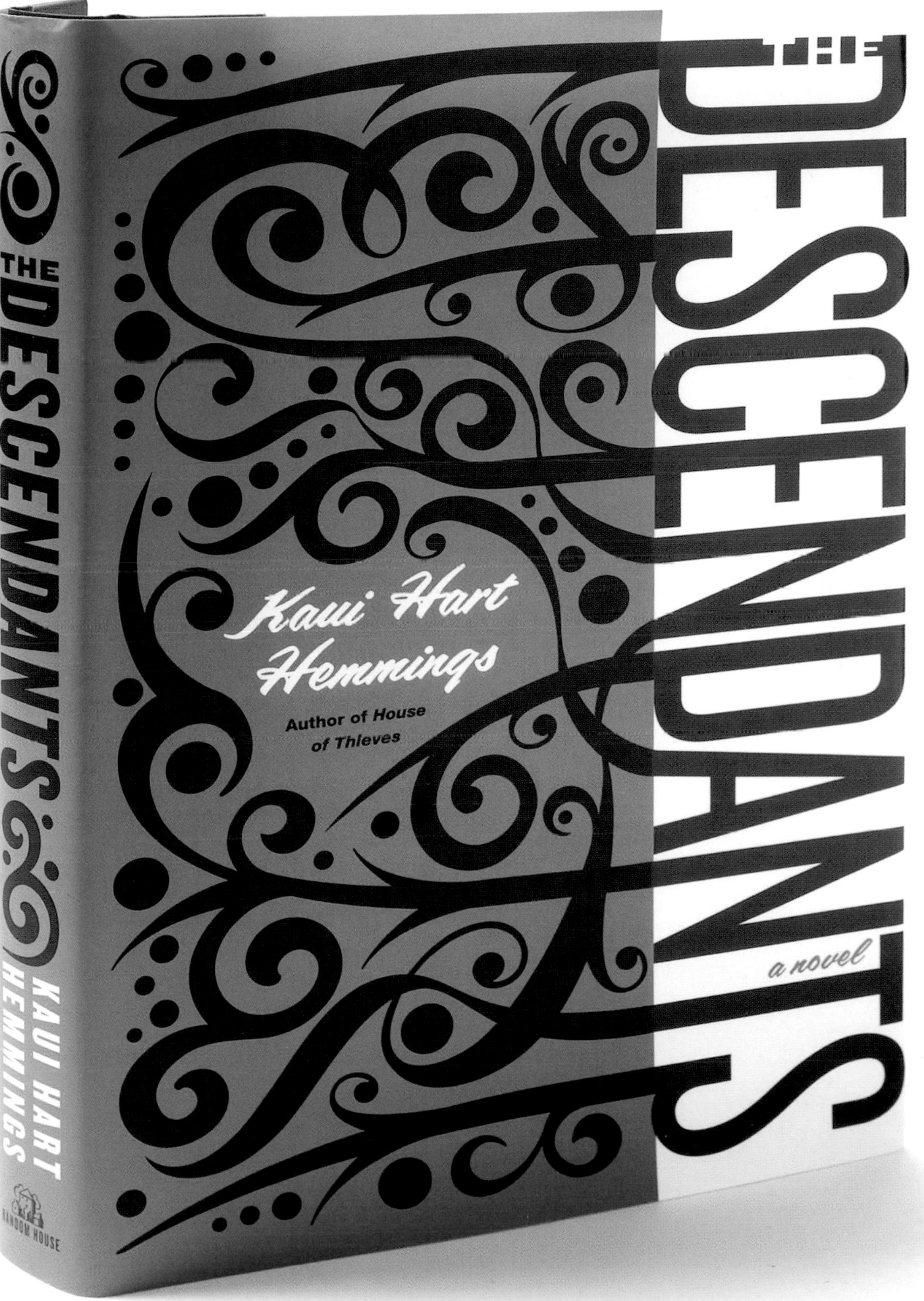

THE DESCENDANTS The design is based on tribal ornaments found in Samoan and Hawaiian tattoos, which also look like the roots of a plant. They make a soothing pattern, distinct from the unornamented typography.
DESIGN FIRM: de Vicq design ART DIRECTOR: Robin Schiff DESIGNER: Roberto de Vicq de Cumptich CLIENT: Random House PRIMARY FONTS: Knockout, La Salle

BRANCHES

THINKING LIFE WILL BE... Stefan Sagmeister found the line, “Thinking life will be better in the future is stupid. I have to live now,” under the heading, “Things I have learned in my life so far,” in his diary. The client graciously agreed to use it on this poster advertising the School of Visual Arts in New York. An entire life cycle of caterpillars and butterflies lives within the twigs. DESIGN FIRM: Sagmeister, Inc. ART DIRECTOR: Silas Rhodes DESIGNERS: Stefan Sagmeister, Irina Thaler, Paul Rustland RETOUCHING: Steve West CLIENT: The School of Visual Arts PRIMARY FONT: Hand lettering

cuisine

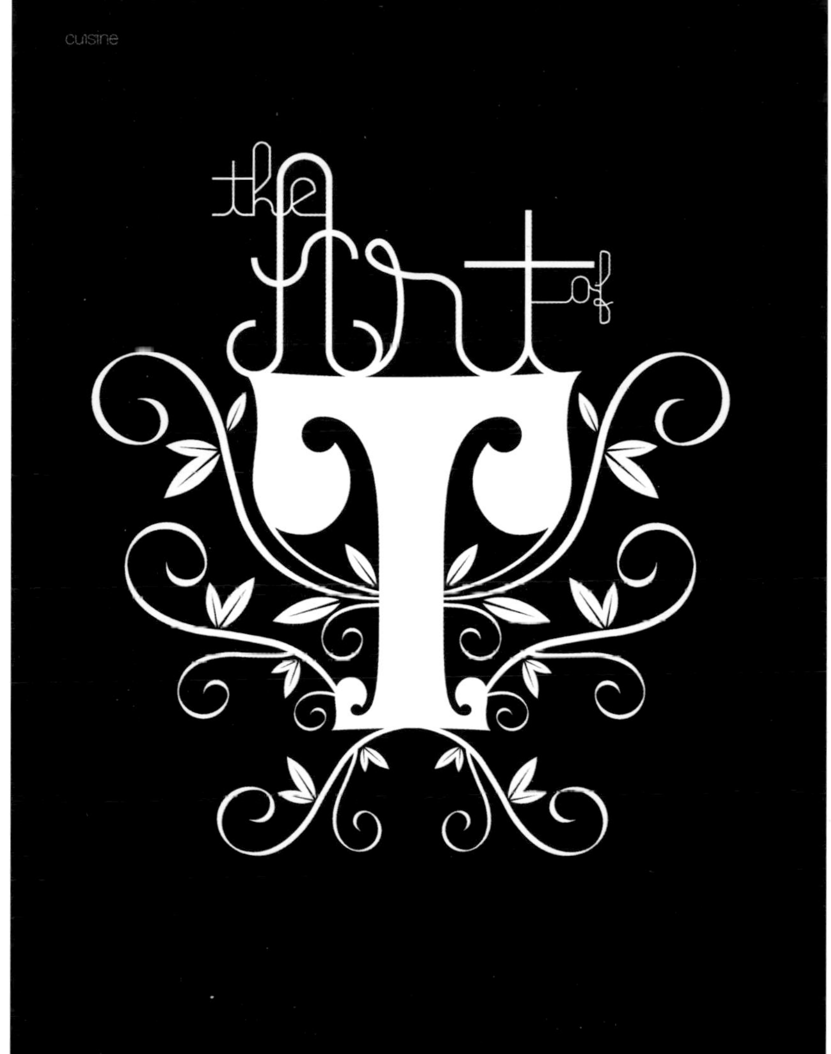

a sensory discourse both tasteful and historic

BY LONELLE SELBO

The legend began nearly five thousand years ago in 2737 BC when the Chinese Emperor, Shen Chung, a learned and scientific man, was served a drink of boiling water. Before he had taken a sip, a gust of wind blew a leaf from a nearby bush into the cup. Upon noticing the water change colour and a pleasant aroma filling the air, the inquisitive emperor sipped the liquid and found it to be fragrant and flavourful and revitalizing. Thus, tea was born and this new drink quickly became a part of Asian culture, and over a few millennia, the world.

The history of tea is intertwined with mysticism, art, political upheaval, medicine and ritual. Its influence has crossed cultural and economic barriers. It has been the source of conflict, an aid to societal progress and it has, in many ways, bridged the East and West.

After tea's fortuitous beginnings in China, it spread throughout Eastern culture into many aspects of society, its role ranging from religious facilitator to medical curative. Tea was first brought to Japan by a Buddhist priest who felt that it enhanced meditation. The Russians too, had an interest in the brew—its warmth and sustenance was well suited to their lifestyle and climate. It took centuries before tea was brought to Europe, but by 1710 tea replaced ale as the national drink of England. The American colonies fell head over heels for the fashionable brew, but the love affair didn't last long. In 1773, a group of Bostonians decided to demonstrate their dissatisfaction with British control and taxation by tossing a shipment off a British tea vessel into Boston Harbour. This event became known as The Boston Tea Party and shortly following this act of rebellion a revolution was declared. In spite of this, the tea bush continued to put down roots. By the late 1880's, trade stabilized and tea quickly became the second most consumed beverage in the world—right behind water.

All teas are made from leaves plucked from the *Camellia sinensis* plant. There are three thousand different types of teas and tens of thousands of blends, but only five main categories: Black tea, Oolong, Green tea, White tea and Pu-erh. Chamomile, peppermint and other brewed fruit or herbal drinks are called tisanes and are not considered teas as they do not come from the Camellia sinensis bush. Many factors affect the quality and taste of tea. The "first flush," or first plucking of spring, yields leaves with more delicate characteristics, while elevation above sea level, the age of the plant, the climate, soil, firing time all play a role in affecting the final brew. A discriminating palate will be intrigued to discover the subtle, yet delightful, differences between teas.

The classification of the tea is determined by the process used to prepare the leaves, while oxidation establishes the flavour, body and colour. With Black tea, the leaves are steamed and rolled to crack and release the juices, then aged and dried through firing. This process allows the tannin oils to ferment and adds body to the brew. Green tea is produced by a similar process, but the leaves are immediately fired before oxidization can take place. This gives the tea a strong herbal, fruity taste that is similar to that of the natural leaf. Oolong is a compromise between black and green teas. It, too, is steamed, rolled, then aged, but the fermentation process is cut short and the leaves are fired before they are fully black. Oolong is vaguely herbal and fruity unlike a Black, but more subdued than a Green. White tea is deemed to be the purist because it is completely unfermented. It is picked only once a year in the spring and is, therefore, quite rare. White teas are made from the best and youngest part of the tea plant. It exudes citrus and floral tones and the flavour is subtle and delicate. The final classification of tea, Pu-erh, is considered to belong to a distinct category as it is the only tea that is intentionally aged, and it becomes more expensive and desirable as it does. Pu-erh is thought of as vintage tea, kept alive and refined by a double fermentation process, the details of which are a highly guarded secret in China.

Today, tea is grown and cultivated in many different areas of the world. Various teas offer numerous flavours, and certain regions are solely responsible for particular types of tea. The art of appreciating fine tea harkens to the admiration and study of wine. An eavesdropper might think a critic was describing a cabernet when speaking of Black tea, or a sauvignon blanc when discussing Oolong. The world's great tea plantations are held in similar regard to well-known vineyards and are attributed the same celebrity. And different types of tea can be paired with food in a manner evocative of wines. White and Green teas are best paired with fish or poultry like a chardonnay, and Oolong is perfect for fatty foods like duck or noodles as it controls oil and helps break down fatty acids. Black tea is comparable to pinot noir in that they are heavier and well-suited to darker meats. The myriad of teas available today are more than comparable to the multitudinous wine selections of the world.

Darjeelings, considered the champagne of teas, are grown in the Himalayan Mountains in the North Eastern part of India. They have a characteristic dryness, a muscatel aroma and are prized for their lingering astringency. It is rare to come across a cup of pure Darjeeling as most of the tea is sold as a blend under the same name. Assams are also grown in this area of India. They are hearty and creamy with a depth of flavour that welcomes the addition of lemon or milk. Ceylon teas come (surprise) from Ceylon, which is the colonial name for Sri Lanka. This tea has a wide spectrum of variations which offer tea connoisseurs the opportunity to detect and appreciate subtle differences in taste and aroma. The experience of becoming a tea drinker is an adventure. One can take a sensory expedition around the world with a variety of delicious blends, from Keemuns to Lapsang Souchangs, to Wu Lungs and Yunnans, not to mention the Jasmines and countless flavoured and spiced teas.

This journey of the senses is boundless, and each culture has a particular way of preparing and serving tea. The Japanese and Chinese enjoy it black or with jasmine, chrysanthemum or rose petals, while Asian Indians combine tea with spices and milk. Europeans and North Americans prefer it black or with cream, milk, sugar, lemon or honey. Those from the Middle East take it black with mint and spices, while the Russians favour a strong brew, highly sweetened with sugar, jam or honey.

Tea has been always been treasured and its rituals are culturally distinct and deeply embedded in tradition. While the Chinese legendarily first discovered tea, the Buddhists of India were the first to harness its mysticism. The Buddhist tea ceremony is symbolic and solemn. It involves the ritual consumption of tea offered by the tea master, in a nearly empty room, while meditating on simplicity and peace. The Japanese Tea Ceremony, also called Cha-no-yu, epitomizes the tea rite in which the simple act of serving tea is elevated to a gracefully perfected art. Influenced by Zen Buddhism, the ritual involves a geisha or skilled

111

THE ART OF TEA "This hand-lettered 'wordmark' was created as a quick substitute for a photograph that was not used in this magazine story," says Paul Sych. "I positioned the large 'T' as the main element and focal point and used decorative tea leaves as an accent."

DESIGN FIRM: Faith ART DIRECTOR/DESIGNER: Paul Sych
CLIENT: *Lush* magazine PUBLISHER: Bassett Publishing
PRIMARY FONT: Hand lettering

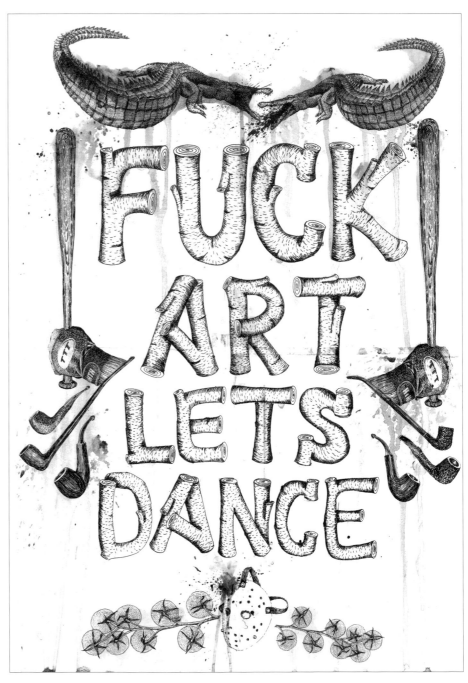

HOT HOT HOT Given carte blanche to design a poster for the club Hot Hot Hot, Grandpeople drew inspiration from the typical Norwegian black metal aesthetic, which in turn derives from nature, folklore and artists such as Theodor Kittelsen. They made a pun out of the title to fit the imagery: "*Hat Hat Hat*" (translated "Hate Hate Hate") is spelled out by the withering branches. Black metal with a sweet, club-pop twist.
DESIGN FIRM: Grandpeople ART DIRECTORS/DESIGNERS: Grandpeople CLIENT: Hot Hot Hot PRIMARY FONT: Hand lettering

FUCK ART LET'S DANCE This quirky self-promotional poster, featuring log cabin lettering and engraving-like illustrations, invokes some of the elements of Russian prison tattoos.
ART DIRECTOR/DESIGNER/ILLUSTRATOR: Fiodor Sumkin
CLIENT: Self PRIMARY FONT: Hand lettering

IN THE WOODS

a novel

TANA FRENCH

IN THE WOODS "Although I did not directly refer to any of their works," says Paul Buckley, "William Morris and Marian Bantjes are two designers from whom I find constant inspiration, whose skills I can only hope to some day glimpse in my own work." DESIGN FIRM: Penguin Art Department/Penguin Group (USA) ART DIRECTOR: Paul Buckley DESIGNER: Jennifer Wang CLIENT: Viking, Penguin Group USA PUBLISHER: Viking PRIMARY FONT: FF Hydra

BELLA LEA For Bella Lea's 2005 "Summer Tour" poster, Diana Sudyka's main inspiration was the natural history illustrator Ernst Haeckel. DESIGNER/ILLUSTRATOR: Diana Sudyka CLIENT: Bella Lea PRIMARY FONT: Hand lettering

ART NOUVEAU, which began in 1896 in France and gained popularity across Europe, saw naturalism as an alternative to stiff academic art. Known in its later stages as "floriated madness," owing to an excessive use of vines and tendrils, not to mention nymphs and satyrs, it is often revived as a decorative conceit. Largely reintroduced through Push Pin Studios and Psychedelic art in the 1960s, the use of flowers, leaves, stamens and pistils is today blooming throughout the design world. In some instances, the flower is a perfect foil for Modernist austerity, while in others it provides the right balance between mechanistic and natural aesthetics.

ROCK 'N' ROLL "As a kid I loved looking at the hand lettering on old rock 'n' roll posters," says Jess Volinski. "In particular, the lettering on Jimi Hendrix concert posters struck me because the forms of the letters actually looked like his music sounded. The idea that the shape of words could communicate sound really blew me away." All Volinski's hand lettering is inspired by those old posters. However, for this piece she went for the exact opposite of Hendrix's bold angular lettering and created an innocent and feminine take on rock 'n' roll with soft, flowing letters.
ART DIRECTOR/ILLUSTRATOR: Jess Volinski CLIENT: Blue Foliage PRIMARY FONTS: Hand lettering, Oberon, Stanzie

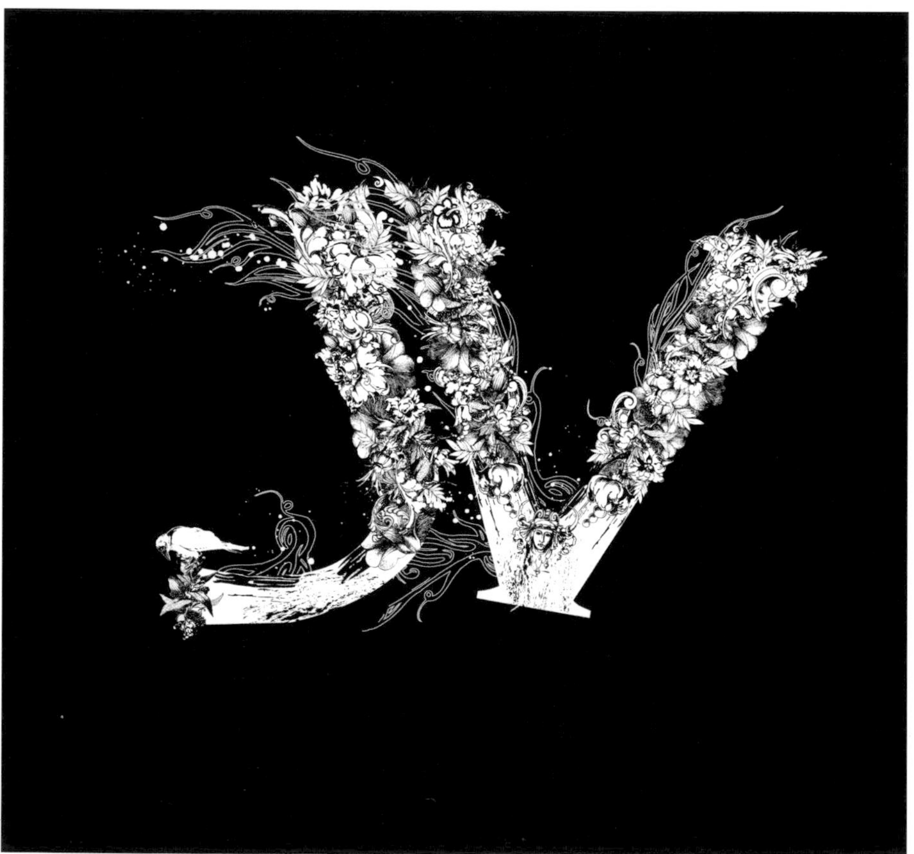

JV Bridal retail company Wedding Essentials commissioned Inksurge to design a concept wedding invitation for a Hollywood couple. JV stands for Johnny Depp and Vanessa Paradis. The dark ornamental embellishments are stunning, mixing an element of the macabre with the beauty of the floral motif.
DESIGN FIRM: Inksurge ART DIRECTORS/DESIGNERS/ILLUSTRATORS: Rex Advincula, Joyce Tai CLIENT: Wedding Essentials PRIMARY FONT: FZ Roman

STYLE SPRINGS TO LIFE This Beardsley-esque approach to floral decoration was common during the nineteenth century. Here, it suggests a marriage of old and new, and a re-blooming, too.
DESIGN DIRECTOR: Deb Bishop
ART DIRECTOR: Lisa Thé DESIGNER: Si Scott CLIENT: *Blueprint* magazine
PUBLISHER: Martha Stewart Omnimedia PRIMARY FONT: Fling

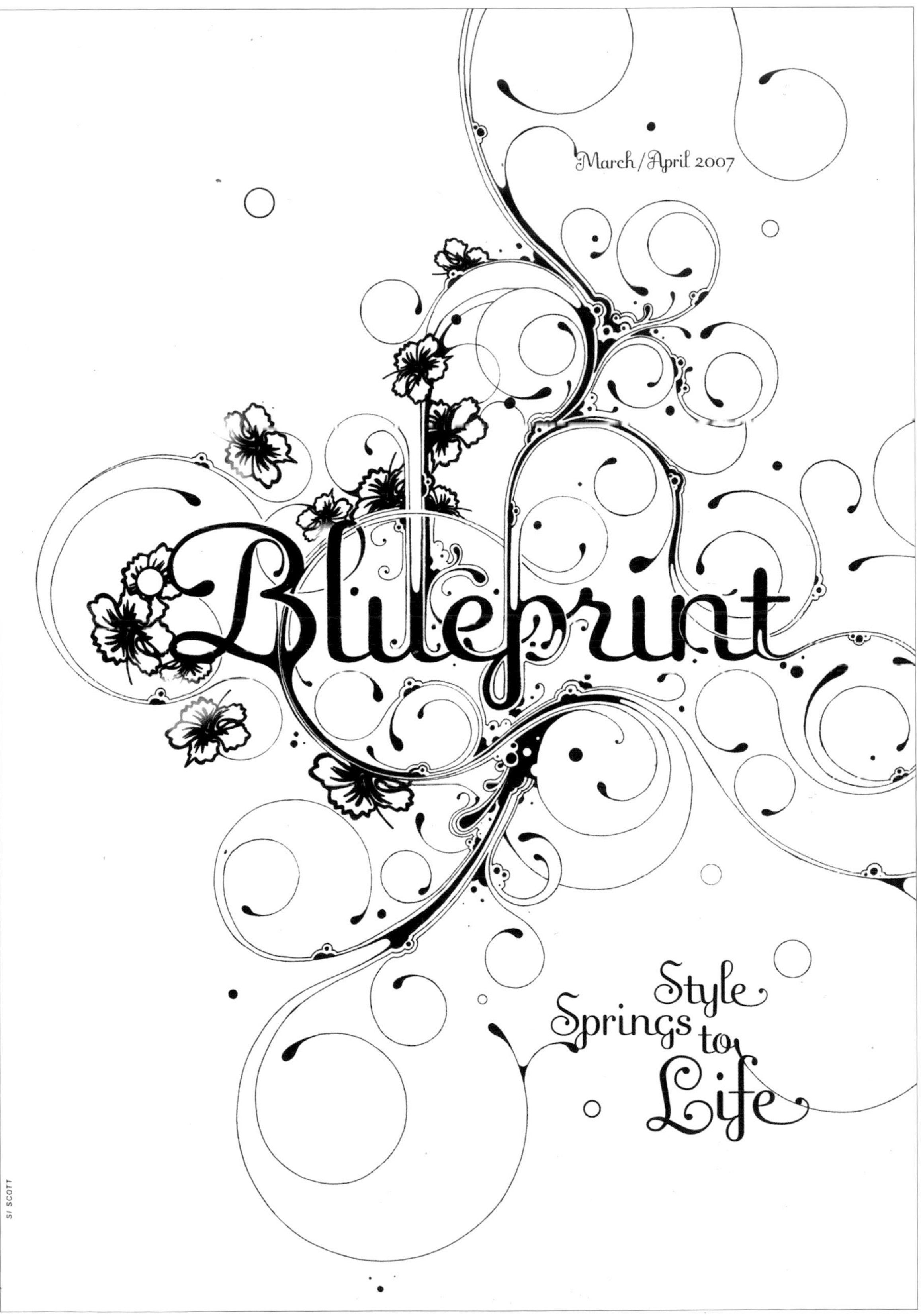

March/April 2007
Blueprint
Style Springs to Life
SI SCOTT

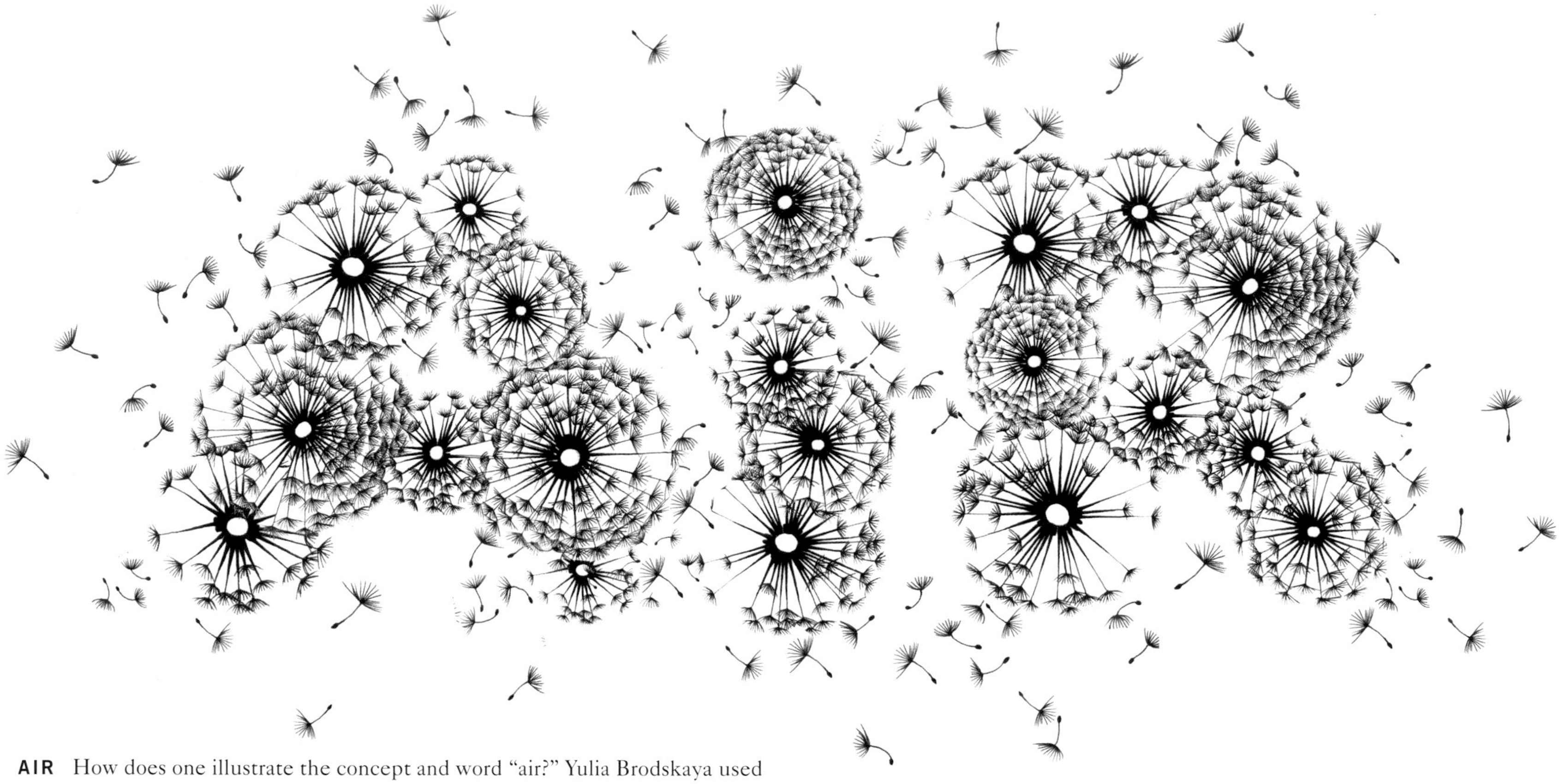

AIR How does one illustrate the concept and word "air?" Yulia Brodskaya used the lighter-than-air dandelion seed as a perfect metaphor for this self-promotion. DESIGN FIRM: Yulia Brodskaya ART DIRECTOR/DESIGNER/ILLUSTRATOR: Yulia Brodskaya CLIENT: Self PRIMARY FONT: Hand lettering

FUNKRUSH The new swash lettering has become more and more florid. This logo in split fountain colors looks like the beginning of fall.
DESIGN FIRM: Aeiko ART DIRECTOR: Pete Harrison DESIGNERS: Pete Harrison, Colin Lee CLIENT: Funkrush PRIMARY FONT: Custom made

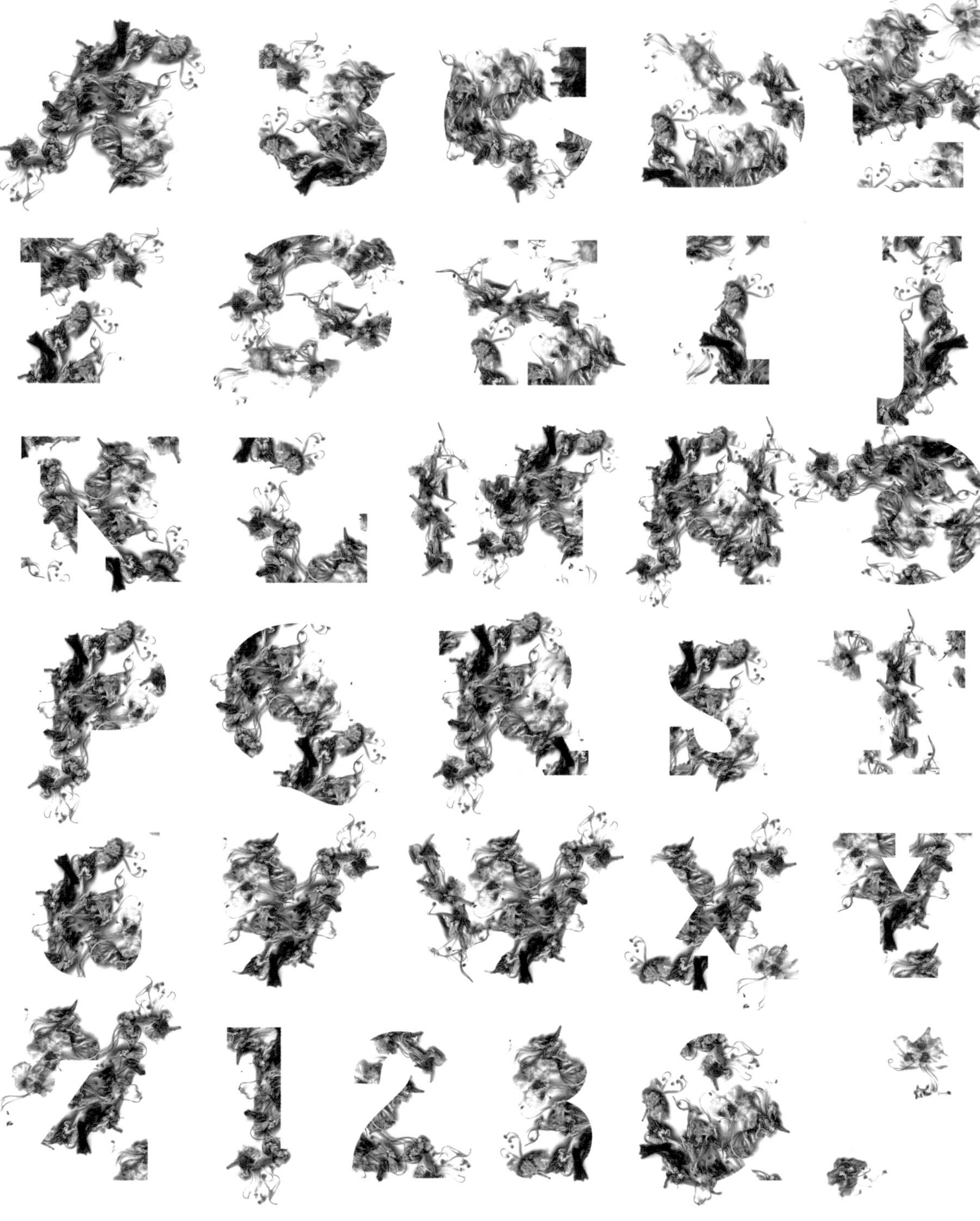

FONTLAB 001: BLOSSOMWELL The Fontlab asked Craig Ward to create some new "Photofonts" to promote their new Bitfonter software, which allows the creation of full-color typefaces for use within Photoshop. "I set about scanning in hair collected from my local barber's floor, some dying blossoms I found on the drive outside my flat and and some ink and water experiments from my sketchbook, and juxtaposed them with Futura Bold, Rockwell and Bodoni," he says. "I was trying to achieve a contrast between the type – which is forced to stick to a grid – and the organic elements that are beyond your control."
DESIGNER/ILLUSTRATOR: Craig Ward
CLIENT: Fontlab PRIMARY FONT: Custom made, based on Futura Bold, Rockwell, Bodoni

TYPE This magazine illustration draws upon the prosaic notion that nature is fluid, and watercolor decoration best expresses that fluidity.
DESIGN FIRM: Shinybinary ART DIRECTOR/DESIGNER/ILLUSTRATOR: Nik Ainley CLIENT: *Computer Arts* magazine PUBLISHER: Future Publishing PRIMARY FONT: Alba

HAIR

IS IT JUST a coincidence that Hair, *the 1960s musical, has recently been revived, and that the use of hair in creating letterforms is currently growing? Maybe. Whereas hair has long been a graphic trope in illustration (the flowing locks of Pre-Raphaelite damsels, for example), having it sprout up in typographic concoctions and alphabets is a fairly recent phenomenon. Is it right to consider this ornamental? Yes – especially when the hair is tied with a florid ribbon or decorative beret clip.*

CHOSEN The notion of using hair as a typographic motif is used ironically in this illustration for *Heeb* magazine. The hair replaces the tattoos that are typically used in this manner.
DESIGN FIRM: Post Typography ART DIRECTORS: Jennifer Daniel (*Heeb*), Nolen Strals, Bruce Willen DESIGNERS: Nolen Strals, Bruce Willen CLIENT: *Heeb* magazine PUBLISHER: Heeb Media PRIMARY FONT: Hand lettering

PAKI/TERRORIST Henna is traditionally used in many Asian cultures to decorate the hands and feet of a new bride, to protect her from harm and negative spirits; this is the inspiration for Satveer Kaur's work, a response to racial prejudice in the UK. "I used gold ink as it is the traditional color of celebration," says Kaur. "All the images were hand rendered in the true style of henna design. I produced a series of three typographic images titled *Paki*, *Terrorist*, and *British Asian*. The decorative henna style of the lettering was meant to create something beautiful out of words so hurtful and controversial. The images were designed to be thought-provoking and to raise awareness on the heightened issue of racism against British Asians. These images tell people I am not a Paki, I am not a terrorist, I am a British Asian." There are different meanings behind shapes and flowers in the design: the lotus is said to represent truth and honesty, while long vines represent prosperity and growth.
ART DIRECTOR/DESIGNER: Satveer Kaur CLIENT: Self PRIMARY FONT: Hand lettering, based on an Arnold Belkin font

HAIR

CAT LADY Matthew Heckart's two fabulously hairy cats, Charles Wallace (light fur) and Dax Jackson (dark fur) provide the raw material for this furry alphabet.
DESIGN FIRM: The School of Visual Arts ART DIRECTOR: Gail Anderson DESIGNER: Matthew Heckart PRIMARY FONT: Hand lettering

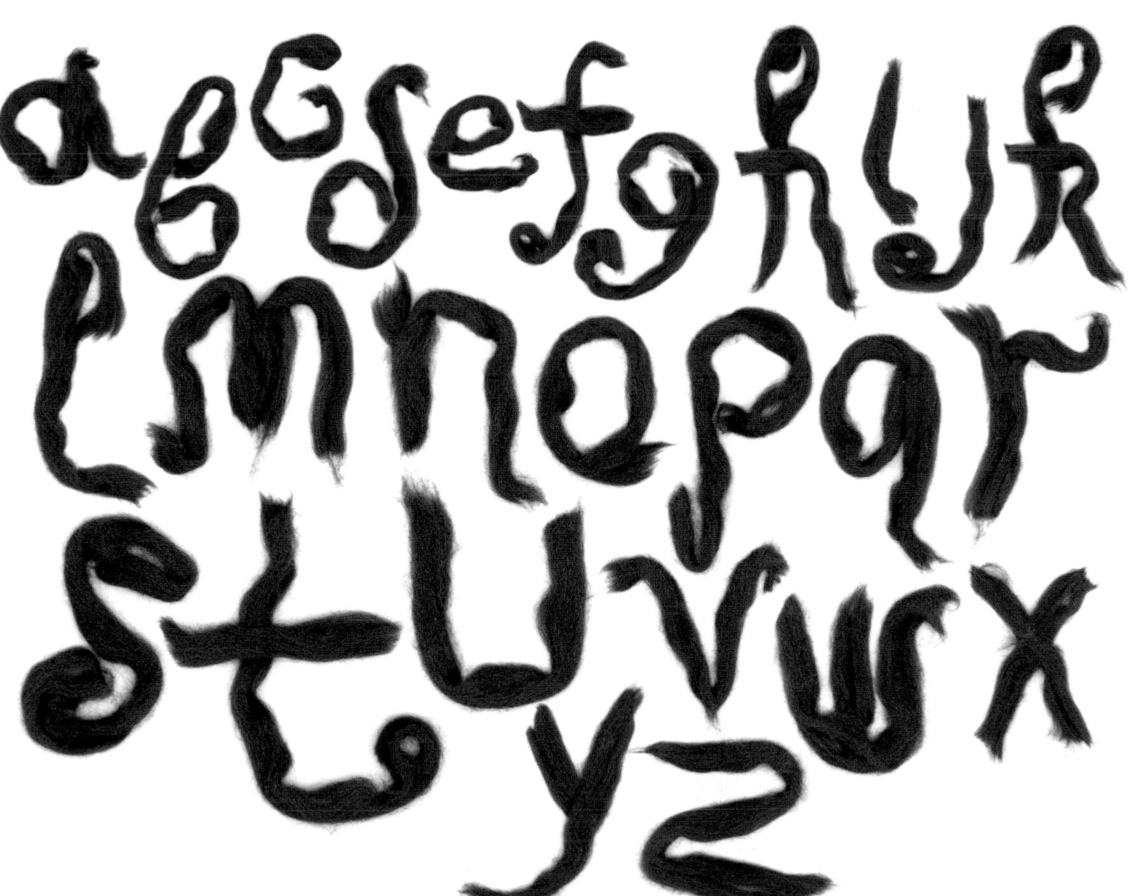

BEARD When it comes to beards, ZZ Top's are unsurpassed. This alphabet pays homage to the hirsute rockers.
DESIGN FIRM: HandMadeFont ART DIRECTORS/DESIGNERS: Vladimir Loginov, Maksim Loginov PHOTOGRAPHER: Vladimir Loginov CLIENT: HandMadeFont PRIMARY FONT: Hand lettering

BEARDS RULE This poster for a Post Typography lecture at Susquehanna University uses the principals' beards as a fitting venue for lettering.

DESIGN FIRM: Post Typography ART DIRECTOR/DESIGNER/ ILLUSTRATOR: Nolen Strals CLIENT: Susquehanna University PRIMARY FONT: Hand lettering

FONTLAB 001: HIRSUTURA "Hirsutura juxtaposes hair from the floor of my local barber," says Craig Ward, "with Futura. It is primarily an experiment in legibility, colliding the clean, designed lines of a classic typeface with the organic and unpredictable."

DESIGNER/ILLUSTRATOR/PHOTOGRAPHER: Craig Ward CLIENT: Fontlab PRIMARY FONT: Custom made, based on Futura Bold

DMBQ Reed Burgoyne and Sarah Mead were influenced by the 1960s rock posters of Victor Moscoso in this poster design, but DMBQ's live performances inspired the final outcome. Their sound, the duo say, was "filled with ferocity and chaos, yet complemented by tamed artistic talent harking back to heavy Psychedelic sounds from the past." DESIGN FIRM: Urban Inks ART DIRECTORS/DESIGNERS: Reed Burgoyne, Sarah Mead ILLUSTRATOR: Dover Books Clip Art CLIENT: Panache Booking PUBLISHER: *Panache* magazine PRIMARY FONTS: Hand-drawn Urban Inks original by Reed Burgoyne, Century Gothic

LIGHTNING BOLTS are used in alphabets and in graphic art to signify raw power. What could be more descriptive? Although not as frequently used as one might think, graphic representations of electricity are certainly not uncommon. As both metaphor and narrative device, electrifying imagery has the power to make the reader feel all tingly.

THUNDERSTRUCK! Brian Smith notes that this character, featured in a yearly collection from the School of Visual Arts's cartooning department, is "one part anime, one part hero, two parts lightning." It is comic all the way.
DESIGN FIRM: Visual Arts Press ART DIRECTOR: Michael J. Walsh DESIGNER: Brian E. Smith LETTERER: Anthony Bloch ILLUSTRATOR: Ben Ross PRIMARY FONT: Hand lettering

GARAMOND POWERLINE This experiment is based on the Garamond typeface and the theme "decorated type." Daniel Adolph created Garamond Powerline as a collage, constructed from digital images of railway power lines. He says it is not intended to be readable or functional: "It is just a homage to the beautiful typeface, a combination of two worlds: industrial heaviness and the fragile beauty of the Renaissance-Antiqua."
DESIGN FIRM: 0c/0m/0y/0k ART DIRECTOR: Daniel Adolph PRIMARY FONT: Garamond

TREY ANASTASIO There are various historical references in this commemorative poster advertising a Halloween night performance by ex-Phish frontman Trey Anastasio. But the main focus was simply to get the lightning to read "Trey," without sacrificing its verisimilitude. The lightning is reminiscent of his high-energy concerts.
DESIGN FIRM: FarmBarn Art Co.
DESIGNERS: Drue Dixon, Mike Pierce
CLIENT: Trey Anastasio/Red Star Merchandise PRIMARY FONTS: Custom made, Bodoni Poster, Akzidenz Grotesk

OCTOBER 31 2006 TREY ANASTASIO STUBB'S BBQ | AUSTIN

LIQUID

BEFORE PHOTOSHOP, it took some considerable effort to get water to look like letters, let alone to make sense as text. The easiest way was to urinate in the snow, but even that was hit or miss. But with digital technology it is now possible to make liquid take on any form and shape. Probably the most adventurous use of liquid as a lettering tool was Stefan Sagmeister's script saying, "Everybody thinks they are right," which he peed into the air, and captured the moment on film (page 104).

SOUL Almost anything can be made into letters, and almost any letter can be made into something else. Alex Trochut says the idea behind this cover for Taiwanese magazine *Xfuns* was to merge meaningful shapes (letters) and abstract shapes as far as possible. The word "soul" emerges from the centre of the composition.
DESIGN FIRM: Alex Trochut ART DIRECTOR/DESIGNER: Alex Trochut CLIENT/PUBLISHER: *Xfuns* magazine PRIMARY FONT: Custom made

NIKE: SUMMER HOOPS Nike wanted this poster campaign to be in the spirit of the old, classic Nike Basket ads – relatively simple, but playful, with some handmade typography and letters that are distant relatives of old-school graffiti. The headings were filled with pictures of basketballs, basket shirts and other details. The accompanying lettering was designed to contrast the headings.
ART DIRECTOR: Michale Spoljaric DESIGNER: Grandpeople PHOTOGRAPHER: Nike DESIGN FIRM: Grandpeople CLIENT: Nike USA PRIMARY FONT: Custom made

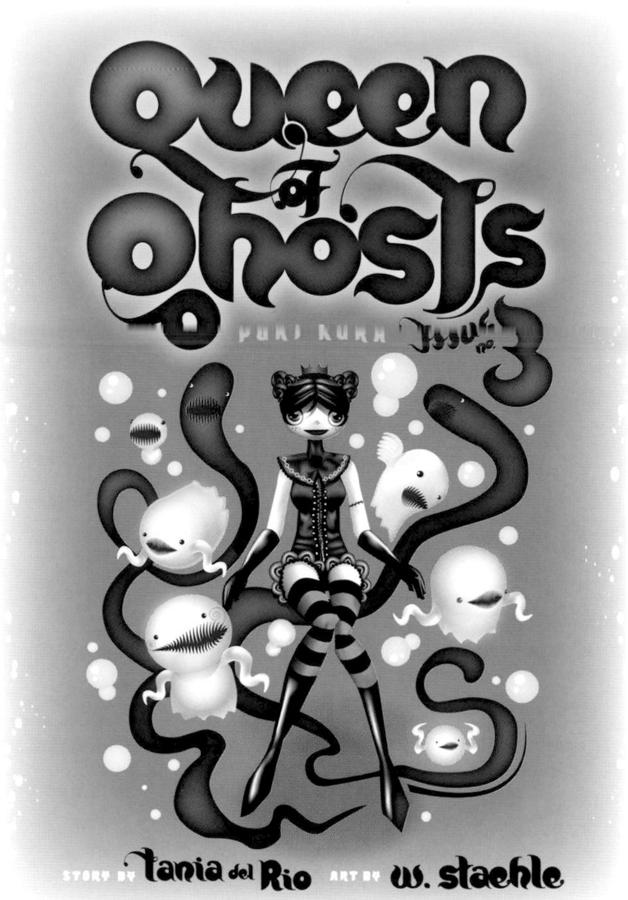

QUEEN OF GHOSTS This poster is an odd mix: half Tokyo-Gothic-*Lolita*, half faux-Art Noveau poster. The lettering, says Will Staehle, "is bubbly and vinyl-feeling, yet it meshes with its thin, sinewy swashes."
DESIGN FIRM: Lonewolfblacksheep ART DIRECTOR/DESIGNER/ILLUSTRATOR: Will Staehle CLIENT: Disney PRIMARY FONT: Hand lettering

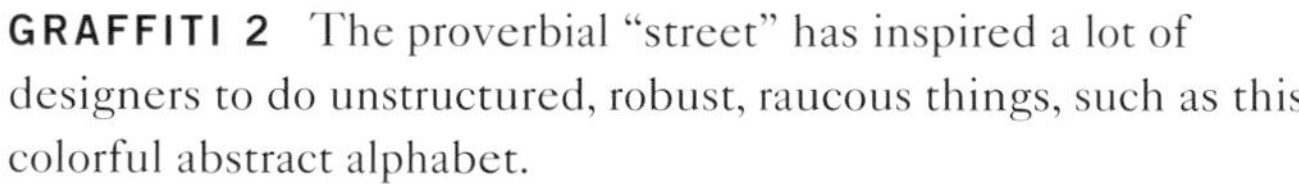

GRAFFITI 2 The proverbial "street" has inspired a lot of designers to do unstructured, robust, raucous things, such as this colorful abstract alphabet.
DESIGN FIRM: Acme Industries DESIGNER/CLIENT: Andrei Robu PRIMARY FONT: Trick Graffiti

NOISECAPE "I think this is my first flyer and at the time I was very much inspired by underground comic artists such as Charles Burns, Daniel Clowes and Chris Ware," says Zeloot. *Monty Python's Flying Circus* is also a partial reference, and the design is rooted in Chinese science textbook images, too.
DESIGN FIRM: Zeloot DESIGNER/ILLUSTRATOR: Zeloot
CLIENT: De Garage PRIMARY FONT: Hand lettering

MODERN LOVES The sinuous quality of these letterforms for a magazine feature is consistent with the ethereality of modern love – indeed, all love.
ART DIRECTOR/DESIGNER/ILLUSTRATOR: Mario Hugo
CLIENT/PUBLISHER: *Faesthetic* magazine PRIMARY FONT: Custom made

LIQUID

GO Gominola is a Barcelona studio that offers "creative" coding and programming for digital and interactive projects, so Michele Angelo designed a clean logo with a modern flavor. "Then I played with it to develop a variety of images and stickers with a funny approach," he says.
DESIGN FIRM: Superexpresso ART DIRECTOR/DESIGNER: Michele Angelo CLIENT: Gominola Creative Media PRIMARY FONTS: Based on Lineto Typ1451

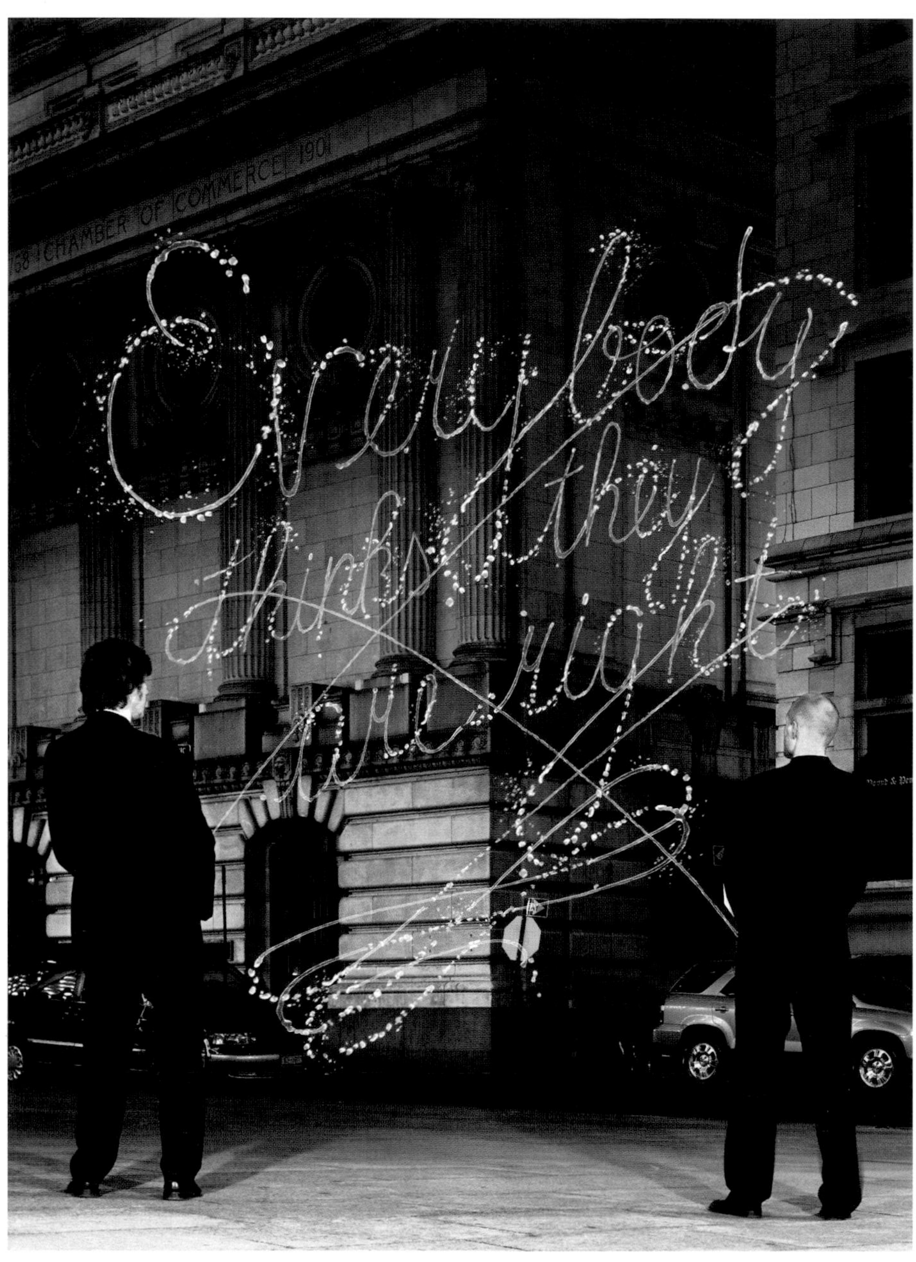

EVERYBODY THINKS THEY ARE RIGHT... About everything, "including predicting the future of media," says Stefan Sagmeister, who used his natural juices in a typographically creative and liquid manner in this image for Japanese *Esquire* magazine.
DESIGN FIRM: Sagmeister, Inc.
ART DIRECTOR: Stefan Sagmeister
DESIGNER: Matthias Ernstberger
PHOTOGRAPHER: Bela Borsodi
CLIENT: *Esquire* magazine PUBLISHER: *Esquire* magazine Japan Co. PRIMARY FONT: Urine

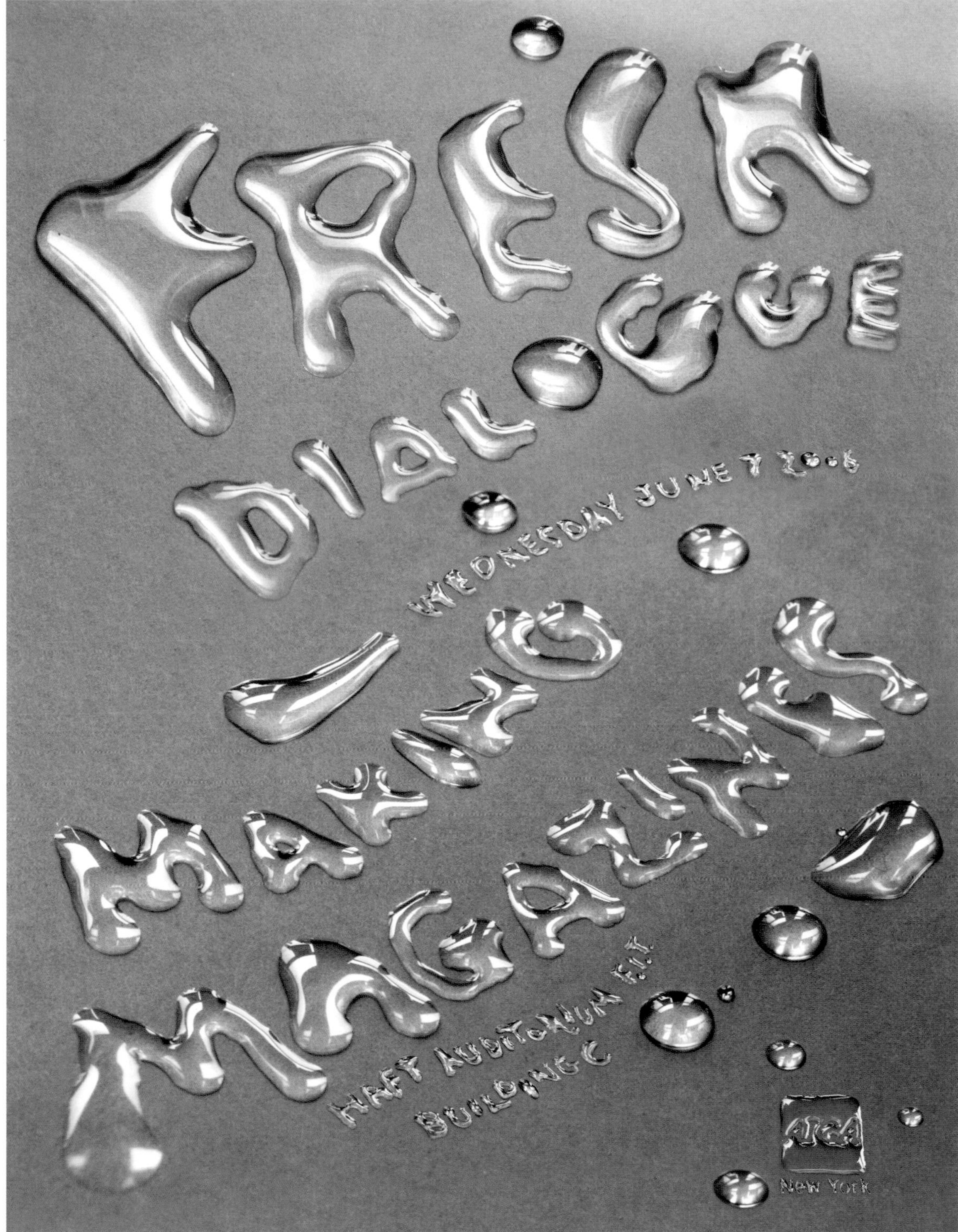

FRESH DIALOGUE Roger Black once designed a magazine cover with elegant black type and blobs of water on top of it. The beads of water distorted the type beautifully. This AIGA poster "is a reinterpretation of that piece taken to its illogical extreme," says Stephen Doyle. "The water becomes the type. When Louis Kahn picked up a brick and asked it what it wanted to be, the brick answered, 'I want to be an arch.' When I looked into my glass of water and asked it what it wanted to be, there was no answer. So, I decided to make it into its own language. It clearly needed a way to communicate. Making letterforms out of water is fleeting and temporary. The photograph becomes the record, a souvenir of a disappearing idea. I love that the letters hold both bright white and solid black, yet they are made of something completely clear. It is visible only because it has reflective properties. Look closely and you can see my window sash and the buildings across Madison Square Park in every single letter."
DESIGN FIRM: Doyle Partners
ART DIRECTOR/DESIGNER/PHOTOGRAPHER: Stephen Doyle
CLIENT: AIGA PRIMARY FONT: Freehand water

IF LIQUID CAN be transformed into letterforms, then smoke and ethereal smoke-like substances are not far behind. Fire, for example, has long been used in lettering. And although they are not smoke per se, dust has a smoky film, and ink and intestines could also be mistaken for fumes.

JACKIE PEPPER LOGO The most common way of making type appear to be smoke is to have the swashes rise upward like flames. The word "pepper" in this Texan musician's name suggests heat.
DESIGN FIRM: The Decoder Ring Design Concern DESIGNER: Ben Barry CLIENT: Jackie Pepper PRIMARY FONT: Hand lettering

ACCEPT & PROCEED (A&P) A major influence for this logo, and for much of Sean Freeman's type-based design, is the work of Non-Format, who put a lot of energy and movement into their pieces. DESIGN FIRM: There Is DESIGNER: Sean Freeman CLIENT: Accept & Proceed PRIMARY FONT: Based on Clarendon Roman

THE TASTE OF INK IS GETTING OLD

THE TASTE OF INK IS GETTING OLD "This is directly inspired by the lyrics of one of my favorite band's songs," says Sean Freeman – "'The Taste of Ink' by The Used. I thought a delicate serif font would work best with the ink and water pieces. It was quite a literal interpretation of the lyrics and a bit more of an experiment than anything else I've done." DESIGN FIRM: There Is DESIGNER: Sean Freeman CLIENT: Self PRIMARY FONT: Based on Adobe Garamond Pro

THE

SMOKE

ELVIS This was Sean Freeman's first experiment playing with type, and was done while he was at the marketing agency Elvis Communications. "I was just seeing how I could work into the type, this time with cotton wool. It has now led on to treatments with flour, ink, milk, and my tongue," he admits. DESIGN FIRM: There Is DESIGNER: Sean Freeman CLIENT: Elvis Communications PRIMARY FONT: Bebas

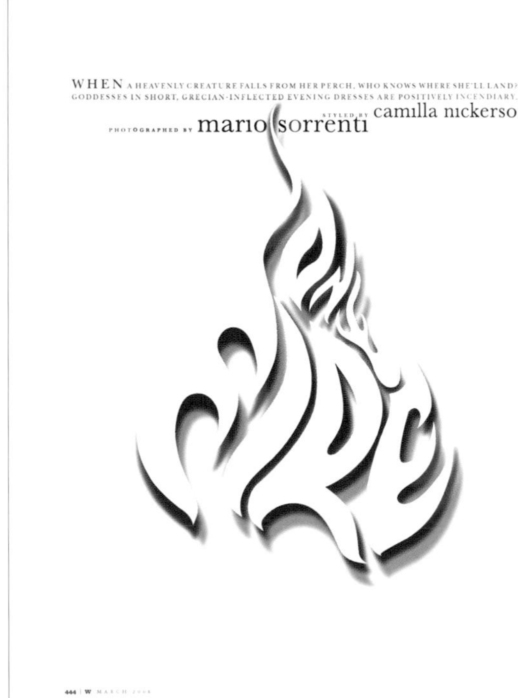

WHEN A HEAVENLY CREATURE FALLS FROM HER PERCH, WHO KNOWS WHERE SHE'LL LAND?
GODDESSES IN SHORT, GRECIAN-INFLECTED EVENING DRESSES ARE POSITIVELY INCENDIARY.
STYLED BY camilla nickerson
PHOTOGRAPHED BY mario sorrenti

ON FIRE The images in this story are literally smoldering. Hairstyles that look like flames and backgrounds filled with smoke conjure up the 1960s poster design hero Wes Wilson. Edward Leida's own hand-lettered flames were first drawn when he was a child. "For this I sketched a type treatment several times in pencil and then it was redrawn in Illustrator for the final." ART DIRECTOR/DESIGNER/ ILLUSTRATOR: Edward Leida PHOTOGRAPHER: Mario Sorrenti CLIENT: *W* magazine PUBLISHER: Condé Nast PRIMARY FONT: Hand lettering

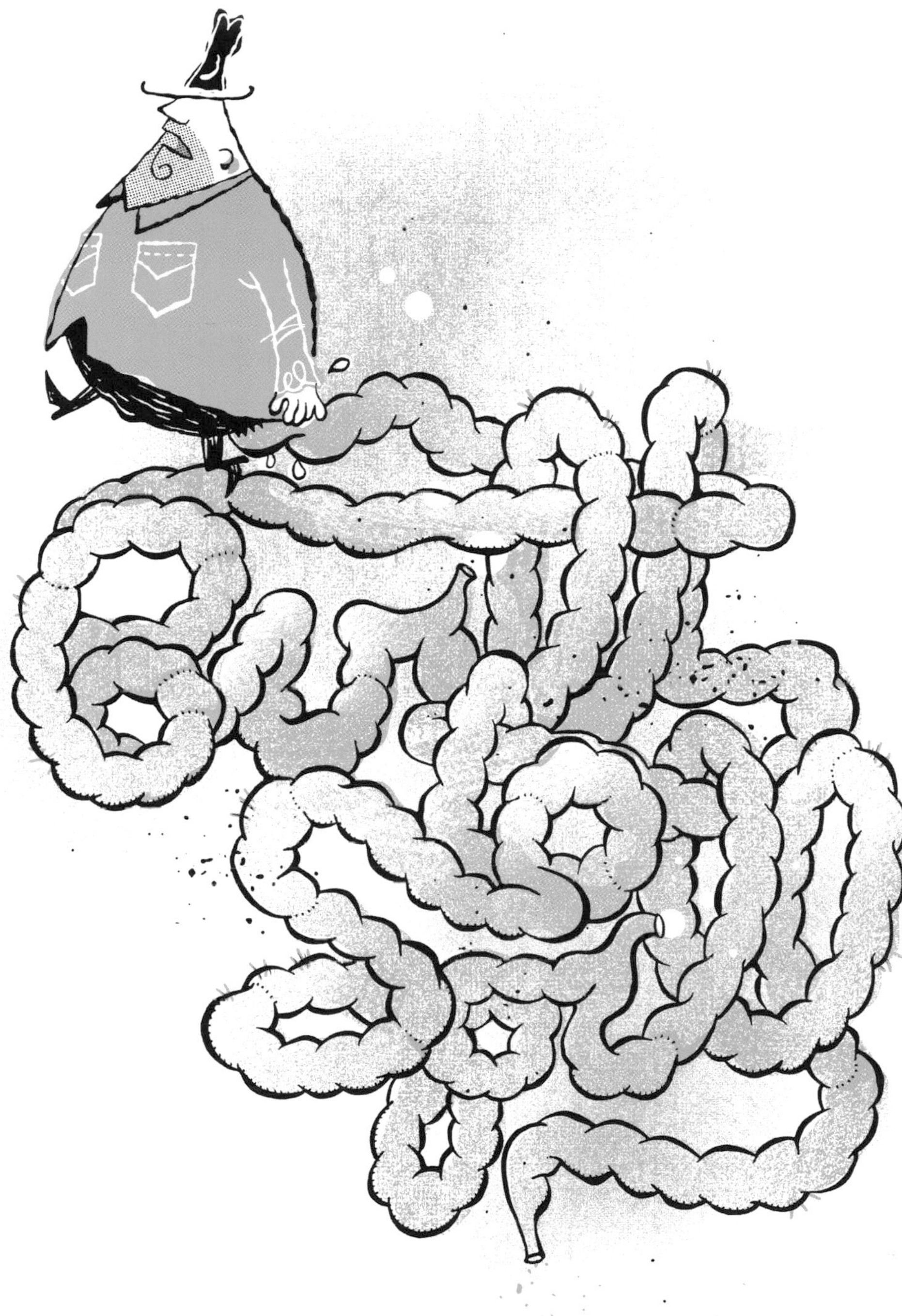

SEPTEMBER 27 2006 NEWPORT MUSIC HALL COLUMBUS OHIO

POSTER BY FARMBARN ART CO

BUILT TO SPILL Not exactly smoke, but where gas comes from in the human body…the designers of this concert poster say they were completing the visual pun of the intestines literally "spilling" from the running cowboy. The idea for the poster started as a silly doodle in a sketchbook; the illustration style is loosely based on the graphic style of 1950s cartoons.
DESIGN FIRM: FarmBarn Art Co.
DESIGNERS: Drue Dixon, Mike Pierce
ILLUSTRATOR: Drue Dixon CLIENT: PromoWest Productions PRIMARY FONT: Hand lettering

WITH THE ENTIRE world concerned about global warming and sustainability, why shouldn't typography be green – not just the color, but also the form it takes? What is more Au Naturel than a lettering lawn? Flora is easy to train, and if watered daily will not only give weeks of good typography, but will also turn carbon dioxide to oxygen.

12|24.06

ON LANGUAGE BY WILLIAM SAFIRE

The comeback word in foreign policy.

By far the hottest word of 2006: the noun *realism*, with its brother noun, *realist*, as a label for its practitioners.

In a Washington Post column titled "This Is *Realism*?" Charles Krauthammer led with "Now that the '*realists*' have ridden into town gleefully consigning the Bush doctrine to the ash heap of history, everyone has discovered the notion of interests, as if it were some new idea thought up by James Baker and the Iraq Study Group."

Contrariwise, Tom Ricks wrote in the same paper: "The Iraq Study Group report might well be titled 'The *Realist* Manifesto,'" a repudiation of the Bush administration's diplomatic and military approach now being challenged by recommendations stemming from "the '*realist*' school of foreign policy."

"We are all *realists* now." That was the lede of George Packer's article in a recent issue of The New Yorker, paraphrasing Milton Friedman's temporary salute to the economic activism of Britain's Lord Keynes. "Iraq has turned conservatives and liberals alike," Packer wrote, "into cold-eyed believers in a foreign policy that narrowly calculates national interest without much concern for what goes on inside other countries."

Then, unexpectedly in a magazine with unabashed Bush-bashing credentials, Packer put his thumb in the eye of triumphalist *realists*: "At some point events will remind Americans that currently discredited concepts such as humanitarian intervention and nation-building have a lot to do with national security — that they originated as necessary evils to prevent greater evils. But, for now, Kissingerism is king."

That equated *realism* with *Kissingerism*, synonymy that Henry the K surely considers insufficiently nuanced. He was long associated, however, with the German word *Realpolitik* (pronounced re-AL-po-li-teek), coined in 1853 by Ludwig von Rochau in an attack on German liberals. In an essay in Time last month headlined "The Return of the Realists," Walter Isaacson noted that "the doctrine of realism, or its Prussian-accented cousin *Realpolitik*, emphasizes a hard-nosed focus on clearly defined national interests, such as economic or security goals, pursued with a pragmatic calculation of commitments and resources. Idealism, on the other hand, emphasized moral values and ideals, such as spreading democracy."

Pragmatism was the word that proponents of *realism* preferred in the Nixon administration to define the opening to Communist China and détente with the Soviet Union, as well as a tolerance for authoritarian (O.K., dictatorial) leaders like Lee Kwan Yew of Singapore who were on our side in the cold war. In that temporary renaming of *realism*, Nixon speech writers liked to quote the famous saying attributed to President Franklin D. Roosevelt about a Central American strongman: "Somoza may be a sonofabitch, but he's our sonofabitch."

(Tangent: That "famous saying" first appeared in Time magazine in an unsigned article — as all were in the era of group journalism — about a 1939 visit to Washington by President Anastasio Somoza García. "To prime President Roosevelt for the visit," Time reported in 1948, "Sumner Welles sent him a long, solemn memorandum about Somoza and Nicaragua. According to a story told around Washington, Roosevelt read the memo right through, wisecracked, 'As a Nicaraguan might say, he's a sonofabitch, but he's ours.'" No source for that "story" was ever found; it must be put down as apocryphal, a word rooted in the Greek "hidden." This debunking denies today's *realists* one of their best lines.)

The old *realism* of the 1960s and '70s derogated diplomatic morality, coined "the balance of terror" and glorified strategic stability. It treated *idealism* as a fatuous word, deriding President Woodrow Wilson's dream of a war to end wars that would "make the world safe for democracy" as hopelessly unpragmatic. In the 1980s, however, under Ronald Reagan, it was the word *realism*'s turn to take a hit: the lexical pendulum swung toward evocation of America as "the city on a hill," an embrace of human-rights rhetoric and the moral denunciation of an "evil empire." Crusading *idealism* was In and amoral *realism* was Out.

In the first Bush era of 1989-93, with "stability" the paramount goal of diplomacy, the word *realism* began to make a comeback. It peaked in the senior Bush's visit to Kiev, just as the Soviet Union showed signs of coming apart in the Baltics and Ukrainians sought their freedom from Moscow rule. Brent Scowcroft, a retired general who had been a longtime Kissinger aide, helped write a stability-first speech for George H.W. Bush urging Ukrainians to stay within the Soviet Union and direly warning of "suicidal nationalism." This caused a vituperative right-wing opinion monger at The New York Times to label the outburst of realism "Chicken Kiev" (and the elder Bush has not talked to me since).

Realism, as word and policy, had its ups and down through the Clinton years, but in the first term of Bush II was battered by what the historian Robert Kagan calls "Americans' belief in the possibility of global transformation — the 'messianic' impulse." As public impatience grew with "the long, hard slog" in Iraq, however, the stock of Wilsonian idealism fell out of bed, and *realism* came back into oratorical vogue and, in last month's elections, into shared political power.

Ascendant *realists* now face the problem introduced in The New Yorker: even amid war-weariness, how to justify a label with a history of unprincipled dickering with dictators and an amoral priority of stability over the export of freedom?

Language has a solution: an adjectival qualifier. Although Krauthammer two years ago pre-empted *democratic realism* to describe his idealistic policy of selective intervention, real old realists are now turning to *ethical realism*, an oxymoron with broad appeal, while liberal internationalists are trying out *progressive realism*. Meanwhile, grim idealists will soon be running the modifiers *prudent* and *practical* past focus groups. Prediction for 2007: Whatever adjectives are chosen to take the edge off the core position, the other side will denounce the label as *unrealistic*. ■

Send comments and suggestions to: safireonlanguage@nytimes.com.

Lettering by Dylan Martorell

20

REALISM Each week, *New York Times* columnist and language expert William Safire writes about a word or phrase that is relevant to the moment. For the past three years, Arem Duplessis and Gail Bichler have invited different artists, designers and illustrators to interpret the words in their own unique way, often with curiously ornamental results.
ART DIRECTOR: Arem Duplessis DESIGNER: Gail Bichler LETTERER: Dylan Martorell CLIENT: *The New York Times Magazine* PUBLISHER: *The New York Times* PRIMARY FONTS: Stymie NYT, Cheltenham NYT

FAST COMPANY MAY 06 The front of each issue of *Fast Company* has a calendar section and every month a different designer or illustrator creates a header image. May being when spring turns into summer, Bruce Willen documented the growth of some carefully planted seeds over the course of a few weeks. A camera was set up in one spot for the duration of the growing period, taking a photo every twelve hours.
DESIGN FIRM: Post Typography ART DIRECTOR: Jana Meier (*Fast Company*) DESIGNER: Bruce Willen CLIENT/PUBLISHER: *Fast Company* magazine PRIMARY FONT: Grass

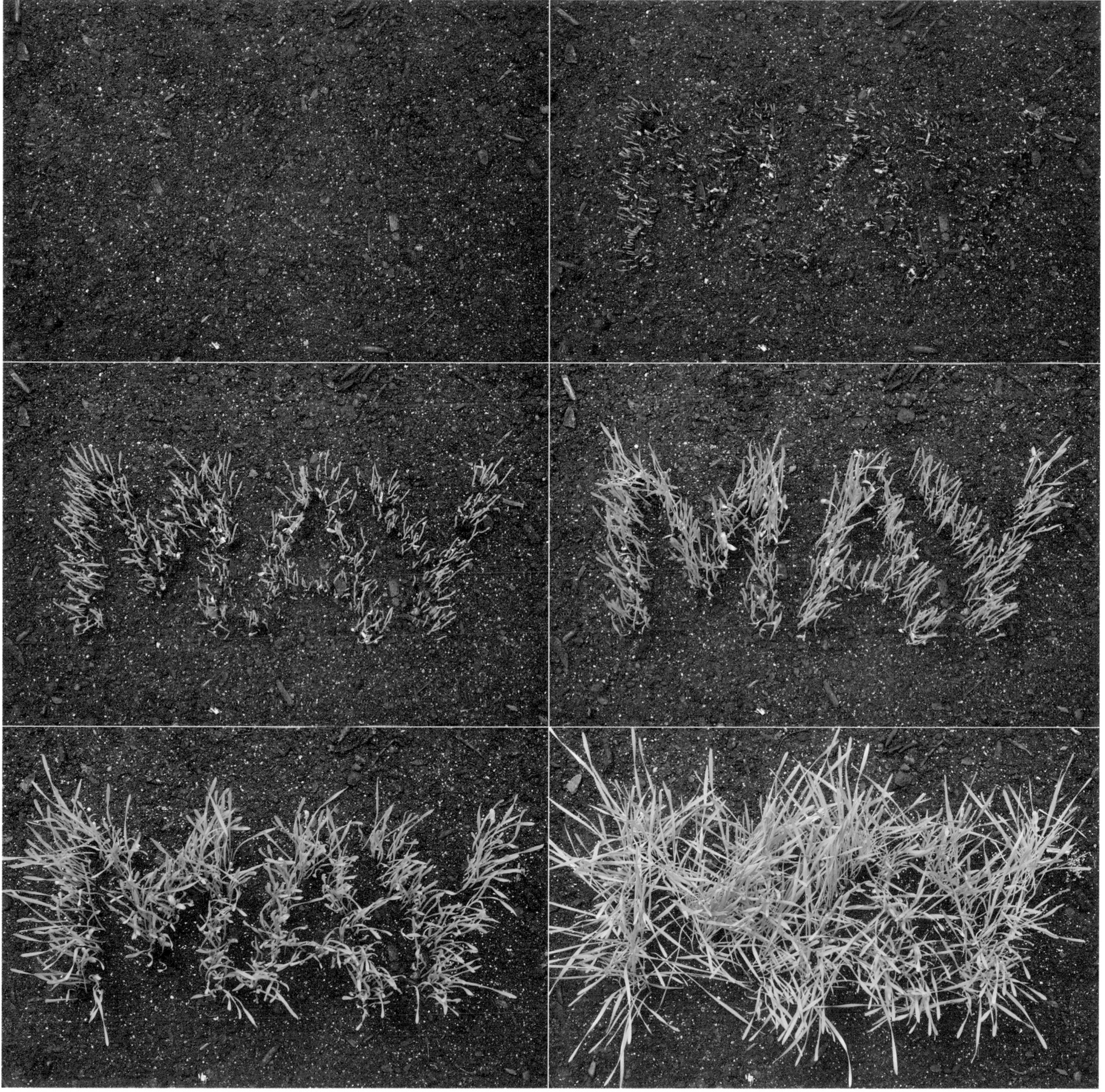
MAY

THE GREEN ISSUE *The New York Times Magazine* "Green Issue" was influenced in part by *The Whole Earth Catalog.* It was a fusion of ideas based around several different "green topics" under headings such as Act, Eat, Invent, Learn, Live, Move, and Build.
ART DIRECTOR: Arem Duplessis DEPUTY ART DIRECTOR: Gail Bichler DESIGNERS: Arem Duplessis, Gail Bichler, Leo Jung, Hilary Greenbaum, Cathy Gilmore-Barnes, Julia Moburg, Ian Allen LETTERER: Gyongy Laky CLIENT: *The New York Times Magazine* PUBLISHER: *The New York Times* PRIMARY FONTS: Sunday NYT (various weights) and Cheltenham NYT

The New York Times Magazine / APRIL 20, 2008

THE GREEN ISSUE

ACT 46 EAT 52 INVENT 54 LEARN 61 LIVE 62 MOVE 68 BUILD 72

Some Bold Steps to Make Your Carbon Footprint Smaller

LETTERING BY GYONGY LAKY PHOTOGRAPHS BY DWIGHT ESCHLIMAN GROWING-FOREST ILLUSTRATIONS BY ANDREW RAE

45

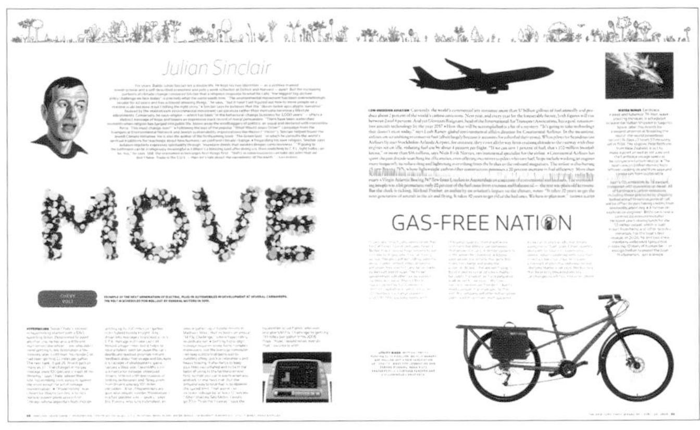
Julian Sinclair

MOVE

GAS-FREE NATION

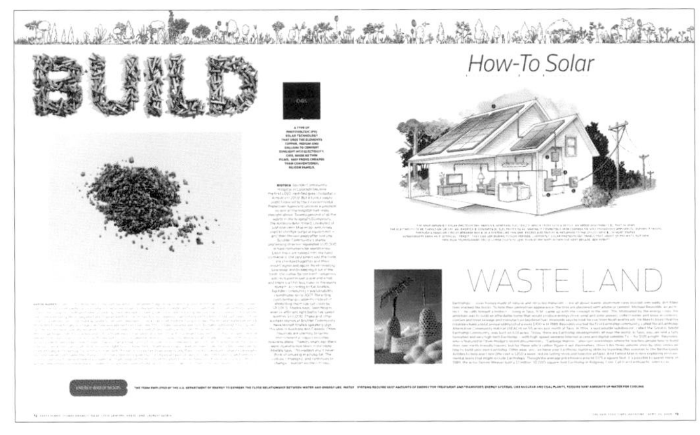
BUILD

How-To Solar

WASTE LAND

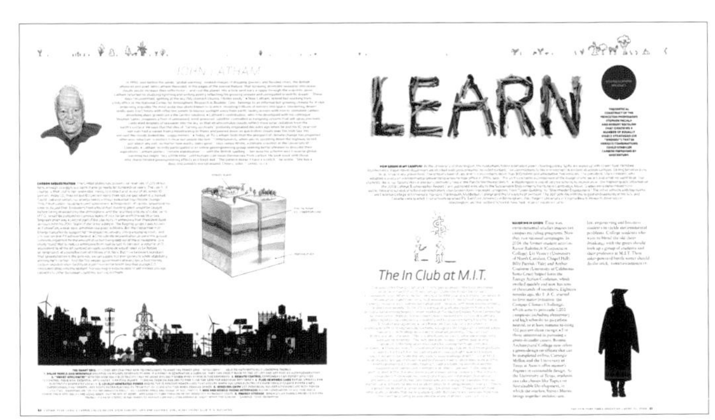
LEARN

The In Club at M.I.T.

SO MUCH GROWS IN BROOKLYN Trees and their trunks make a serpentine bramble of letters and words for this self-promotional piece.
DESIGN FIRM: Mike Perry ART DIRECTOR/DESIGNER/ ILLUSTRATOR: Mike Perry CLIENT: Self PRIMARY FONT: Hand lettering

TRYING TO LOOK GOOD LIMITS MY LIFE "My grandfather was educated in sign painting and I grew up with many of his pieces of wisdom around the house – traditional calligraphy carefully applied in gold leaf on painstakingly carved wooden panels," says Stefan Sagmeister. "One of his panels, still hanging in our hallway in Austria, reads: 'This house is mine, and it isn't mine. The next guy won't own it either. They will carry out the third one, too. So tell me, my friend, whose house is it?' I am just following this tradition with *Trying to Look Good Limits My Life*. The title of this work is among the few things I have learned in my life so far (some of the others are: having guts always works out for me, and everything I do always comes back to me). Broken up into five parts and displayed in sequence as typographic billboards, the giant photographs [displayed in the "Art Grandeur Nature" exhibition, 2004] work like a sentimental greeting card left in a park north of Paris."
DESIGN FIRM: Sagmeister, Inc.
ART DIRECTOR: Stefan Sagmeister
DESIGNERS: Stefan Sagmeister, Matthias Ernstberger PHOTOGRAPHER: Matthias Ernstberger CLIENT: "Art Grandeur Nature" PRIMARY FONTS: Custom made

EVERYTHING I DO ALWAYS COMES BACK TO ME These six double-page spreads for the Austrian magazine *.copy* are dividing spaces, each opening a new section. Each month the magazine commissions a new studio with the design. Stefan Sagmeister started with the backgrounds, sourcing them from clothing wholesalers and the wallpaper company Wolf-Gordon. He then found objects to create the type from the butchers, in Chinatown and in grocery and hardware stores, before adding more detail in Photoshop.
DESIGN FIRM: Sagmeister, Inc. ART DIRECTOR: Stefan Sagmeister DESIGNERS: Eva Hueckmann, Matthias Ernstberger, Doris Pesendorfer, Stefan Sagmeister PHOTOGRAPHER: Matthias Ernstberger MODEL MAKING: Eva Hueckmann BACKGROUNDS: Wolf-Gordon Inc. CLIENT: *.copy* magazine PUBLISHER: Telekom Austria PRIMARY FONTS: Custom made

HANDMADE

THE DO-IT-YOURSELF (DIY) AESTHETIC has grown exponentially in the post-computer epoch. Whether it is the need to keep hands occupied or the desire to keep art from becoming overly mechanical, handwritten letterforms are on the rise. It is also something that everyone can do – and even done poorly, it can be appreciated in an Art Brut kind of way. Handwritten typography comes in many forms, but the vast majority of practitioners get satisfaction – as if they were doodling – from drawing heavy drop shadows on their slab serif and sans serif letters.

DEVIL MAY CARE Jonny Hannah loves badly drawn shop signs, and books such as *Sign Language* by John Baeder and *Sensacional* about Mexican street graphics. This blend of lettering was inspired by Kevin Bradly at Yee-Haw, the Ramones, and pin-up girls, Hannah says. The image is a linocut.
DESIGN FIRM: Cakes & Ale Press ART DIRECTOR/DESIGNER/ ILLUSTRATOR: Jonny Hannah PUBLISHER: Cakes & Ale Press PRIMARY FONT: Hand lettering

MAGIC CLUB This design was created for use on kids' T-shirts. The theme was "magic" and the image took inspiration from old posters for magic shows and circus performances.
DESIGN FIRM: Maki ART DIRECTOR: Chris Coleman
DESIGNERS/ILLUSTRATORS: Kim Smits, Matthijs Maat
CLIENT: WGSN PRIMARY FONT: Hand lettering

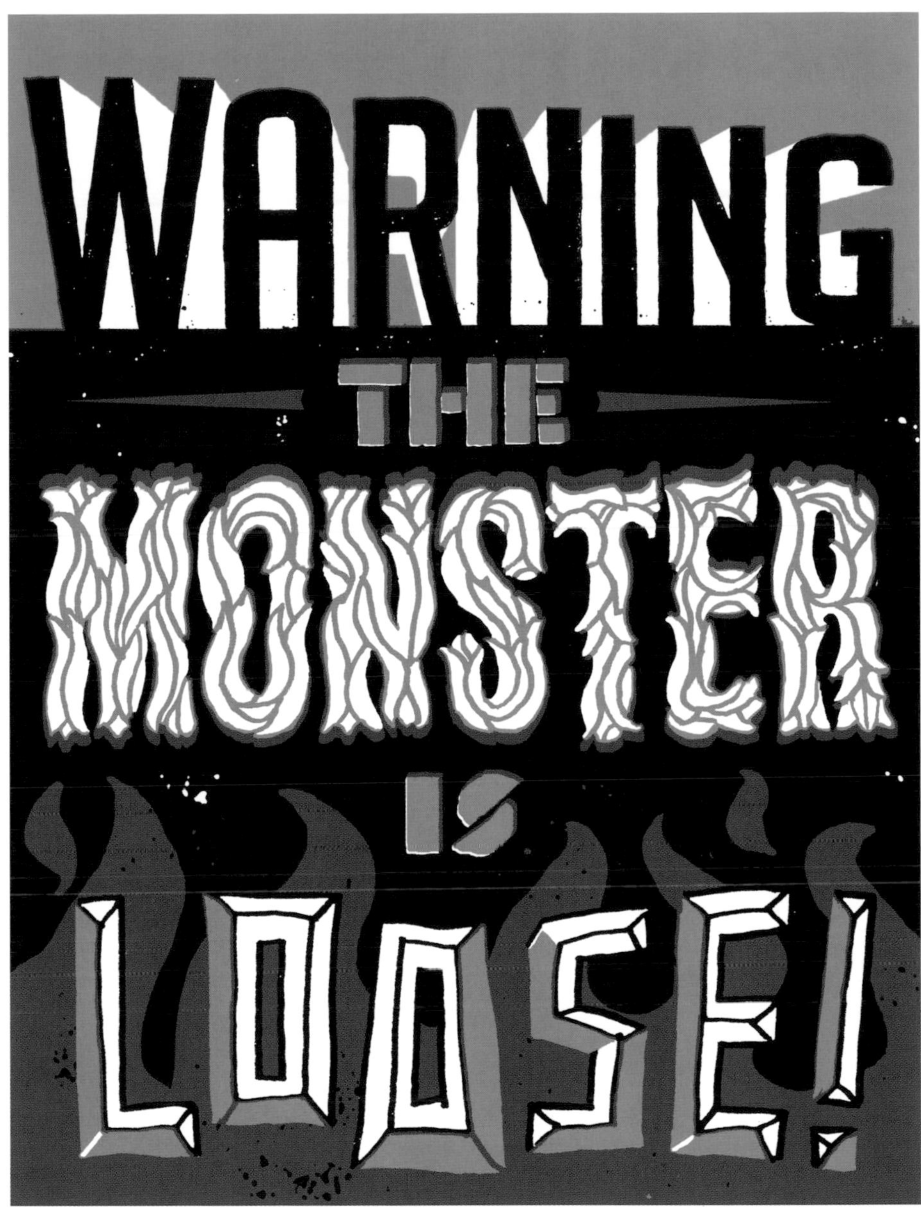

WARNING: THE MONSTER IS LOOSE! Andy Smith wanted to produce a self-promotional poster using only two base colors and the color that was produced from overlaying them. The lettering for this piece was inspired by vintage horror posters and comic book fonts.
DESIGN FIRM: Andy Smith ART DIRECTOR/ILLUSTRATOR: Andy Smith CLIENT: Self PRIMARY FONT: Hand lettering

YOU WERE PLAN B T-shirt company Threadless asked Maki to create a design with this slogan on it. They combined bold letters with smaller line drawings. Although the reader can interpret the message in many different ways, the design "lets our criminal minds do the talking," Maki say.
DESIGN FIRM: Maki ART DIRECTOR: Ross Zietz DESIGNER/ILLUSTRATOR: Maki CLIENT: Threadless PRIMARY FONT: Hand lettering

EXPLOSIONS IN THE SKY Since the imagery, illustrations, and textures were assembled from sketchbook drawings and torn pieces of paper, Nate Duval decided that he would "hand-draw eight or nine different fonts (A–Z) and piece together the type on this poster by selecting different letters from each 'alphabet' as I saw fit," he says.
DESIGN FIRM: NateDuval.com ART DIRECTOR/DESIGNER/ILLUSTRATOR: Nate Duval CLIENT: Constant Artist Management PRIMARY FONT: Hand lettering

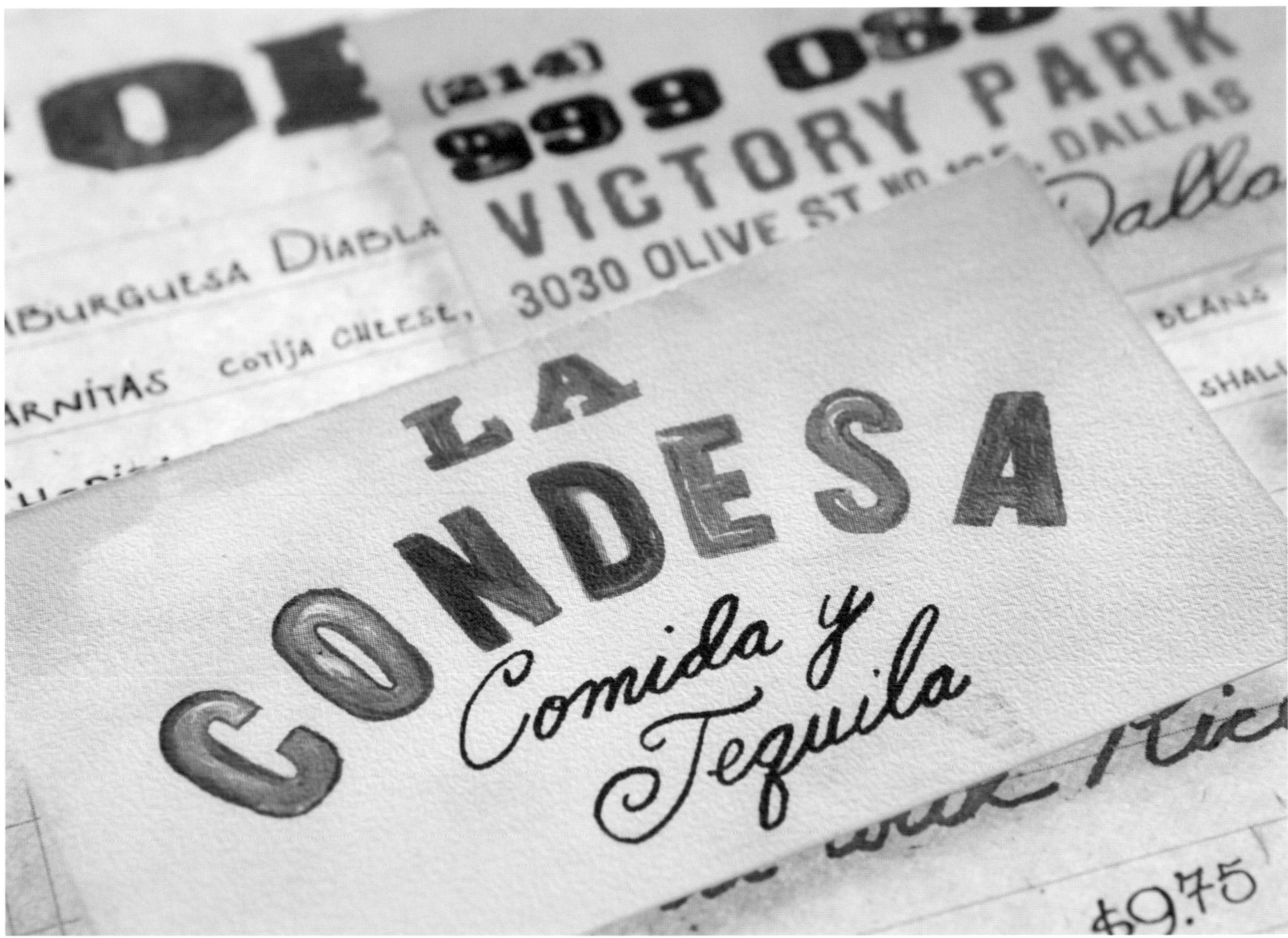

LA CONDESA La Condesa is a neighborhood in Mexico City, filled with a charming mix of old and new culture. Although most of the architecture dates from the 1920s and 1930s, the walls of all the markets have been repeatedly hand-painted with menus, lists of services, and colorful graffiti, each layer covering the last. Based on research from the area, Mucca created hand-painted typography for every headline, and a typeface for the text that appears to be real handwriting. The business cards were also hand-painted, and printed on a paper that mimics the texture of a cement wall.
DESIGN FIRM: Mucca Design ART DIRECTOR: Matteo Bologna DESIGNERS: Christine Celic Strohl, Lauren Sheldon CLIENT: The Icon Group PRIMARY FONTS: Hand lettering, custom OpenType typography

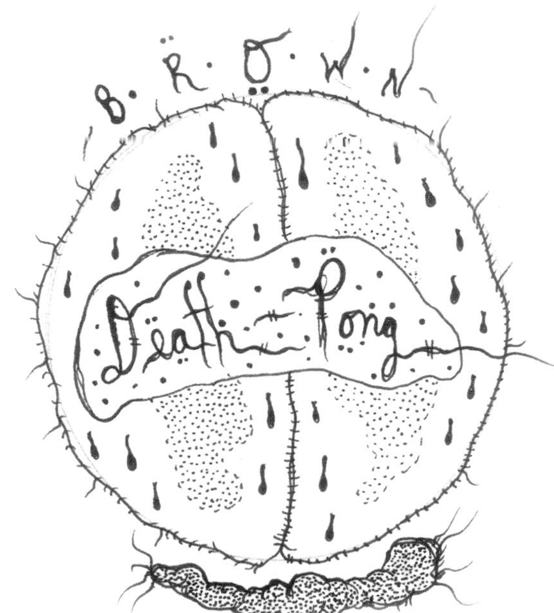

DEATH PONG, DOG SORES, DONKEY CRUST, MEAT CREAM, DUCK BUTTER, PIG BLISTERS, DIRT SLUG
The influences for these circles derive from 1960s underground Psychedelic art, R. Crumb comics, cartoons and DIY publications, as well as biomorphic abstraction, graphic scatology, and medical illustration.
DESIGNER: Paul Nudd CLIENT: Self
PRIMARY FONTS: Hand lettering

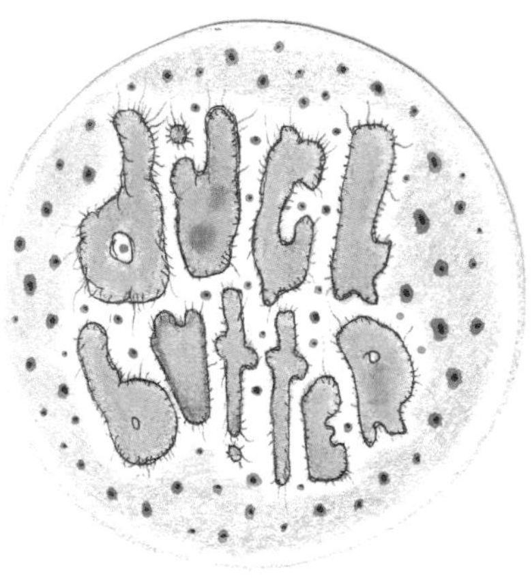

YALE UNIVERSITY ART GALLERY

This logo is a crazy patchwork quilt of doodled letterforms that can be read only when the reader's eyes are carefully focused.
DESIGN FIRM: Christopher Sleboda
ART DIRECTOR: Christopher Sleboda
DESIGNER/ILLUSTRATOR: Mike Perry
CLIENT: Yale University Art Gallery
PRIMARY FONT: Hand lettering

BEN HARPER + JACK JOHNSON

Michael Strassburger notes that the inspiration for this poster came from Ed Fella's typography work, specifically his notebooks (see page 126), combined with the idea of using pencils to represent acoustic guitar playing.
DESIGN FIRM: Modern Dog Design Co. ART DIRECTOR/DESIGNER/ILLUSTRATOR: Michael Strassburger
CLIENT: House of Blues PRIMARY FONT: Hand lettering

HANDMADE

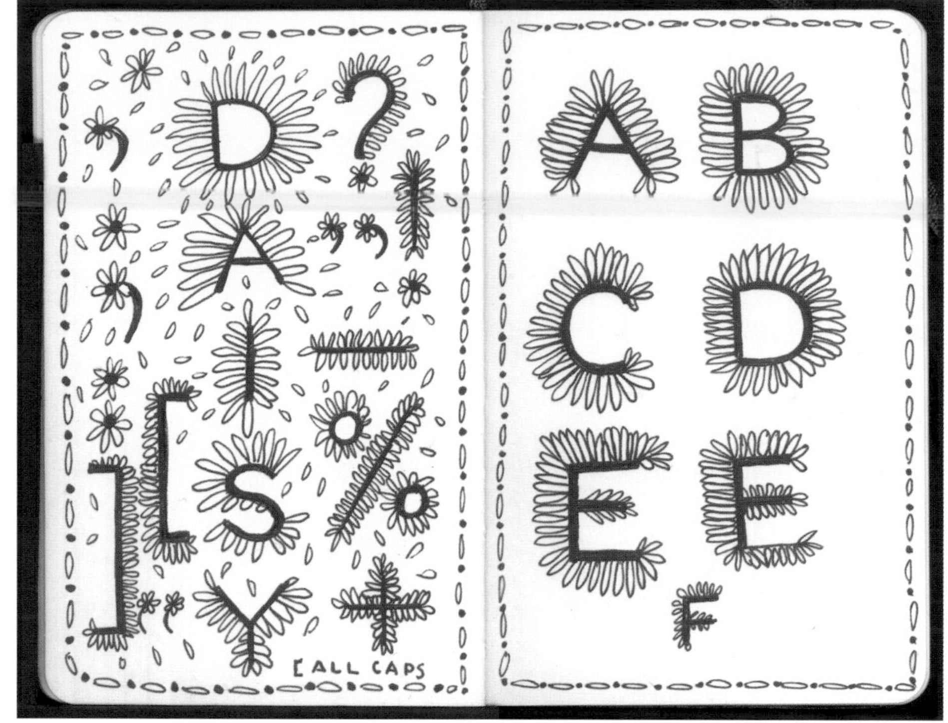

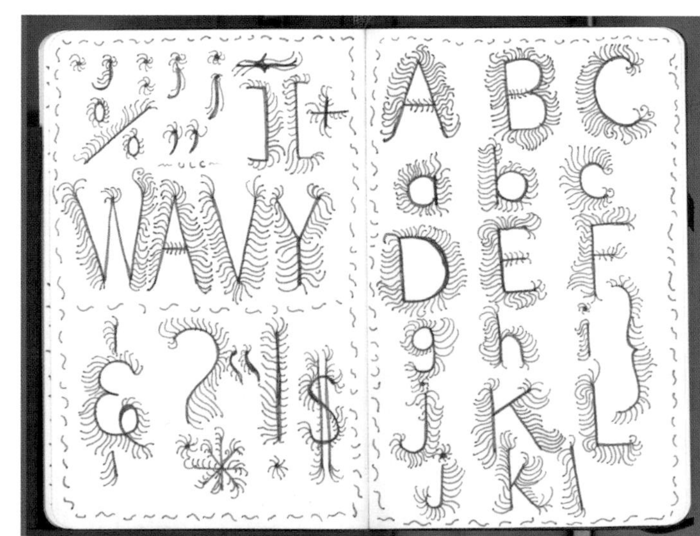

PAULA SCHER'S SKETCHBOOK

Although the similarity may be hard to see, the letterforms in this sketchbook are all influenced by the fluidity and wit of Saul Steinberg, legendary cover artist for the *New Yorker*.

DESIGN FIRM: Paula Scher/Pentagram
ART DIRECTOR/DESIGNER/ILLUSTRATOR: Paula Scher/Pentagram
PRIMARY FONTS: Hand lettering

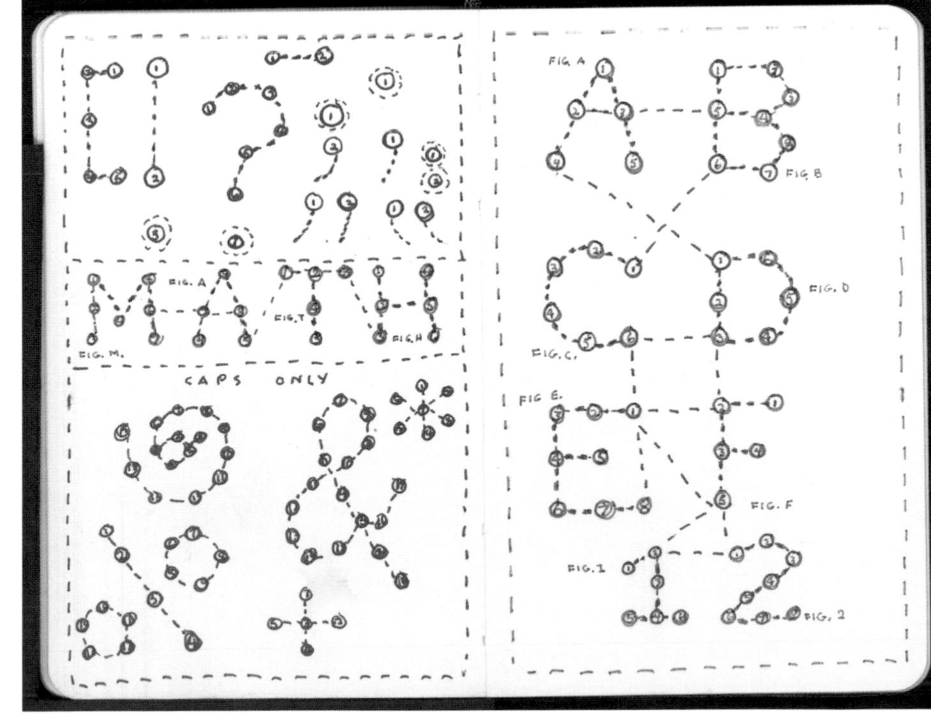

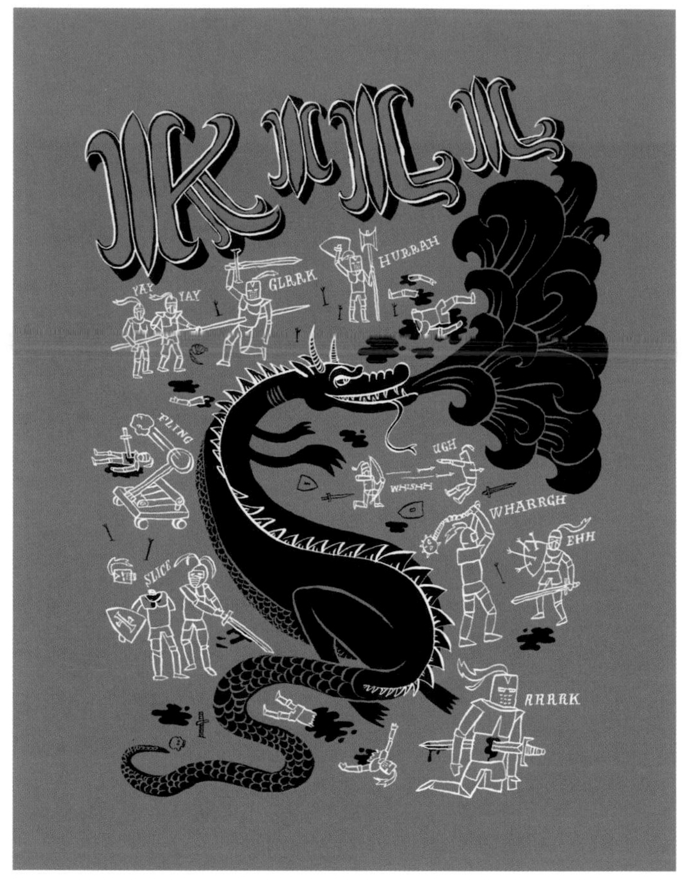

KILL The typefaces were inspired by Tuscan letterforms, while the image was inspired by a simple and free childlike sensibility.
ILLUSTRATOR: Ray Fenwick CLIENT: Self PRIMARY FONT: Hand lettering

EX MODELS The main theme is the circle/target, and the idea of infinite repetition that accompanies it. The outer squareness of each letterform makes it stand out from the rest of the design, while the circles and the repetitions inside hold the whole composition together.
DESIGN FIRM: Seripop ART DIRECTORS/DESIGNERS/ILLUSTRATORS: Yannick Desranleau, Chloe Lum CLIENT: Ex Models PRIMARY FONT: Hand lettering

COMPLETE SHAKESPEARE Jonny Hannah says that he put together a big mix of hand-drawn letterforms – all he could muster on a Sunday morning – to get this piece ready for a Monday deadline. He was so pleased with the result that he turned this one into a screen print.
DESIGN FIRM: *The Sunday Telegraph* ART DIRECTOR/DESIGNER: Alex MacFadyen ILLUSTRATOR: Jonny Hannah CLIENT: *The Sunday Telegraph* PUBLISHER: Telegraph Media Group Limited PRIMARY FONT: Hand lettering

FALL ARTS PREVIEW This is a lighthearted "header" for the *San Francisco Chronicle*'s "Fall Arts" section, which recalls the Hatch Show Print posters.
ART DIRECTOR: Matt Petty
ILLUSTRATOR: Nate Williams
CLIENT: The *San Francisco Chronicle*
PUBLISHER: Hearst Communications
PRIMARY FONT: Hand lettering

ED FELLA REINVIGORATED hand lettering in the 1990s with a blend of whimsy and theory. His colored pencil drawn illuminated letters, sayings, and announcements done by hand at the height of computer-driven typographic experimentation inspired many designers who were looking for that bridge between commercial art and personal expression. As a former commercial artist from the bullpens in Detroit, Fella found that he did not have to adhere to Modernist or Post-Modernist dogma, but rather used his lettering prowess as a way to express himself.

LETTER "B" "Bunch had designers from all over the world do a letter 'B' for them to use in their studio promotions," says Fella.
CLIENT: Bunch Design

MOZART SIGNATURE All this lettering is done mostly with templates and Prismacolor pencil. It is inspired by what Fella calls "the commercial art vernacular," such as showcard lettering.
CLIENT: Giorgio Camuffo Studio

LUCY 60 Original lettering for Fella's wife's sixtieth birthday present.
CLIENT: Lucy Fella

AIGA SCHOLARSHIP CERTIFICATE
PROJECT DIRECTOR: Tony Manzella
CLIENT: AIGA

A BEAUTIFUL ADDICTION For this wordmark, Paul Sych wanted to experiment with a traditional hand-lettered script with a hint of Psychedelic art thrown in for good measure, hence this slogan for a beauty salon in New York.
DESIGN FIRM: Faith ART DIRECTOR/ DESIGNER: Paul Sych CLIENT: Established PRIMARY FONT: Hand lettering

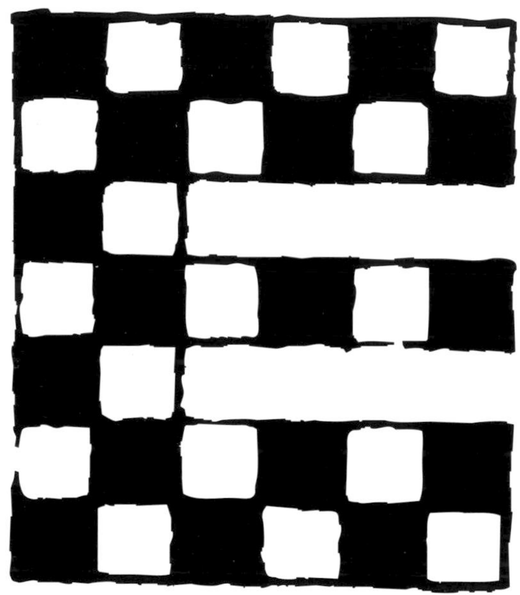

CERTAINLY ALL THE TYPOGRAPHY in this book is eclectic – after all, what else can one call lettering and type that does not conform to the centuries-old standards? What's more, this is designed as a compilation of unusual and delightful alternatives to conventional practice. But, to paraphrase George Orwell in *Animal Farm*: everything is eclectic, but some things are more eclectic than others.

Eclecticism is in the eye of the beholder – wackiness or weirdness are not always an accurate measure. Who is to say that Stefan Sagmeister's bread font on page 130 is more idiosyncratic than Ed Fella's hand lettering on page 126? For Fella this mannerism is his "normal" way of writing; Sagmeister routinely thinks out of the breadbox, so his results are also appropriate to who he is. As outlandish as certain letterforms may appear on the surface, they might well be rooted in deeper history or be blessed with some other kind of pedigree. For a piece of typography to fit into this section, it has to be one of a kind. It should not be made with a template, even an eclectic one. It has to move type and lettering beyond both convention and common reason, yet remain rational. Letters made from objects have to be eccentric and yet still work within their context.

Viktor Koen's alphabet made from weapons spelling out "Lies" (page 134), with former president George Bush's head dotting an "I" made from an ammunition clip, has a clear rationale. Similarly, the word "shame" made from tools of pain and torture (page 134) illustrates the concept as it shocks the reader. On a more comic note, "The National" made from clothes on hangers (page 139) is fitting, funny, and conveys a welcome lightheartedness.

There are many ways in which something may be considered eclectic, but the trick is in making it smart, not merely sensational. Some eccentricities are not radically over the top, but they are unexpected. Jason Rubino's cross (page 143), made from script letterforms, is as sublimely elegant as it is exceptionally crafted. But it is also a total surprise. In the Chaotic section, Marian Bantjes's "Sustainability" poster (page 146) is not the most obvious interpretation of the word, yet it communicates an alternative vision of how it can be perceived. Her eclectic sensibility is clearly showing.

Few things may be more surprising than the Puzzle section, where the typography is either made from puzzle parts or is itself a perception puzzle. Bruce Willen's conjoined font (page

150) is a crazy but sensible notion that earns its eclectic brand because few would put in the effort to make such an eccentric composition. Turning to embellishment, it takes a true eclectic to find new ways of freshening up the venerable decorative art of over-ornamentation. Jonathan Kenyon, John Glasgow, and Daryl Waller's "V49" (page 155) puts Rococo and Victorian tropes in a Cusinart and the result is unseemly. Likewise, Si Scott's rendering of the *Notion* magazine logo (page 157) takes liberties with legibility that surprise and delight.

Designers have often used sewing and embroidering as a means of making letterforms eclectic. But as stitching goes, little is as inventive as Sagmeister's "Self-Confidence Produces Fine Results" (page 165); rather than string or yarn, rather than sewing with a needle and thread, his typography is stitched together with bananas. As they turn color they reveal the saying, and as they turn brown, it disappears. Now, that's eclectic at its most intense.

THE BISHOPS A delightful hand-drawn swash and flourish logo that owes its look to the popular nineteenth-century Spencerian Script. DESIGN FIRM: Mike Perry ART DIRECTOR/ DESIGNER/ILLUSTRATOR: Mike Perry CLIENT: *Amelia's* magazine PUBLISHER: Amelia Gregory PRIMARY FONT: Hand lettering

OBJECT AS LETTER

SEEING LETTERFORMS in objects is one of the many perceptual games played by designers as they walk the streets. It has also been the subject of books and slide shows galore. Objects as letters are sublime visual puns – virtually anything can be made into type. The trick is to create an alphabet that is actually functional. Some objects just don't make the cut. But, looking at the cut records on page 137, it is easy to see how simple it is to transform something that has another purpose altogether into a "W" or "H" or "Y".

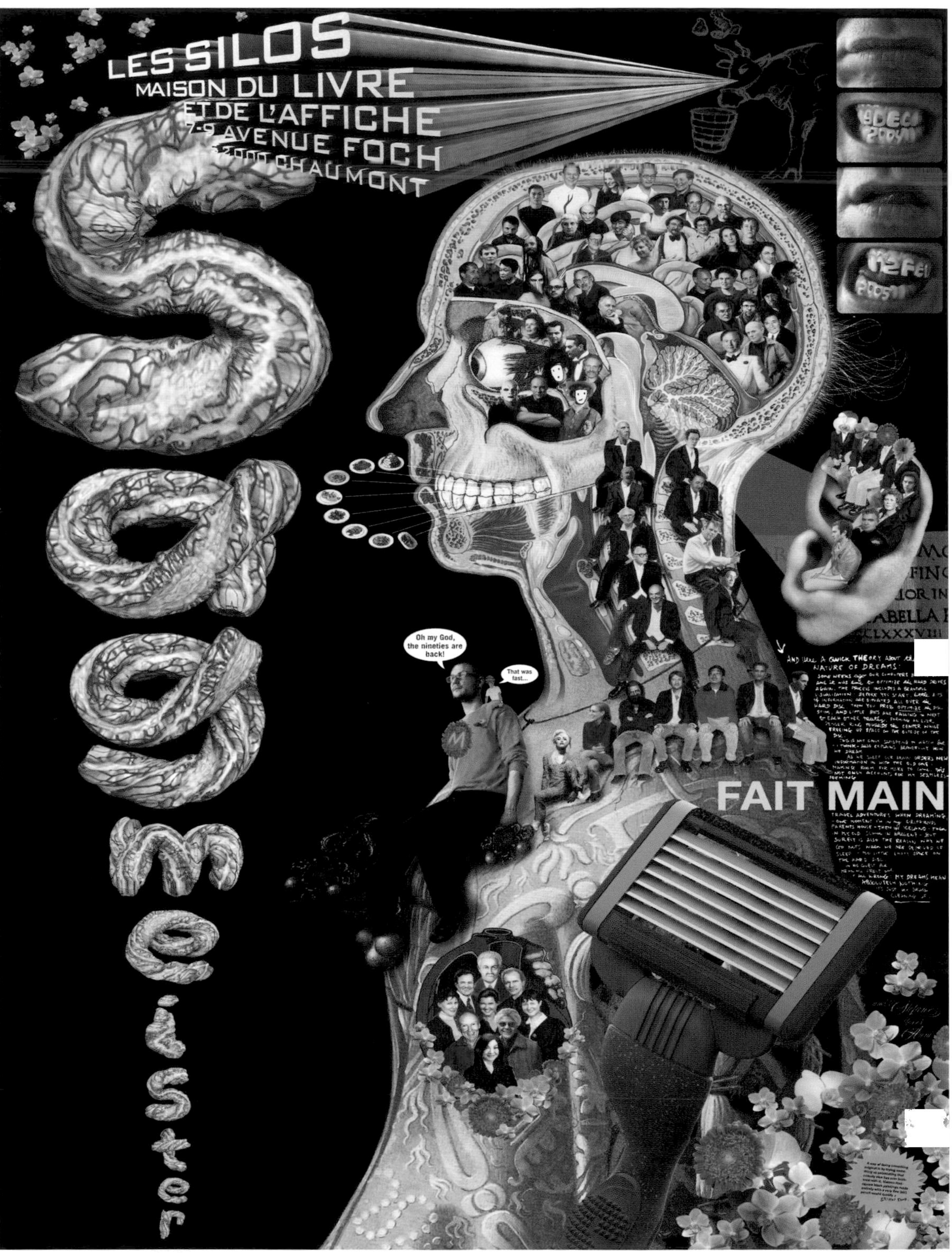

CHAUMONT The poster for Stefan Sagmeister's 2004 exhibition at Chaumont, France, features people who have had a significant influence on his work. Its imagery includes intestines, which spell his name in the most unappetizing way.
DESIGN FIRM: Sagmeister, Inc.
ART DIRECTOR: Stefan Sagmeister
DESIGNER: Matthias Ernstberger
3-D ILLUSTRATION: Aaron Hockett
ILLUSTRATOR: Gao Ming, Mao
CLIENT: Chaumont PRIMARY FONT: Intestines

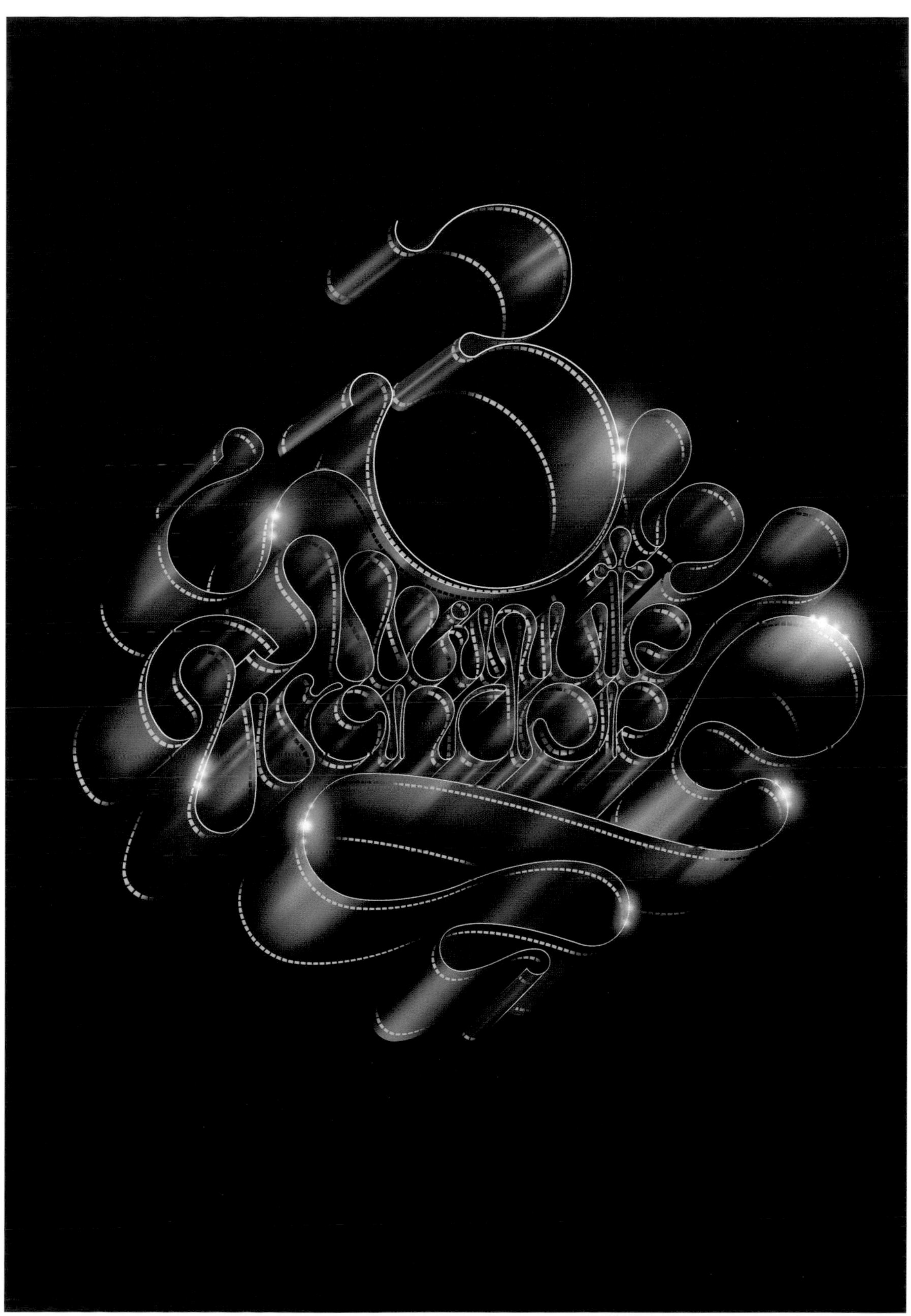

3 MINUTE WONDER Film strips are easily transformed into letters. This eccentric extravaganza for a British television channel shows what can be done with a lot of patience and the influence of yards of ribbon.
DESIGN FIRM: Alex Trochut ART DIRECTOR: Richard Haart DESIGNER: Alex Trochut CLIENT: Channel 4 PRIMARY FONT: Custom made

OBJECT AS LETTER

2009 CALENDAR In 2006, *The New York Times* asked Post Typography to design a typographic cover for the "Arts & Leisure" section's "Year in Culture" issue. During the course of the project they developed sketches that never saw print. After finishing the cover design, they decided to rework and expand their sketches into a wall calendar – one design for each month of the year. Post Typography's "Two Thousand and Nine 2009" interprets the number 2009 through twelve meditative and mind-bending typographic illustrations and lettering treatments. DESIGN FIRM: Post Typography ART DIRECTORS/DESIGNERS/ILLUSTRATORS: Nolen Strals, Bruce Willen PUBLISHER: teNeues Publishing Group PRIMARY FONT: Hand lettering

PIERRE BASTIEN Pierre Bastien generates his experimental music from self-constructed machines. In the poster design for his "Tour de Norvège," Grandpeople wanted to combine the mechanical theme with an acoustic feel. The ancient blueprints of Byzantine water dispensers from which the type is constructed almost look like resonance boxes. DESIGN FIRM: Grandpeople ART DIRECTORS/DESIGNERS: Grandpeople CLIENT: Rikskonsertene PRIMARY FONT: Custom made

"A" CAKE These are letters a designer could really sink his teeth into. And they come in delicious flavors.
DESIGN FIRM: Seb Lester ART DIRECTOR/DESIGNER/ILLUSTRATOR: Seb Lester CLIENT: Self PRIMARY FONT: Hand-drawn "A," digitized

OBJECT AS LETTER

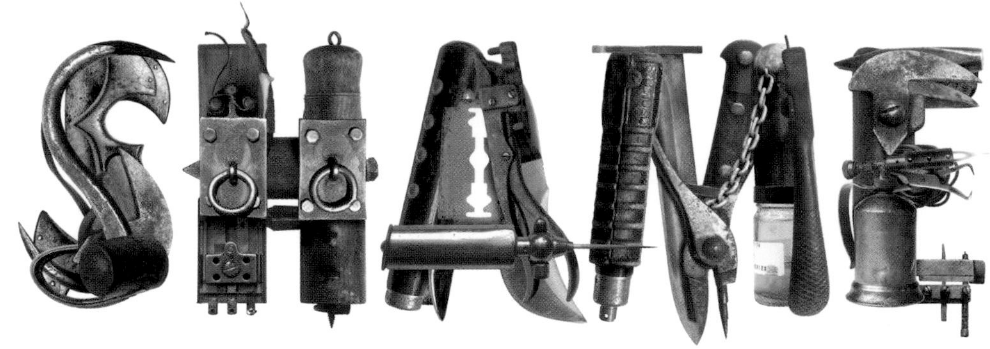

SHAME These letters were constructed using an array of torture implements. "The idea was simple," says Viktor Koen: "the communication of two different things by spelling only one."
ART DIRECTOR: Minh Uong ILLUSTRATOR: Viktor Koen
CLIENT: The *Village Voice* PUBLISHER: Village Voice Media
PRIMARY FONT: Custom made

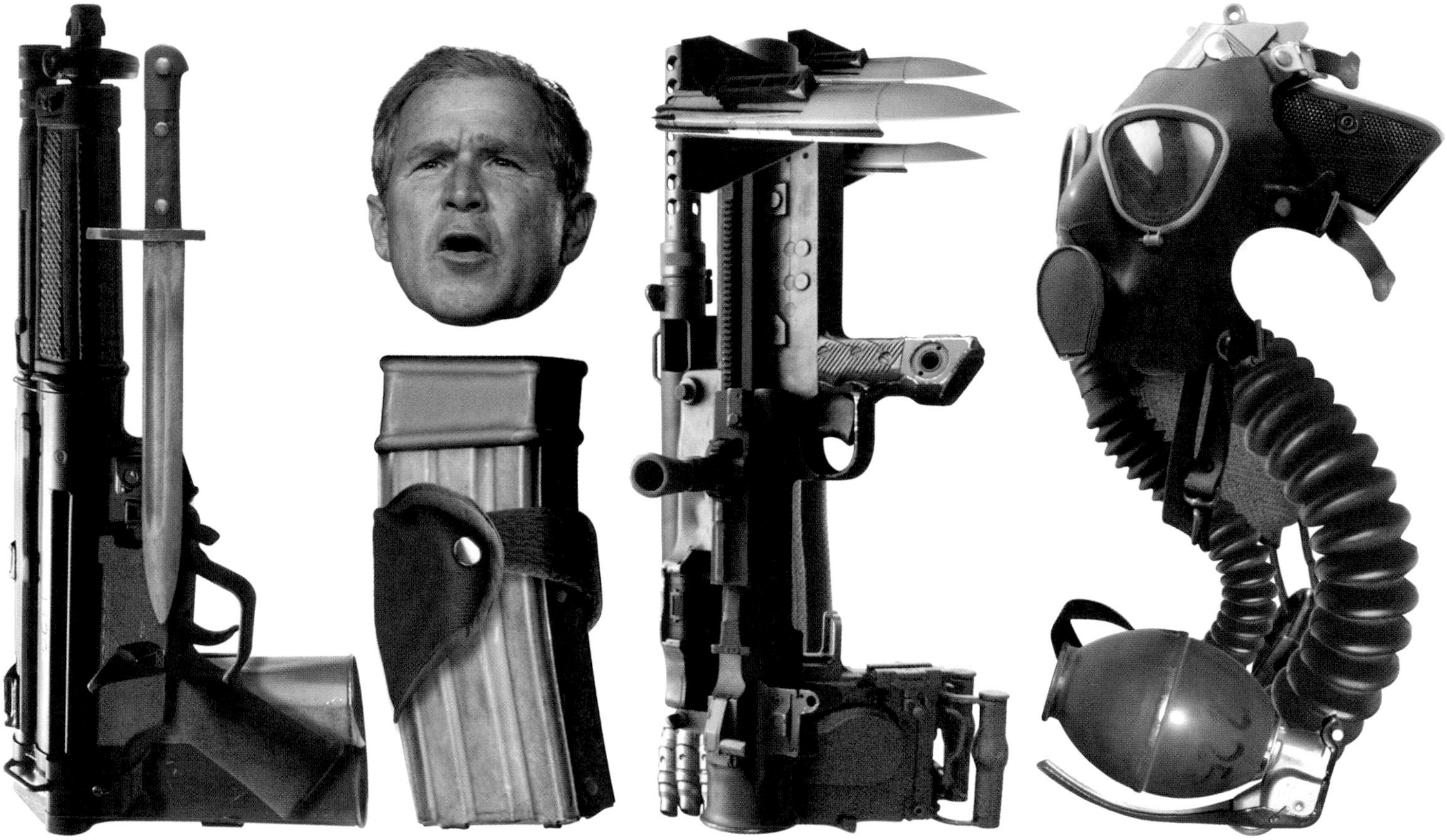

LIES These letterforms, for a cover of the *Village Voice* on weapons control, are surprisingly easy to read.
ART DIRECTOR: Minh Uong ILLUSTRATOR: Viktor Koen
CLIENT: The *Village Voice* PUBLISHER: Village Voice Media
PRIMARY FONT: Custom made

TOYPHABET Viktor Koen has long been working on a series of prints titled "Dark Peculiar," based around the surreal use of toys. A toy alphabet made perfect sense not only because of the abundance of materials he had in his hands (he photographed hundreds of vintage toy parts), but because he was interested in exploring the combination of these otherwise unrelated shapes while braiding them into something as structured and functional as type. The letters don't represent a toy molded into a letterform. They are a fusion of elements that connect with each other only through their common theme, creating a homogenous aesthetic lexicon that characterizes this "typeface," and Koen's work in general.
ILLUSTRATOR: Viktor Koen CLIENT: Self PRIMARY FONT: Custom made

OBJECT AS LETTER

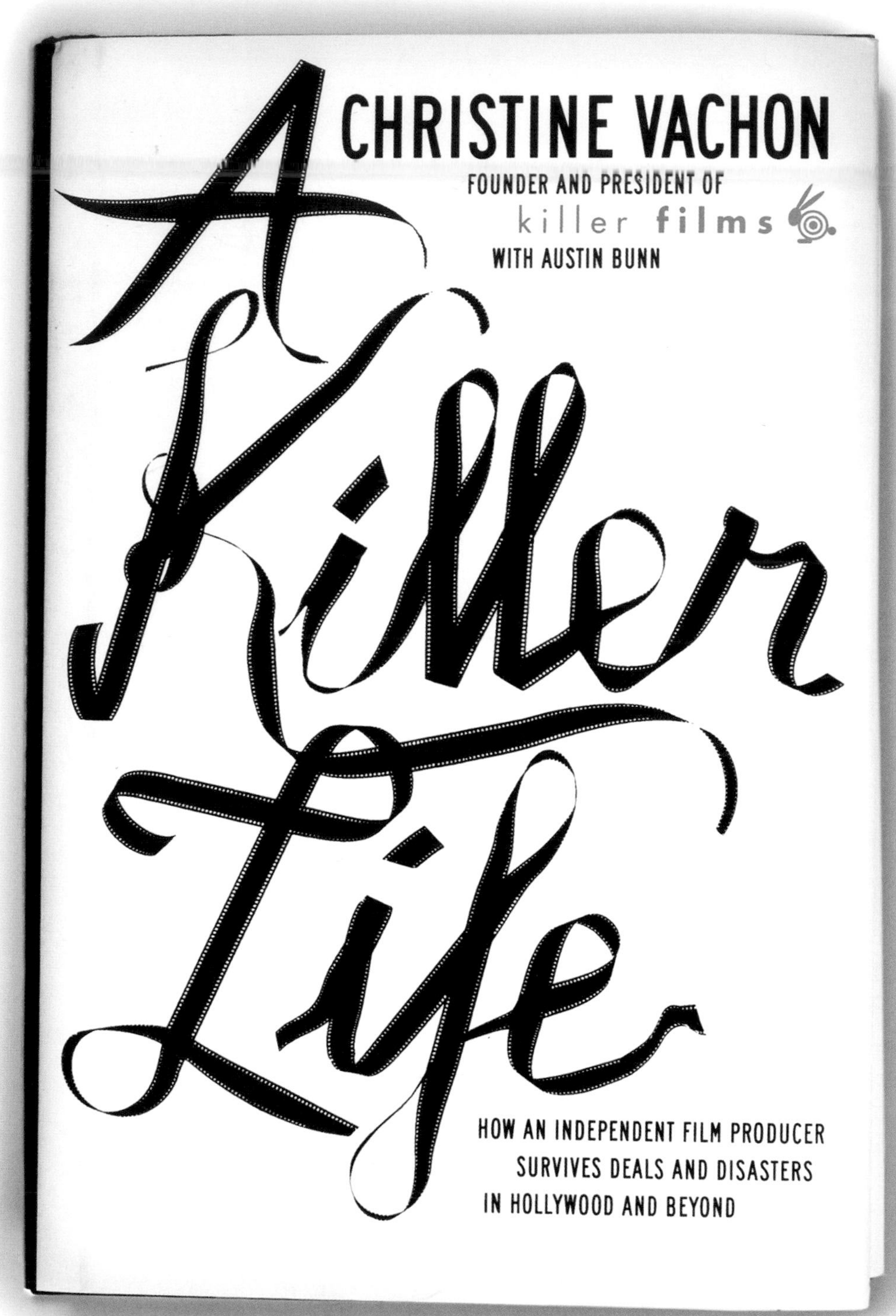

CHRISTINE VACHON
FOUNDER AND PRESIDENT OF
killer films
WITH AUSTIN BUNN
A Killer Life
HOW AN INDEPENDENT FILM PRODUCER
SURVIVES DEALS AND DISASTERS
IN HOLLYWOOD AND BEYOND

A KILLER LIFE "I have always loved film as a medium, and I enjoy making type out of objects," says Darren Cox. "When it came to making the cover for *A Killer Life*, a book about the founder of Killer Films, I thought it would be a great solution to make the title out of film. Since I began working in design, I have admired Alvin Lustig's work and have often drawn inspiration from him and his contemporaries. I loved the way he introduced type made out of actual objects into his book-cover solutions." DESIGN FIRM: SpotCo ART DIRECTOR: Gail Anderson DESIGNER: Darren Cox PUBLISHER: Simon & Schuster PRIMARY FONT: Film strips

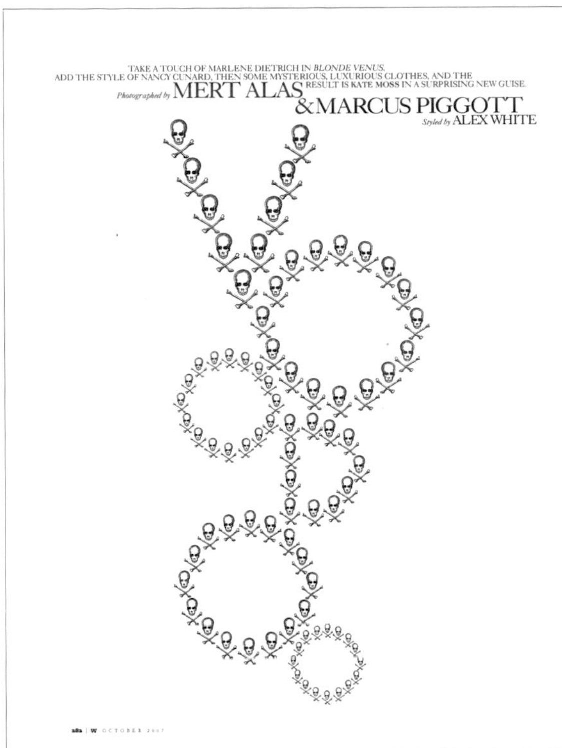

TAKE A TOUCH OF MARLENE DIETRICH IN BLONDE VENUS,
ADD THE STYLE OF NANCY CUNARD, THEN SOME MYSTERIOUS, LUXURIOUS CLOTHES, AND THE
RESULT IS KATE MOSS IN A SURPRISING NEW GUISE.
Photographed by MERT ALAS
& MARCUS PIGGOTT
Styled by ALEX WHITE

VOODOO In the original 1933 movie *King Kong*, a film director chooses the mysterious "Skull Island" as a location to complete his film. This cult classic inspired Edward Leida's type solution: "I tracked down a skull and crossbones engraving in a vintage 1930s type book from my personal collection and proceeded to create the letterforms that spell out 'Voodoo.'"
ART DIRECTOR/DESIGNER/ILLUSTRATOR: Edward Leida
PHOTOGRAPHERS: Mert Alas, Marcus Piggott CLIENT: *W* magazine
PUBLISHER: Condé Nast PRIMARY FONT: Skulls

ALOPECIA
RECORD RELEASE
why?
MARCH 6, 2008 | DOSE ONE + CRYPTACIZE + ODD NOSDAM + JEL | GREAT AMERICAN MUSIC HALL | PRESENTED BY PERFORMER

WHY? "Whenever I get a job where the band has a short name I'm inspired to try something type related," says Jason Munn. "When Why? mentioned a record release, I knew what I wanted to experiment with." Type was made from scanning and cropping some old 45s.
DESIGN FIRM: The Small Stakes
DESIGNER: Jason Munn CLIENT: Why?
PRIMARY FONT: Custom made

OBJECT AS LETTER

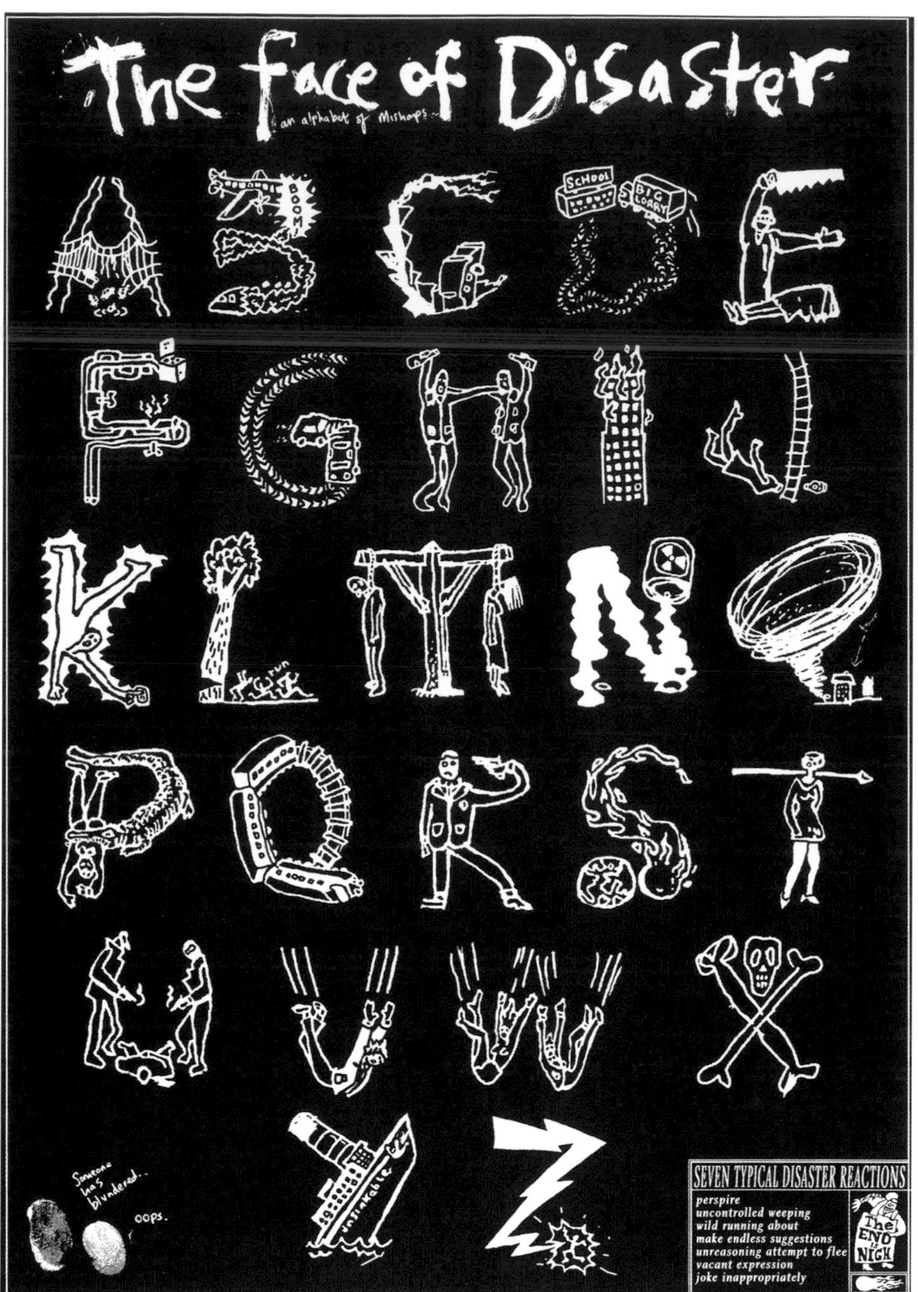

LEGO RED What better way to display the word "brickfilms" – animated films made with LEGO bricks – than with an alphabet made from the bricks themselves?
DIRECTORS/DESIGNERS: Vladimir Loginov, Maksim Loginov CLIENT: LEGO PRIMARY FONT: Custom made

THE FACE OF DISASTER Andy Smith wanted to produce a self-promotional poster that was similar to the illustrated alphabet posters that adults buy for children, but this time made for adults.
DESIGN FIRM: Andy Smith ART DIRECTOR/ILLUSTRATOR: Andy Smith CLIENT: Self PRIMARY FONT: Hand lettering

THE NATIONAL This is a case of typography parlant, where letterforms are made to look like an object they are associated with. In this case pants on hangers. John Solimine used this imagery for the band's name "because quite a few of their lyrical metaphors deal with clothing."
DESIGN FIRM: Spike Press ART DIRECTOR/DESIGNER/ILLUSTRATOR: John Solimine CLIENT: The National PUBLISHER: Spike Press PRIMARY FONT: Hand lettering

A LETTER AS OBJECT

CONSTRUCTIVE or concrete poetry is the transformation of readable words, sentences, or paragraphs into objects by making them conform to the shape of something else, such as a bomb, key, or garden fence. When letters become objects they provide the reader with an extra level of comprehension.

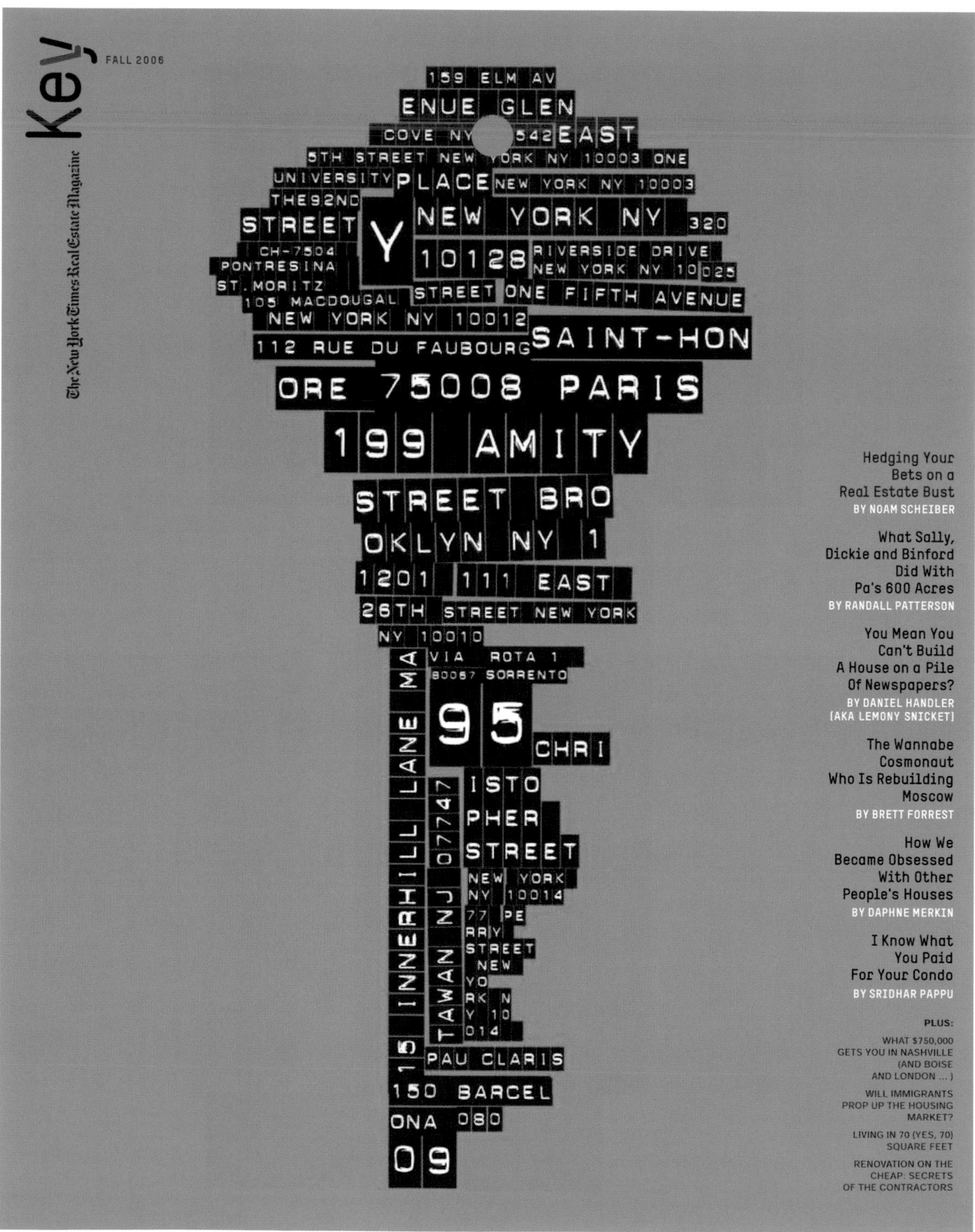

KEY MAGAZINE Using machine-made embossed labels, Carin Goldberg fashioned a key, the recurring visual theme of this real estate magazine, from related words.
ART DIRECTOR: Arem Duplessis
DESIGNER: Carin Goldberg CLIENT: *The New York Times Magazine*
PUBLISHER: *The New York Times*
PRIMARY FONT: FFDynamoe

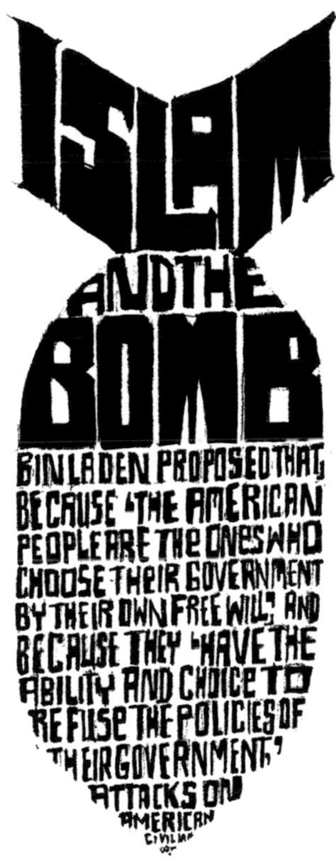

How to think – and not think – about the unspoken issue of the Second Nuclear Age.
By Noah Feldman

ISLAM AND THE BOMB (LEFT), ISLAM, TERROR... (ABOVE)

Scrawling words to fit the shape and form of an object is both a pun and a signpost. These letter-pictures convey a visual and textual message.

ART DIRECTOR: Arem Duplessis DESIGNER: Gail Bichler LETTERING: James Victore CLIENT: *The New York Times Magazine* PUBLISHER: *The New York Times* PRIMARY FONTS: Hand lettering, Stymie NYT, Cheltenham NYT

LETTER AS OBJECT

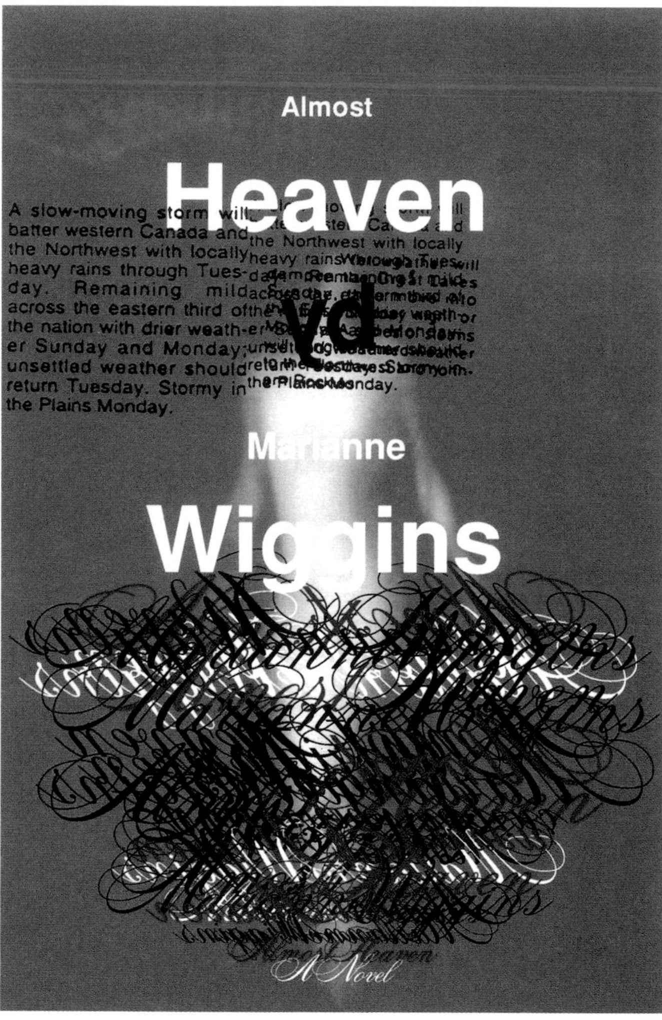

ALMOST HEAVEN This unpublished book cover uses the human object as an armature for typographic design.
DESIGNER: Carin Goldberg PRIMARY FONT: Helvetica

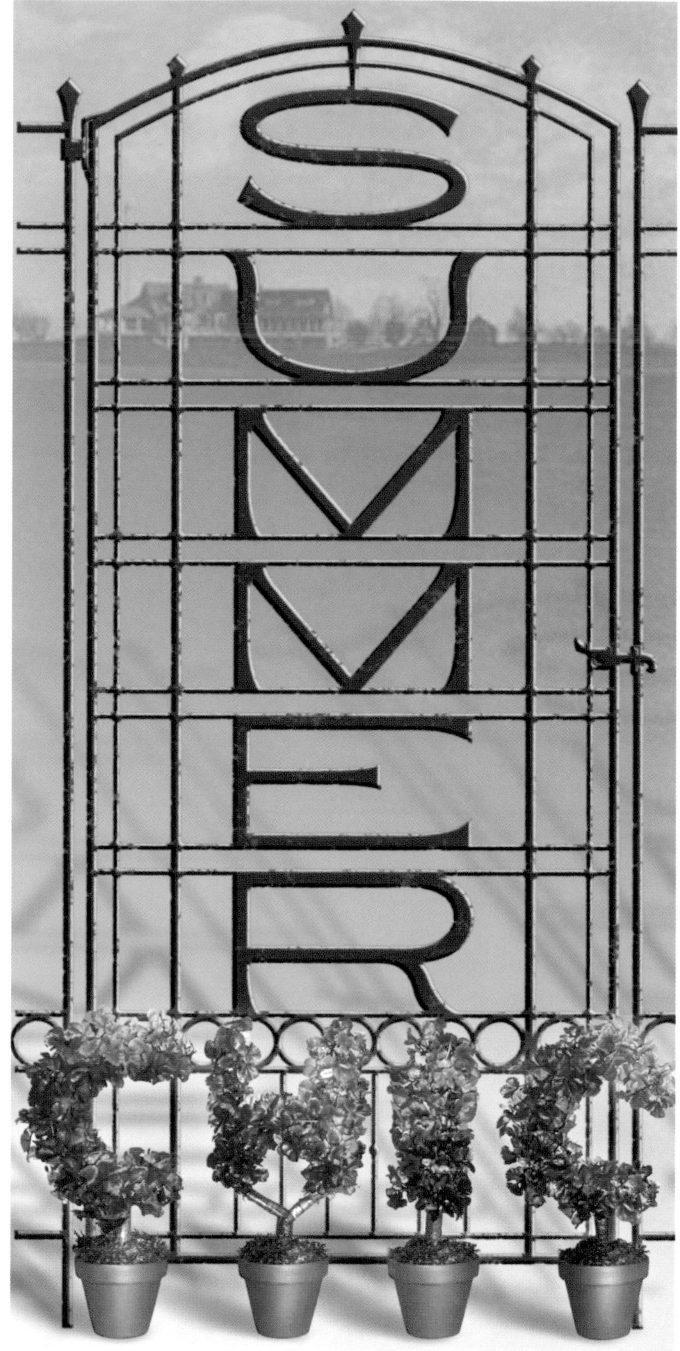

SUMMER CHIC This idea began with a photograph of ironwork on the gates of a country club. "We created the topiary 'chic' from silk-esque boxwood branches secured in little clay pots," says Elizabeth Morrow McKenzie. The ironwork gate typography is heavily modified Atlantis.
DESIGN FIRM: Morrow McKenzie Design DESIGNERS: Elizabeth Morrow McKenzie, Mette Hornung Rankin CLIENT: Carl Greve Jewelers PRIMARY FONTS: Custom made, Atlantis

DECADENCE AND EXCESS The references for this piece come from Catholicism, Old English and Gothic art. Jason Rubino wanted to unify all those elements into one composition. Each part of the cross is constructed from individual letters from the Edwardian Script typeface. The entire cross is purely typographic.
DESIGN FIRM: Jason Rubino Design ART DIRECTOR/DESIGNER/ ILLUSTRATOR: Jason Rubino CLIENT: Self PRIMARY FONT: Edwardian Script

Chaotic

TYPOGRAPHIC ORNAMENTATION has always tended towards the chaotic, but in the current design climate, chaos is a specific and popular trope. It is a means of conveying multiple messages, but also telegraphing a code to a select group of readers. Like 1960s Psychedelic type, chaos requires intense attention. Such attention demands that the reader be invested in the words.

TRICK TYPEFACE Andrei Robu calls this a "type experiment," but more than that it is a sublime pattern of brushed, translucent, colorful letterforms that may have no greater purpose than to be soothing to the eye.
DESIGN FIRM: Acme Industries
DESIGNER/CLIENT: Andrei Robu
PRIMARY FONT: Trick

FLAUNT An 1897 German advertising display typeface called Propaganda was the main influence for this redesigned logo, set against the chaos of an abstract collage.
DESIGN FIRM: Vault 49 DESIGNER: Jonathan Kenyon, John Glasgow
CLIENT/PUBLISHER: *Flaunt* magazine
PRIMARY FONT: Custom made

THIS IS IT! "This is it!" was a memorable sentence from the legendary *Style Wars* documentary, directed by Tony Silver, about graffiti in the 1980s and 1990s. The lettering is a typographic interpretation of graffiti.
DESIGN FIRM: Blikdsgn ART DIRECTOR/DESIGNER/ILLUSTRATOR: Daniel Blik CLIENT: Self PRIMARY FONT: Custom made

CHAOTIC

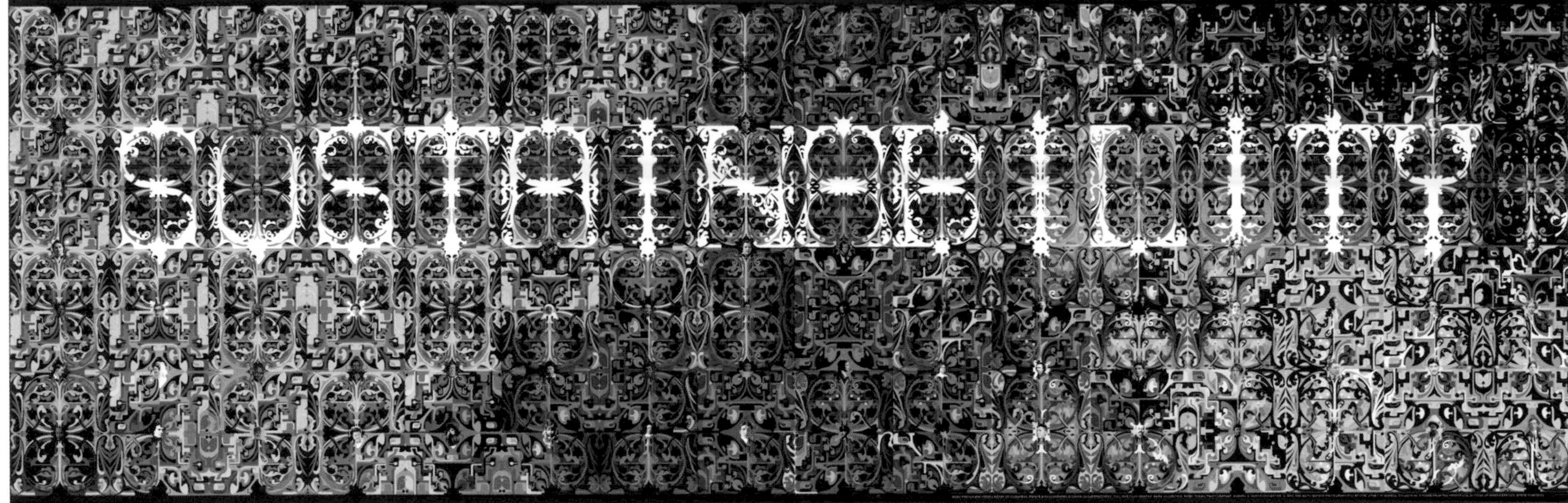

SUSTAINABILITY This poster for the Stora Enso paper company contains two variable repeating patterns and many archival photos (mostly from the US Library of Congress). The theme is "time, families and preserving things for generations," says Marian Bantjes.
DESIGNER: Marian Bantjes CLIENT: Winterhouse/Stora Enso PRIMARY FONT: Vector art

L'APARADOR LEAFLET *Aparador* means "shop window" in Catalan. It is the name of a multidisciplinary cultural space for young people based at Joan Abelló Museum in Mollet del Vallès (Barcelona, Spain). This leaflet/folded flyer was created for an opening exhibition at the Barcelona Contemporary Culture Center and depicts the diversity of proposals that were exhibited.
DESIGN FIRM: Andreu Balius Studio DESIGNER: Andreu Balius CLIENT: Joan Abelló Museum PRIMARY FONT: Mecano

BEASTIE BOYS This illustration to accompany an article on the Beastie Boys was inspired by the cover of the book *Peanuts & Cracker Jacks* by David Cataneo. It combines Victorian hand lettering with a mélange of photos, colors, and other overprints. DESIGN FIRM: Vault 49 DESIGNERS: Jonathan Kenyon, John Glasgow CLIENT: *NME* magazine PUBLISHER: IPC Media PRIMARY FONT: Hand lettering

DAUGHTERS + CHINESE STARS IN CLEVELAND The designers say this concert poster is a "mash-up of two coloring books – type graphics put on top of each other in such a way that the characters are beyond recognition. It provokes a sensation of Baroque, cuteness, and trashiness that we reproduced in the show info." DESIGN FIRM: Seripop ART DIRECTORS/DESIGNERS: Yannick Desranleau, Chloe Lum CLIENT: Daughters, the Chinese Stars PRIMARY FONT: Hand lettering

PUZZLE

TYPOGRAPHY IS OFTEN a game in which the reader is forced to decipher the message through many veils and curtains of graphic devices. This form of ornamentation, like the chaotic kind, demands attention and interaction. But unlike the chaotic kind, there is a reward at the end of the process.

theguardian Monday 24.12.07

12A *

Killer sudoku, whodunnit?, giant crossword . . . plus Christmas TV and radio guide

PUZZLE SPECIAL This special edition of *The Guardian*'s "G2" section was designed to draw the eye away from the mundane into a world of optical deception and delusion. And it works, too.
ART DIRECTOR: Richard Turley
DESIGNER: Marian Bantjes CLIENT: "G2" (*The Guardian*) PRIMARY FONT: Vector art

SAKS FIFTH AVENUE As a Valentine's Day logo, this heart is both sign and puzzle, at first a chaotic maze of lines and on second glance a loving message. But can you read it?
DESIGNER: Marian Bantjes CLIENT: Saks Fifth Avenue
PRIMARY FONT: Vector art

NEPTUNE The idea for this poster, say the designers, "was to work out an image that pulled off references to Neptune's style, being an experimental industrial band. We ended up knocking out the lettering against a 'machinery' background."
DESIGN FIRM: Seripop ART DIRECTORS/DESIGNERS: Yannick Desranleau, Chloe Lum CLIENT: Neptune PRIMARY FONT: Hand lettering

PUZZLE

CONJOINED FONT The concept for this sublimely impractical typeface was to retain its conjoined qualities. But, like Siamese twins, to really function it must be separated (at birth).
DESIGN FIRM: Post Typography ART DIRECTOR/DESIGNER: Bruce Willen PRIMARY FONT: Custom made

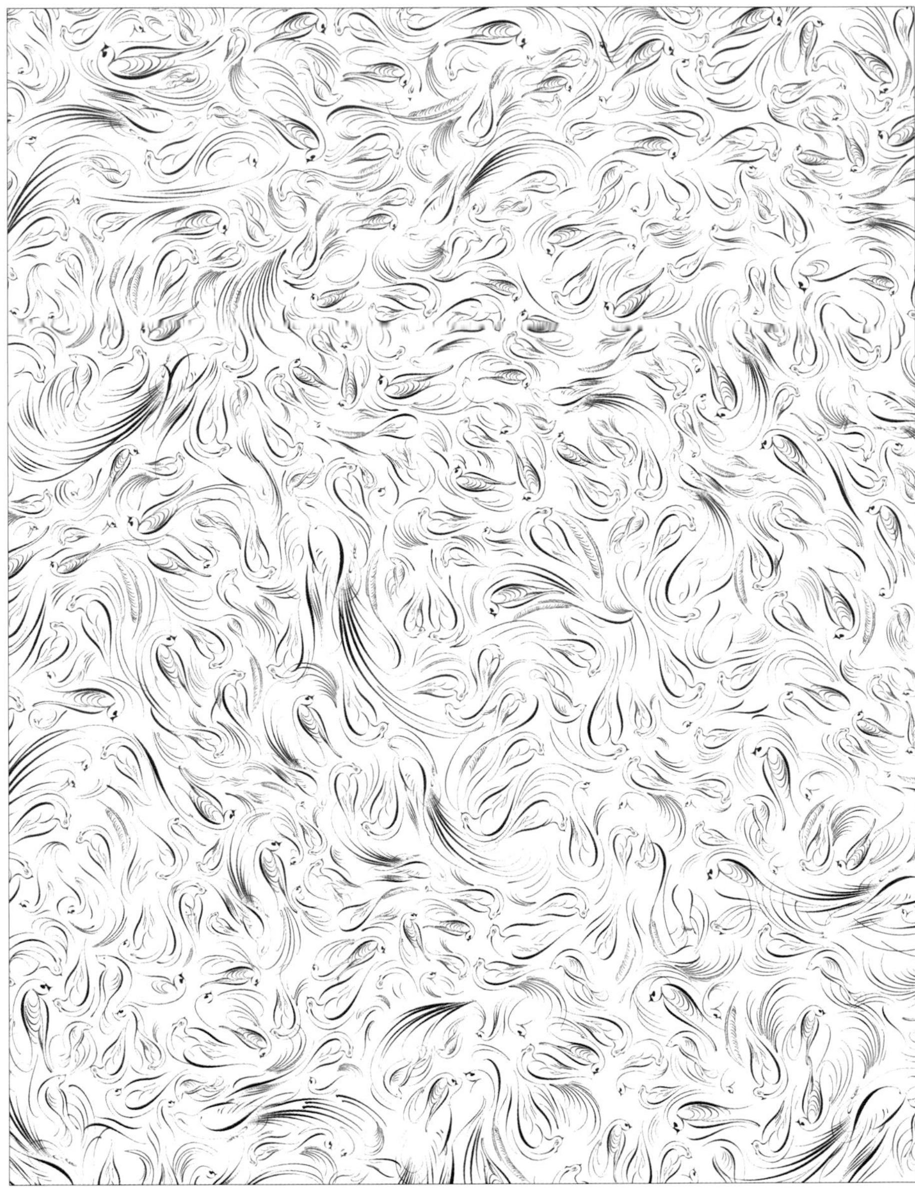

BIRD SERIES, ENGRAVED CARRIER BOX Dustin Arnold cites such influences as Op Art, magic eyes, and Rorschach inkblot tests for this almost indecipherable treatment.
DESIGN FIRM: Dustin Edward Arnold ART DIRECTOR/DESIGNER: Dustin E. Arnold PHOTOGRAPHER: Jonathan Ryans CLIENT: Dustin Edward Arnold PRIMARY FONT: Custom made

NEGATIVE FONT This maze-like font was designed for creating text-based patterns. But it also serves as a challenging puzzle.
DESIGN FIRM: Post Typography ART DIRECTOR/DESIGNER: Bruce Willen PRIMARY FONT: Custom made

MODEST MOUSE The typography in this poster for the band Modest Mouse was inspired by the maze games seen in children's books.
DESIGN FIRM: The Decoder Ring Design Concern DESIGNER/ILLUSTRATOR: Christian Helms CLIENT: Modest Mouse PRIMARY FONT: Hand lettering

EMBELLISHED

LETTERS WITH FANFARE and flourish have long been a major part of the typographic lexicon. Embellishments are employed to provide a sense of opulence and extravagance. The swashes and curlicues of embellished letters went out of fashion with the advent of the Modern era, but now they are back, adding a romantic quality to the typographic message.

"S" This "inital cap" was inspired by eighteenth-century black letter scripts and flourishes. The idea, says Ian Brignell, "was to create a unified letter and swash design that was at once historical in its execution, but somewhat modern in its overall feel."
DESIGN FIRM: Ian Brignell Lettering Design ART DIRECTOR/DESIGNER/LETTERER: Ian Brignell PRIMARY FONT: Hand lettering

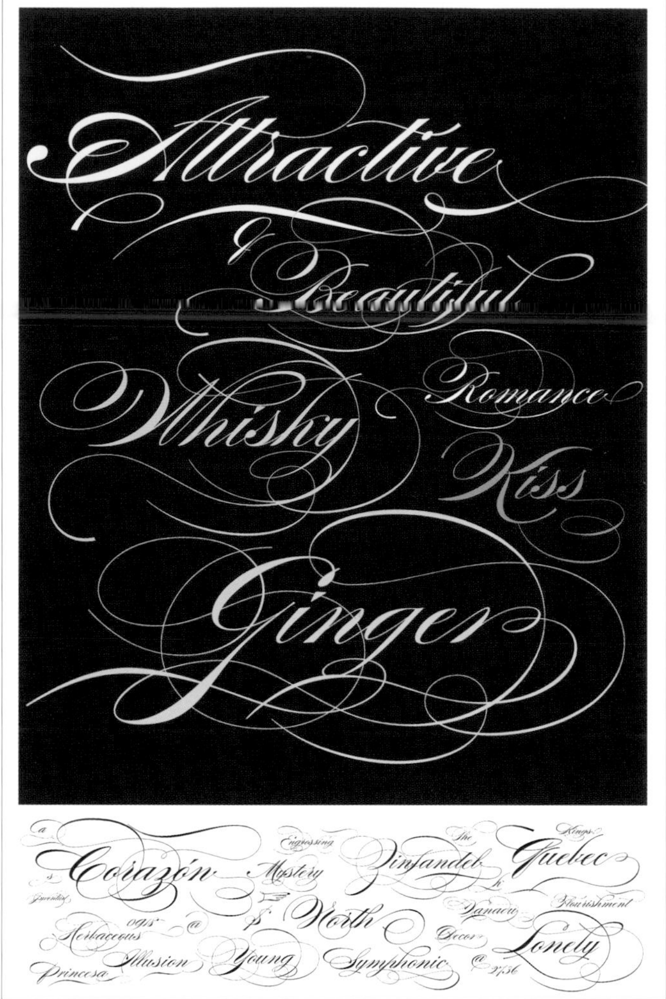

BURGUES SCRIPT Burgues script, says Alejandro Paul, is an "ode" to the legendary late-nineteenth-century American calligrapher Louis Madarasz, who has inspired schools of penmanship for over 100 years. "His talent has led some people to call him 'the most skillful penman the world has ever known.' I use the word 'ode' in a colloquially ambitious manner. If I was an actual poet, my words would be about things I desire but cannot attain, objects of utter beauty that make me wallow in humility, or people of enormous talent who look down at me from the clouds of genius."
DESIGN FIRM: Sudtipos ART DIRECTOR: Alejandro Paul CLIENT: Sudtipos PUBLISHER: Sudtipos-Veer PRIMARY FONT: Hand lettering

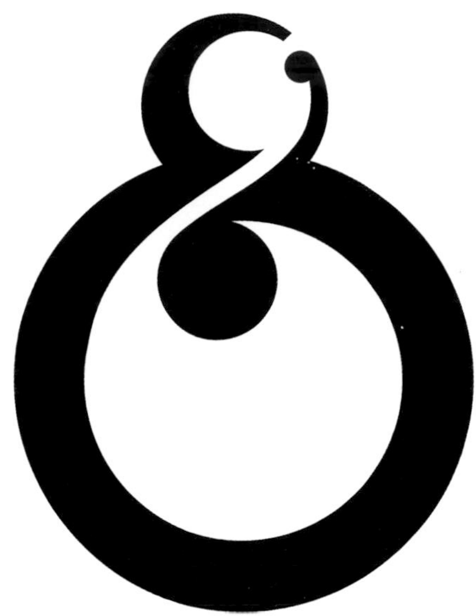

AMPERSAND The source for this delightful form is the ampersand itself – at once easily recognized and curiously abstract.
DESIGN FIRM: Acme Industries
CLIENT: Andrei Robu PRIMARY FONT: The New New

CUNT As this advocacy poster says, "Words look much nicer when they're hand lettered." This profane word comes off as a veritable valentine in this form.
DESIGN FIRM: Mark Denton Design ART DIRECTOR: Mark Denton
DESIGNERS: Mark Denton, Alison Carmichael ILLUSTRATOR: Alison Carmichael CLIENT: Alison Carmichael
PRIMARY FONT: Hand lettering

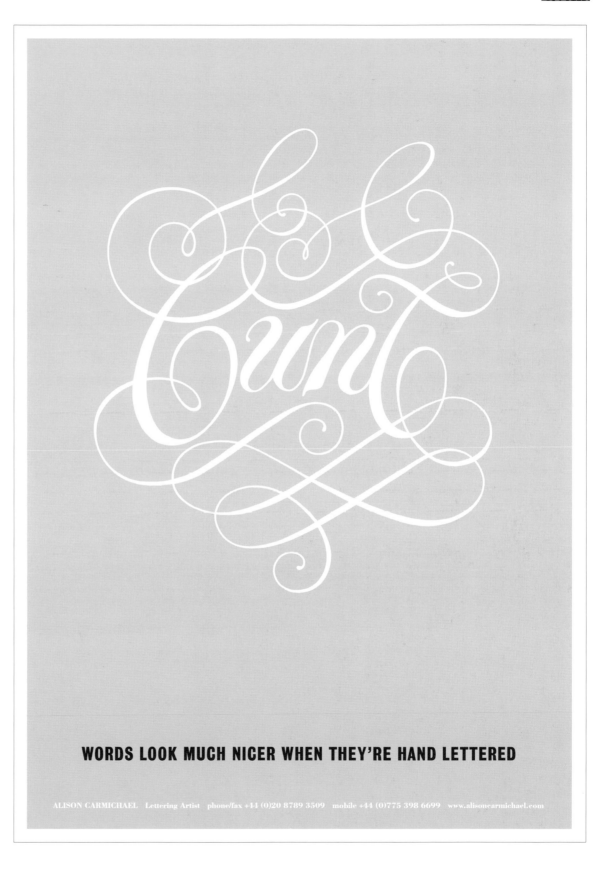

Cunt

WORDS LOOK MUCH NICER WHEN THEY'RE HAND LETTERED

ALISON CARMICHAEL Lettering Artist phone/fax +44 (0)20 8789 3509 mobile +44 (0)775 398 6699 www.alisoncarmichael.com

SELFLESS

INSPIRING WORD SERIES This series of limited-edition prints was developed as a response to working with the communications agency Global Tolerance, who are focused on promoting positive messages in the media. The design of the words was inspired by a beautiful collection of eighteenth-century "initial caps" found in a decorative alphabet reference book published by Booking International.
DESIGN FIRM: Ginger Monkey ART DIRECTOR/DESIGNER/ ILLUSTRATOR: Tom Lane PRIMARY FONT: Baskerville (Semibold)

DARK WAS THE NIGHT – PLAY SAFE The *Dark Was The Night* album celebrated twenty years of fighting Aids through pop culture. The music influenced this folksy, Baroque-style illustration, which takes the old and makes it current.
DESIGN FIRM: Funny Garbage/Red Hot ART DIRECTORS: Andy Pratt, John Carlin DESIGNER/ILLUSTRATOR: Ryan Feerer CLIENT: Red Hot – *Dark Was The Night* music compilation LABEL: 4AD PRIMARY FONT: Hand lettering

V49 Early twentieth-century carnival posters are the basis for this otherwise jarringly raucous typographic pyrotechnic.
DESIGN FIRM: Vault 49 DESIGNERS: Jonathan Kenyon, John Glasgow, Daryl Waller CLIENT: "The Greatest Show On Earth" exhibition (2006) PRIMARY FONT: Custom made

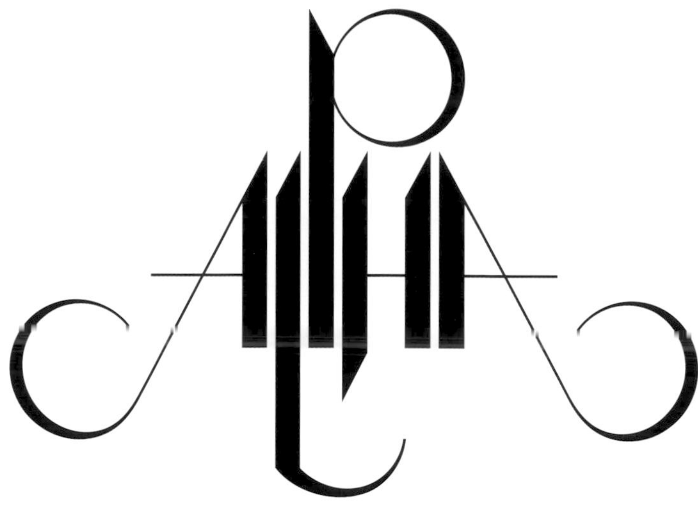

ALPHA This hand lettering was conceived for a client targeting the "alpha" male audience. "I wanted the lettering to be masculine while still maintaining a sense of fashion," reports Paul Sych.
DESIGN FIRM: Faith ART DIRECTOR/DESIGNER: Paul Sych
CLIENT: Alpha PRIMARY FONT: Hand lettering

WANT IT! The signature piece for Saks's "Want It!" campaign was created with Michael Bierut and Terron Schaefer. "The client asked for a very frenetic, over-the-top 'Want It!', using a Spencerian script to go with their logotype, but with, as Michael Bierut put it, 'more swing,'" says Marian Bantjes.
ART DIRECTORS: Michael Bierut, Terron Schaefer DESIGNER: Marian Bantjes CLIENT: Pentagram/Saks Fifth Avenue
PRIMARY FONT: Hand lettering

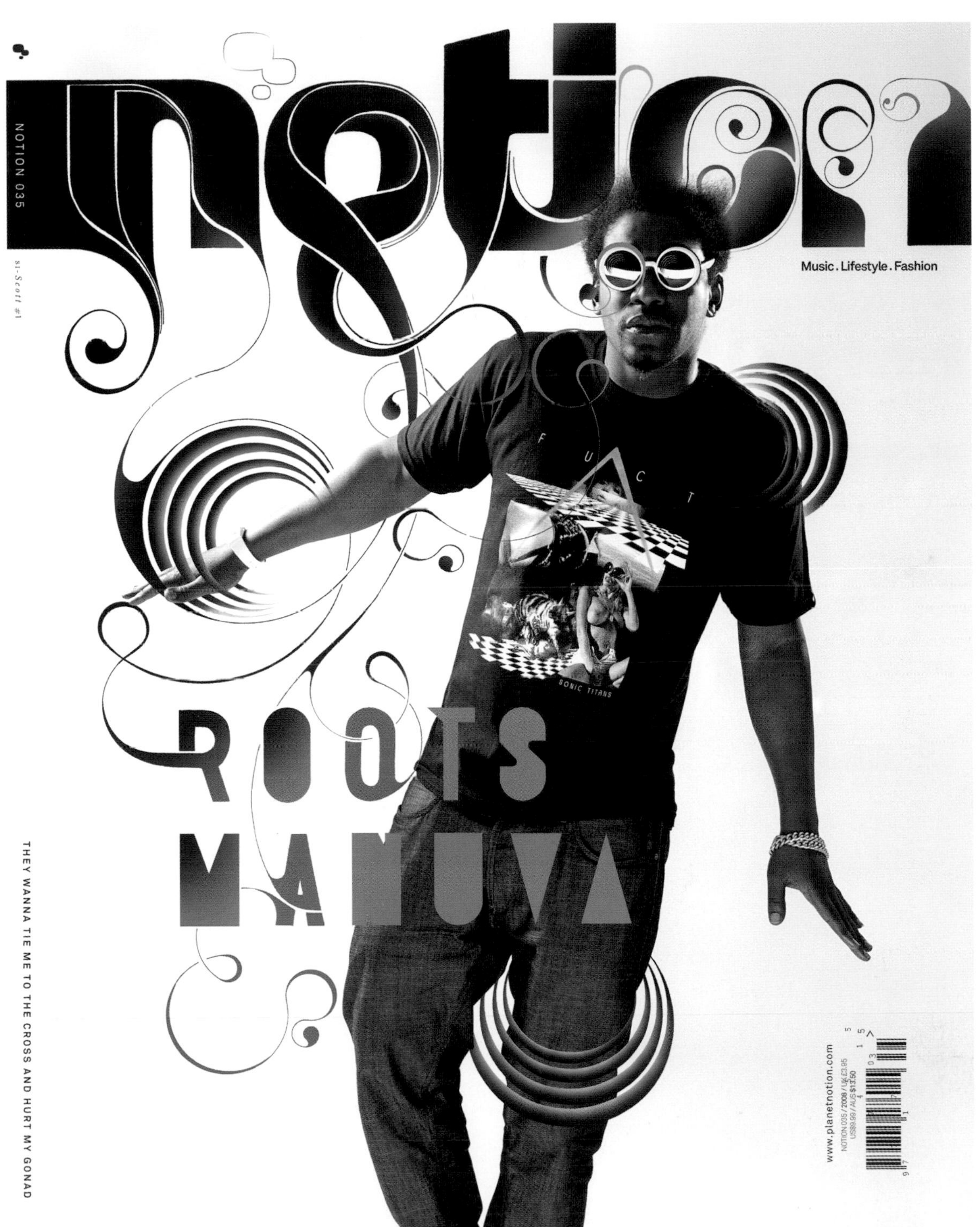

NOTION 035
Music . Lifestyle . Fashion
ROOTS MANUVA
THEY WANNA TIE ME TO THE CROSS AND HURT MY GONAD
www.planetnotion.com

NOTION How is a logo for a magazine made to look different on the newsstand? Embellish it so it is barely readable, then more people will attempt to read it. This design for *Notion* met the challenge. DESIGN FIRM: Si Scott Studio Ltd ART DIRECTORS/DESIGNERS: Liam Gleeson, Si Scott ILLUSTRATOR: Si Scott PHOTOGRAPHER: Jake Green CLIENT: *Notion* magazine PUBLISHER: Planet Notion PRIMARY FONT: Custom made

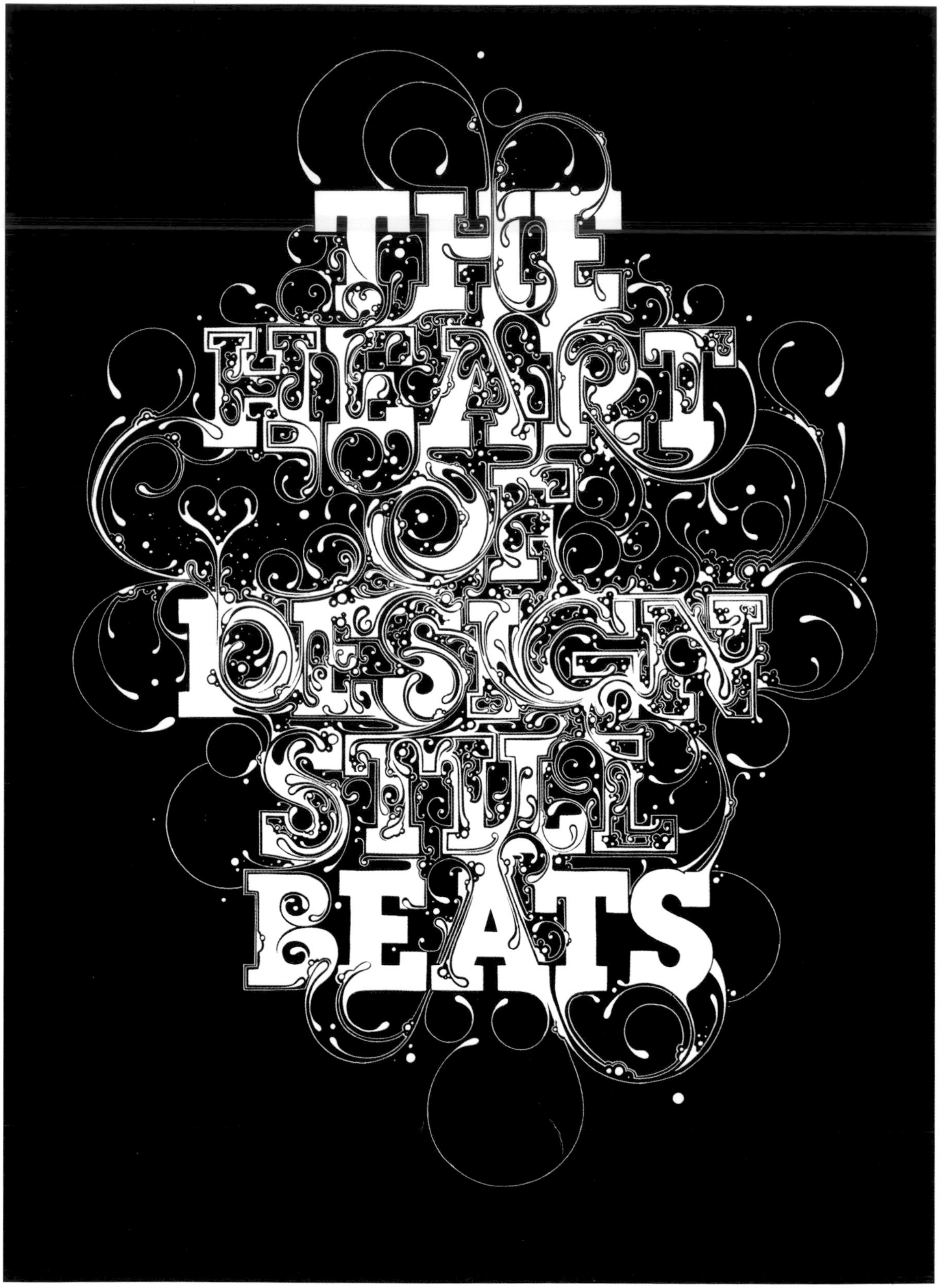

THE HEART OF DESIGN STILL BEATS Embellishing Herb Lubalin's signature slab serif would have warmed the cockles of the famous typographer's heart. In this image for Tokyo Design Week, the swirls take on a fluid quality. DESIGN FIRM: Si Scott Studio Ltd ART DIRECTOR/DESIGNER/ILLUSTRATOR: Si Scott CLIENT: Designers Block PRIMARY FONT: Lubalin

ROSEVILLE This logo for a restaurant in San Diego is a beautifully replicated early twentieth-century script with embellishments that return to the eighteenth century. DESIGN FIRM: Louise Fili Ltd ART DIRECTOR: Louise Fili DESIGNERS: Louise Fili, Jessica Hische CLIENT: Roseville PRIMARY FONT: Hand lettering

TYPE Hints of the past five decades – and the technologies that define them – come together in this homage to digital type in *Computer Arts* magazine. DESIGN FIRM: Shinybinary ART DIRECTOR/DESIGNER/ILLUSTRATOR: Nik Ainley CLIENT: *Computer Arts* magazine PUBLISHER: Future Publishing Limited PRIMARY FONT: Alba

A SUBSET OF EMBELLISHED type is this delightfully, though not exclusively, feminine approach to decorative lettering. All the tools of calligraphic opulence are brought to bear – swashes, squiggles, cartouches, and even little birds.

TXIKITO This intricately crafted restaurant logo is designed to look like a metal sign found on Catalan restaurants.
DESIGN FIRM: Louise Fili Ltd ART DIRECTOR: Louise Fili DESIGNERS: Louise Fili, Jessica Hische CLIENT: Txikito PRIMARY FONT: Hand lettering

BITCH Like "Cunt" (page 153), here words take on a new cadence, if not also new meaning, when they are typeset in script and embellished with swashes. DESIGNER: Mr. Keedy CLIENT: R Wines PRIMARY FONT: Lettering by Mr. Keedy

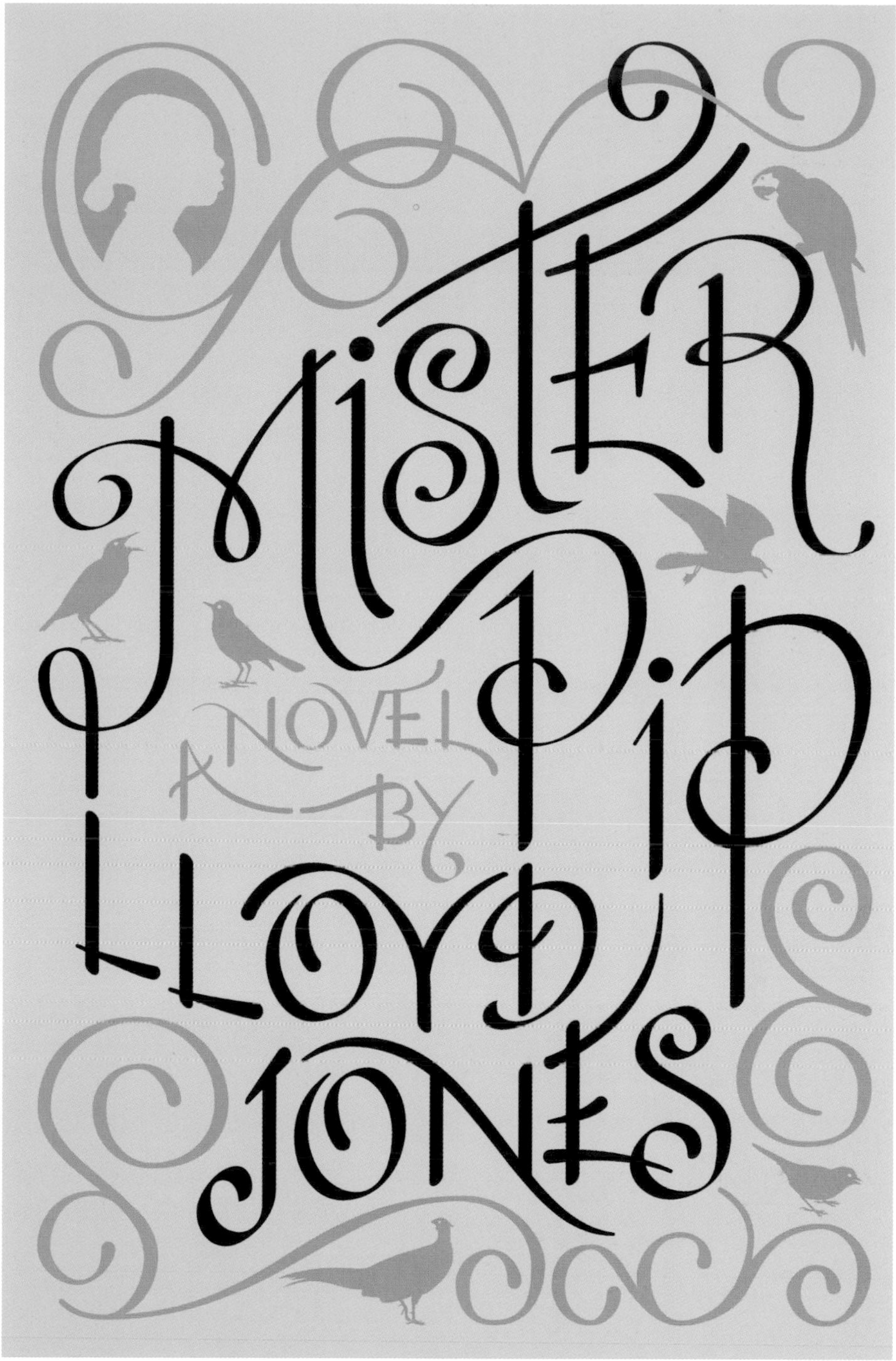

MISTER PIP This book jacket builds on the typographic sensibility by using retro ornament, but with a minimalist quality that can only be contemporary. DESIGN FIRM: de Vicq design ART DIRECTOR: Paola Pepe DESIGNER/ ILLUSTRATOR: Roberto de Vicq de Cumptich CLIENT: Dial Press PUBLISHER: Random House PRIMARY FONT: Hand lettering

THE WHIZBANG Here is a unique big bang explosion of nineteenth-century Japanese characters, Willy Wonka packaging, and Speed Racer branding.
DESIGN FIRM: Dustin Edward Arnold CREATIVE DIRECTOR: Cleon Peterson LETTERER: Dustin E. Arnold CLIENT/PUBLISHER: *Swindle* magazine PRIMARY FONT: Custom made

The New York Times Magazine

Constance Baker Motley
Frank Perdue Wellington Mara
Luther Vandross
John Z. DeLorean Fakher Haider Uli Derickson
Rose Mary Woods
James Stockdale Teresa Wright
Miriam Rothschild Gene Baylor Fred Korematsu
Sandra Dee
Thurl Ravenscroft Georgeanna Jones

The Lives They Lived

THE LIVES THEY LIVED Every year *The New York Times Magazine* publishes an issue dedicated to famous people who passed away that year. As homage to the deceased, the designers invite an artist or typographer to interpret the names in some distinctive and creative typographic manner.
ART DIRECTOR: Arem Duplessis DESIGNER: Nancy Harris Rouemy LETTERER: Deanne Cheuk CLIENT: *The New York Times Magazine* PUBLISHER: *The New York Times* PRIMARY FONTS: Hand lettering, Stymie NYT Extra Bold

BIG MAGAZINE This venerably hip magazine returned to Spencerian Script and Ornamental Script for one of its issues.
DESIGN FIRM: Dustin Edward Arnold
CREATIVE DIRECTOR: Toni Torres
ART DIRECTOR/DESIGNER: Kevin Wolahan PHOTOGRAPHER: James Macari LETTERER: Dustin E. Arnold
CLIENT/PUBLISHER: *Big* magazine
PRIMARY FONT: Custom Helvetica

MEDIEVAL TAPESTRIES USED stitched lettering, but the earliest contemporary form was found in the typographic samplers hung in colonial parlors and bedrooms in eighteenth-century America. Today, as part of the DIY craft trend, sewing, weaving, embroidering, and stitching have been digitized to evoke the "down home" look in a futuristic manner.

ALTMOCROSS This embroidery font was designed for the student association ESAABouge, to adorn some of their party posters.
DESIGNER: Merci Bernard CLIENT: ESAABouge PRIMARY FONT: Hand lettering

A B C D E F G
H I J K L M N
O P Q R S T
U V W X Y Z
abcdefghijklmnopqrstuvwxyz
1 2 3 4 5 6 7 8 9 0

Matilde Script
Pablo canta como un ruiseñor
CARIBE
La novia de Luis se lo monta
con la amiguita de Montsita
Borja Mari se comprará un Golf
BARCELONA
la llama lleva lana
rata remo risa rosa ruso
sapo seta sisa sosa sube
tasa tela tila toma tuno
Type Republic

MATILDE Matilde Script was first featured within the Library #5 of experimental type project Garcia fonts & co. in 1993. Now it has been renovated and "tuned" for commercial distribution at Typerepublic foundry. Matilde Script is a little homage to all those old ladies who were the real pioneers of digital type – they were the first to construct letters as a map of pixels in their stitching.
DESIGN FIRM: Andreu Balius Studio
DESIGNER: Andreu Balius CLIENT: Typerepublic.com PRIMARY FONT: Matilde Script

SELF-CONFIDENCE PRODUCES FINE RESULTS "At the opening of our exhibition at Deitch Projects in New York," says Stefan Sagmeister, "we featured a wall of 10,000 bananas. Green bananas created a pattern against a background of yellow bananas spelling out: 'Self-confidence produces fine results.' After a few days the green bananas turned yellow too, and the type disappeared."
ART DIRECTOR: Stefan Sagmeister
DESIGNER: Richard The, Joe Shouldice
CLIENT: Deitch Projects PRIMARY FONT: Bananas

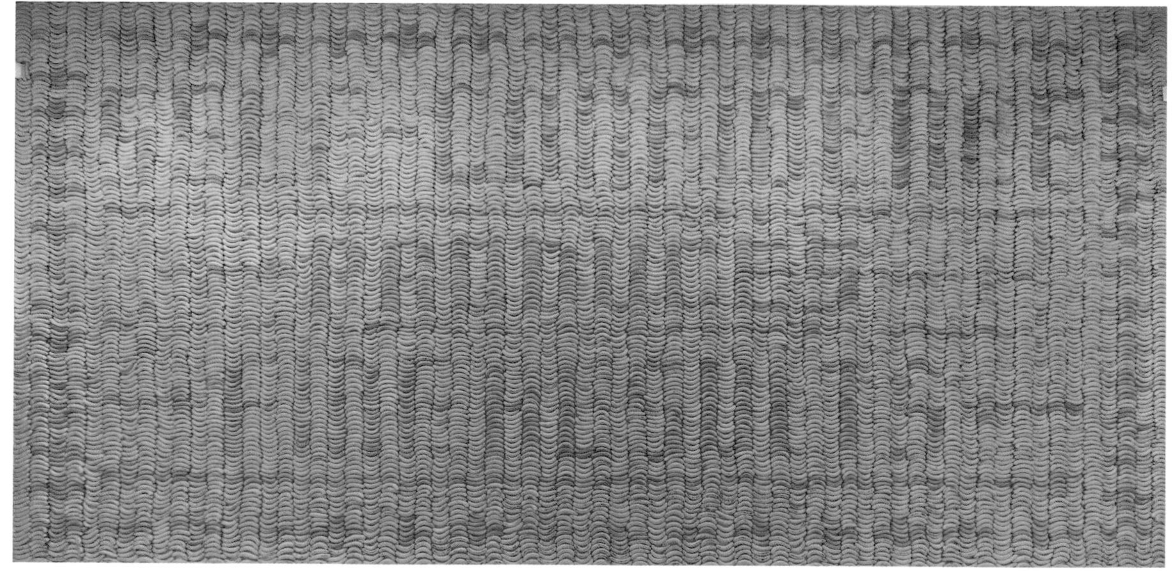

THE BEST NEW DESIGNERS What more appropriate way to design a headline for a feature on new fashion designers than to stitch it?

DESIGN DIRECTOR: Fred Woodward DESIGNER: Anton Ioukhnovets
PHOTOGRAPHER: Peggy Sirota CLIENT: *GQ* magazine PUBLISHER: Condé Nast
PRIMARY FONTS: Stitching, Omnes

IN OUR SECOND ANNUAL SALUTE TO THE INDUSTRY'S MOST PROMISING EMERGING TALENTS, WE HIGHLIGHT THE NAMES THAT SHOULD BE ON YOUR RADAR. IT'S TIME YOU GOT TO KNOW YOUR GILDED AGE FROM YOUR RAG & BONE

PEGGY SIROTA

THE BEST NEW DESIGNERS IN AMERICA 2008

RAG & BONE

Rag & Bone started as a modest jeans-and-tees label, yet in a blindingly brief period, founders Marcus Wainwright and David Neville have become two of New York's young design hotshots.

The collection now reaches far beyond engineered Japanese denim to include everything from sweaters, pants, and boots to short-cut suits and even a tuxedo. These are clothes made for a young James Bond–008, you might say. In other words, a young killer who looks sharp no matter what the situation.

FEB GQ 109

A NEW MODERNISM FOR A NEW MILLENNIUM This study for a book cover for the Logan Collection is what inspired the production of RoarType, one of the many digital typefaces Bob Aufuldish has produced over the past two decades.
DESIGN FIRM: Aufuldish & Warinner ART DIRECTOR/ DESIGNER: Bob Aufuldish ILLUSTRATOR: George Condo
CLIENT/PUBLISHER: The Logan Collection, Vail, Colorado
PRIMARY FONTS: RoarType beta, Dalliance, Helvetica Neue

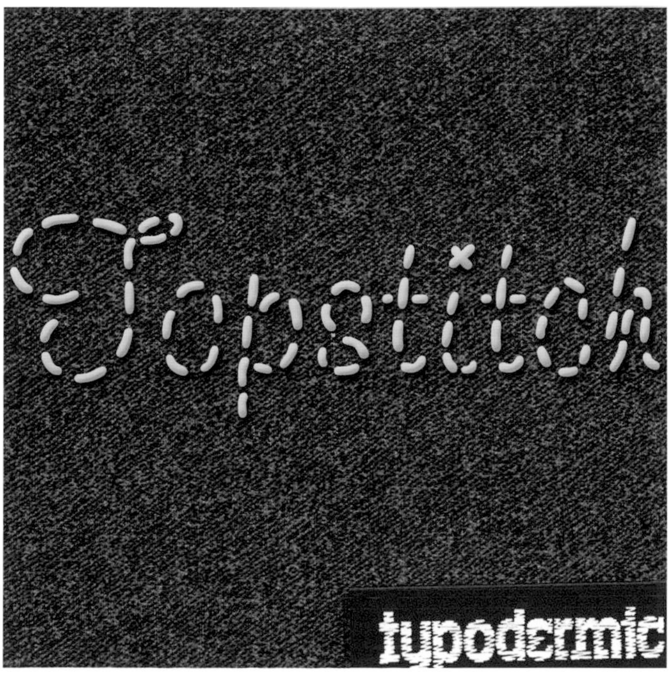

TOPSTITCH This logo for the design firm Typodermic Fonts is made to look like a jeans label. Topstitch is one of their signature fonts.
DESIGN FIRM: Typodermic Fonts
DESIGNER/ILLUSTRATOR: Ray Larabie
PRIMARY FONT: Topstitch

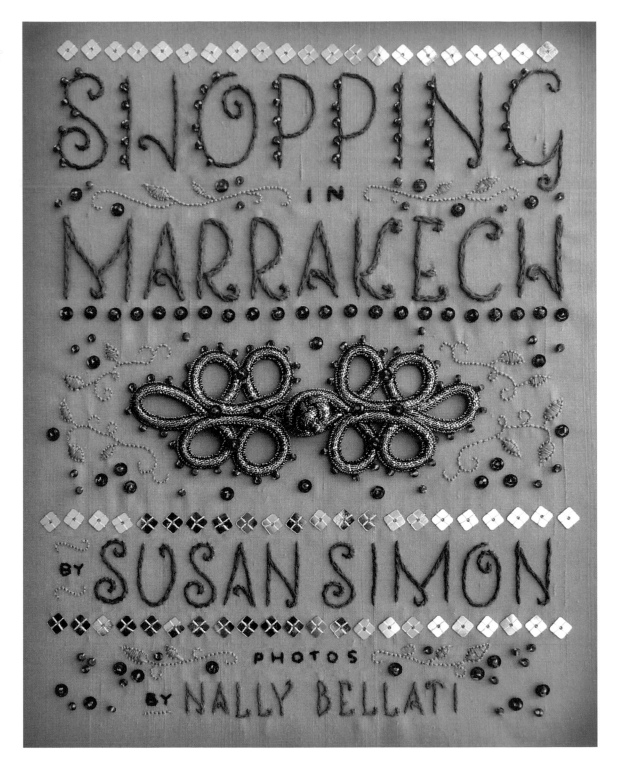

SHOPPING IN MARRAKECH To convey the aura of Marrakech for this book cover, Louise Fili chose embroidered fabric as an apt metaphor, and Jessica Hische carried through the embroidery.
DESIGN FIRM: Louise Fili Ltd
ART DIRECTOR: Louise Fili
DESIGNERS: Louise Fili, Jessica Hische EMBROIDERER: Jessica Hische
PUBLISHER: The Little Bookroom
PRIMARY FONT: Hand embroidered

BUSHISM PILLOWS There are six Bushism pillows: *Levees*, *Mushroom Cloud*, *Decider*, *Liberators*, *Mission Accomplished*, and *Leak Out of My Administration*. The magazine *Vanity Fair* wanted them to look very traditional, "as if they were created by someone's grandmother." In that way, the hominess of each pillow would draw in the viewers and then the satirical effect would be amplified when they read the message. "In some cases, I used all caps to make the sampler's words 'shout' out the pillow's message," explains Margaret Cusack. "As with most of the pillows, I wanted the typeface to be very legible. On the *Levees* pillow, I wanted the typeface to look like a third-grader's script writing. I created a playful, curvy border with a water motif that mocked the sampler's naive statement. With the *Mushroom Cloud* pillow, I summoned all the grandmotherly qualities of samplers by using a decorative initial cap for the 'W' (subconsciously referring to George W. Bush). I included a stately border and an ornate decorative motif above and below the type to create a 'story book' quality that would attract the viewers. I created the *Mission Accomplished* typeface years ago, based on a fragment of a sampler in a stitchery catalog. For the *Liberators* pillow, I wanted to camouflage Cheney's statement with hearts and decorative Xs. The traditional cross-stitch typeface that I chose has a somewhat illegible quality, which was helpful in forcing the reader to work to decipher the words."
ART DIRECTOR: Julie Weiss
ILLUSTRATOR: Margaret Cusack
CLIENT: *Vanity Fair* magazine
PUBLISHER: Condé Nast PRIMARY FONT: Stitching

ANTHROPOMORPHIC

TYPE AS ANIMALS, animals as type, and people as type all fall into the category that goes back to the difficult days when early Egyptian slaves used anthropomorphism to satirize their masters. (And hoped they were not caught.) Today it is common practice to make letters perform the job of illustration in both metaphoric and literal ways. But it is not only animals and humans who get this treatment – see the typographic pun on Stacked *(page 179)*.

DIRTY MIND In his book on language, *The Stuff of Thought*, Steven Pinker theorizes that cursing is hard-wired into a primordial part of the brain – and that even animals "curse" in the form of a yelp when you step on their tail. Post Typography's illustration for a review of Pinker's book weaves a series of curse words into the folds of the cerebral cortex. Influences: our own brains. DESIGN FIRM: Post Typography ART DIRECTOR: Christy Sheppard, *Wired* magazine DESIGNER/ILLUSTRATOR: Nolen Strals CLIENT: *Wired* magazine PUBLISHER: Condé Nast PRIMARY FONTS: Hand lettering

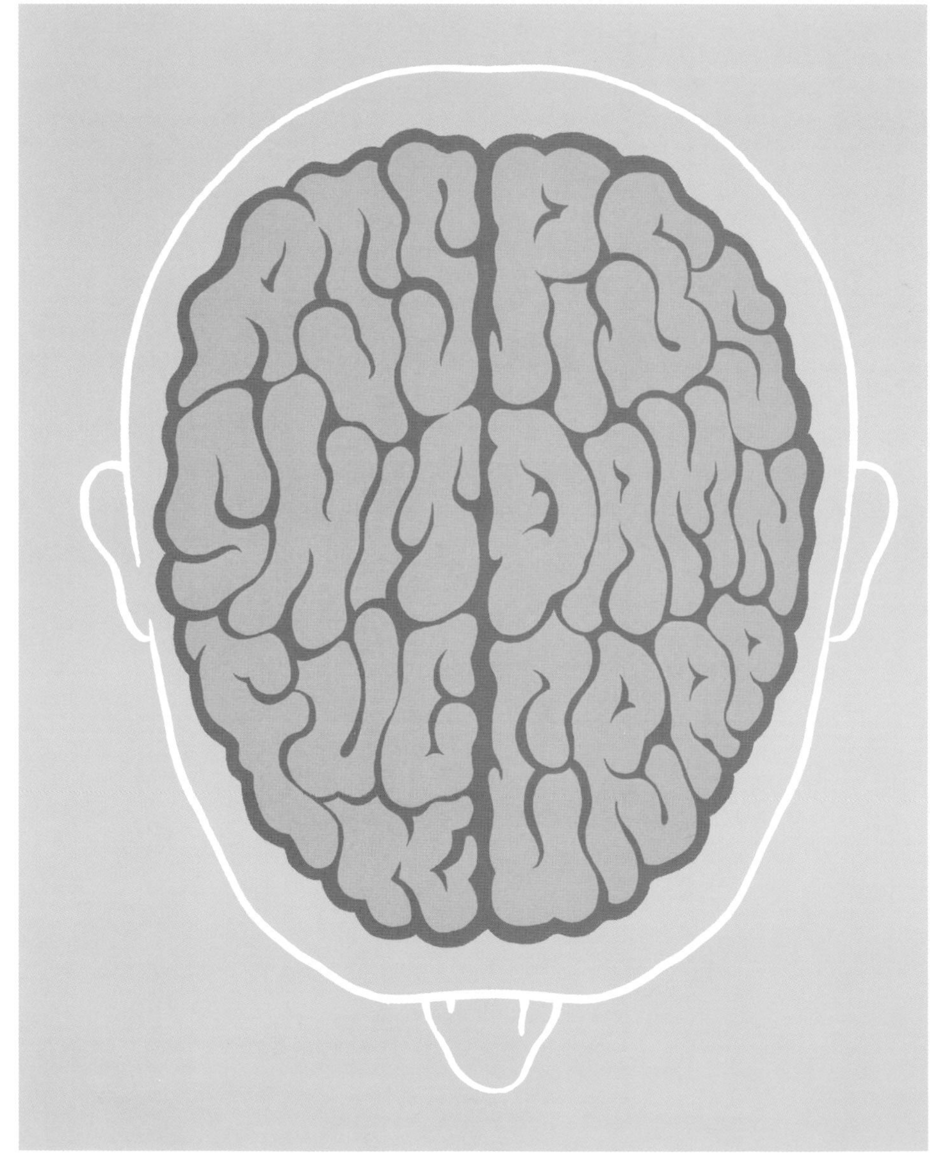

TOTALLY LONDON Making animals from words is one of the most common forms of word-a-morphosis. This one is stuffed to the gills.
DESIGN FIRM: Studio Oscar ART DIRECTOR: Neil Durber, RKCR/Y&R, London DESIGNER: Oscar Wilson CLIENT: Visit London PRIMARY FONT: Hand lettering

MAN MAN Man Man make wild, fun music and Nate Duval's goal for this poster was to recreate their onstage presence by creating their name out of imaginary characters.
DESIGN FIRM: NateDuval.com ART DIRECTOR/DESIGNER/ ILLUSTRATOR: Nate Duval CLIENT: Iron Horse Entertainment Group PUBLISHER: Nate Duval PRIMARY FONT: Hand lettering

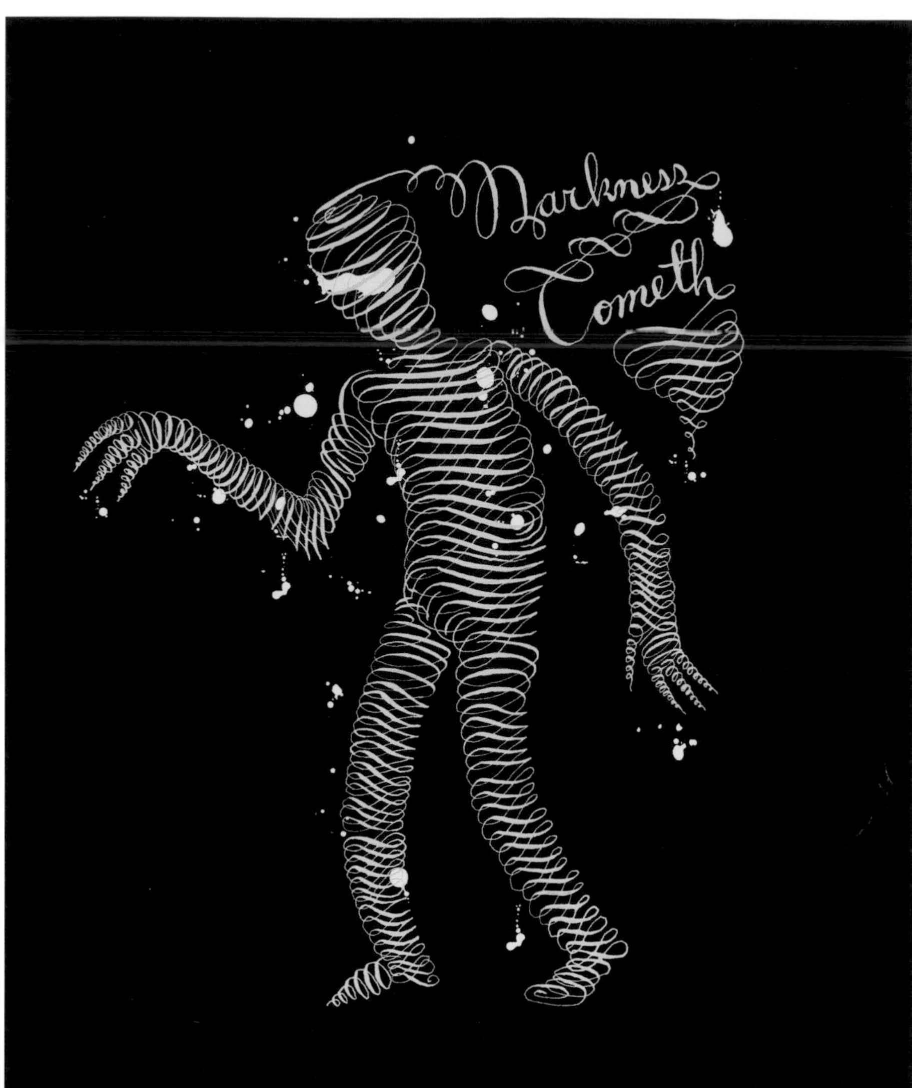

DARKNESS COMETH Ray Fenwick was tickled by a book of ornamental calligraphic birds, "where each bird was made from a series of pen loops, and they struck me as kind of ghoulish. So I made a ghoul."
ILLUSTRATOR: Ray Fenwick CLIENT: Self PRIMARY FONT: Hand lettering

DEEP PURPLE Roberto de Vicq de Cumptich cites Giuseppe Arcimboldo (the Italian painter of faces as mélanges of vegetables and animals), as well as the Bauhaus master Oskar Schlemmer's abstract dance costumes, as influences for this metamorphosed object.
DESIGN FIRM: de Vicq design ART DIRECTOR/DESIGNER/ILLUSTRATOR: Roberto de Vicq de Cumptich CLIENT/ PUBLISHER: HarperCollins PRIMARY FONTS: Stereopticon, Nuptial Script, Baskerville

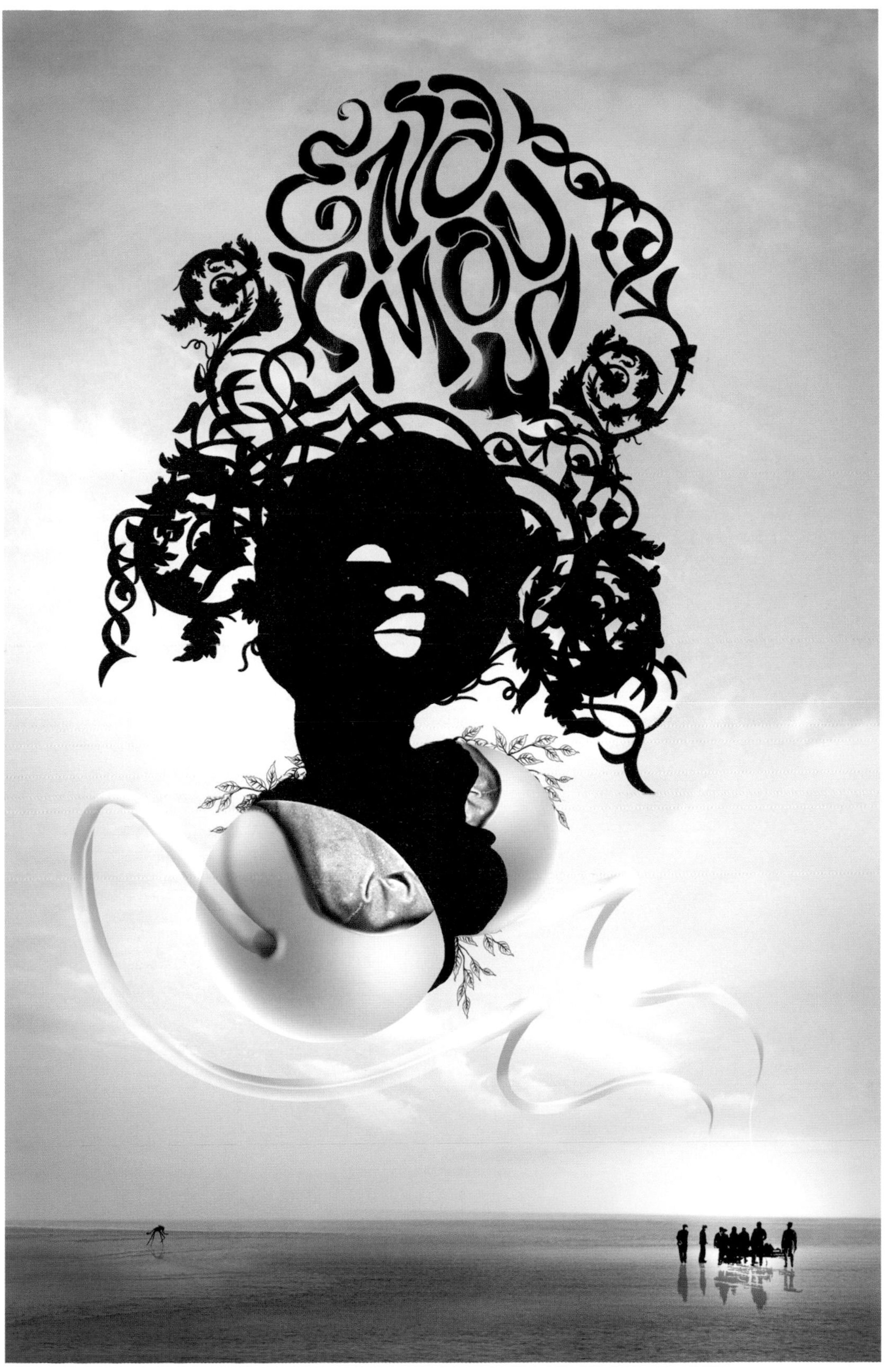

ENORMOUS The Enormous Room is a club in Cambridge, Massachusetts, that features live music several nights of the week. "There is irony in its name," says Adam Larson, "in that the club itself is not that big – it's actually rather small. For a promotional postcard, I wanted to create something that spoke of the club's activities, but shared the same sense of irony. The final image features an impossibly large character with hand-drawn type for hair that was inspired by 1960s Psychedelic concert posters."
DESIGN FIRM: Adam&Co. ART DIRECTOR/DESIGNER/ILLUSTRATOR/ PHOTOGRAPHER: Adam Larson
CLIENT: The Enormous Room
PRIMARY FONT: Hand lettering

TWENTY-SIX TYPES OF ANIMAL (C, E, F, P, W) Animals and letterforms go together like letterforms and animals. They are a perfect fit, as demonstrated here.
ART DIRECTOR/DESIGNER/ILLUSTRATOR: Jeremy Pettis CLIENT: Self PRIMARY FONT: Custom made

DUE The primary influences here, says Michele Angelo, are Mickey Mouse and Felix the Cat cartoons. This poster was made for the second anniversary of the Mosquito Acid Valley nightclub. "I wanted to put emphasis on the number 2, at the same time playing with it and treating it like an organic element." DESIGN FIRM: Superexpresso ART DIRECTOR/DESIGNER: Michele Angelo CLIENT: Mosquito Acid Valley PRIMARY FONT: Custom made

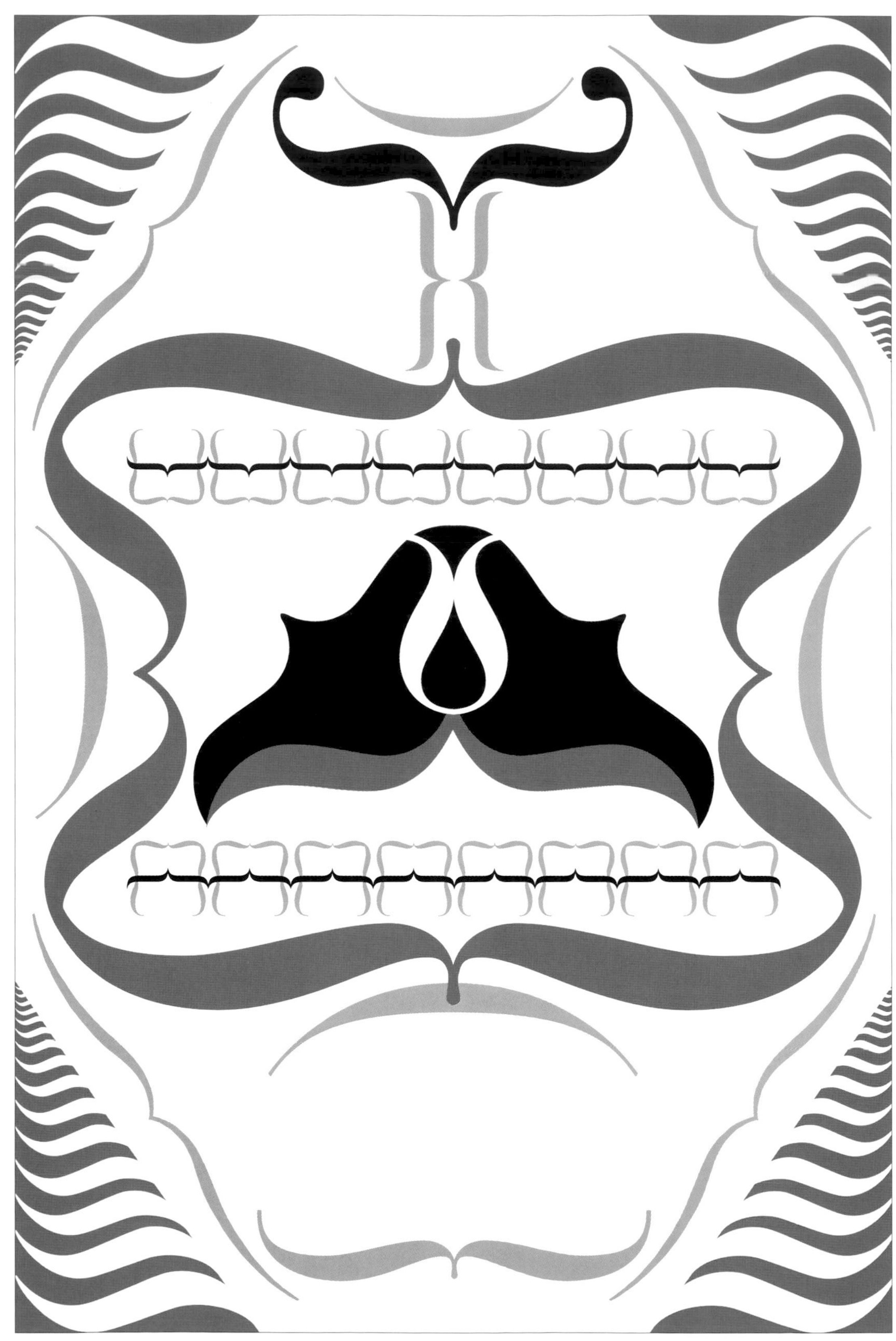

BRACE For Roberto de Vicq de Cumptich, this poster conjures up the back page of any typical high-school yearbook. Several graphic designers were given a punctuation mark (in this case, the bracket) and asked to create a poster for a show called "Punc't," promoting Neenah Paper and raising funds for the non-profit foundation Books for Kids. DESIGN FIRM: de Vicq design ILLUSTRATOR: Roberto de Vicq de Cumptich CLIENT: Punc't PUBLISHER: Neenah Paper PRIMARY FONTS: Edison Bracket, Didot

BIRDS BANNER This banner was inspired, explains John Solimine, "after reading many children's books from the 1960s and soaking up the illustration styles of the time."
DESIGN FIRM: Spike Press ART DIRECTOR/DESIGNER/ILLUSTRATOR: John Solimine CLIENT: Spike Press PUBLISHER: Spike Press PRIMARY FONT: Hand lettering

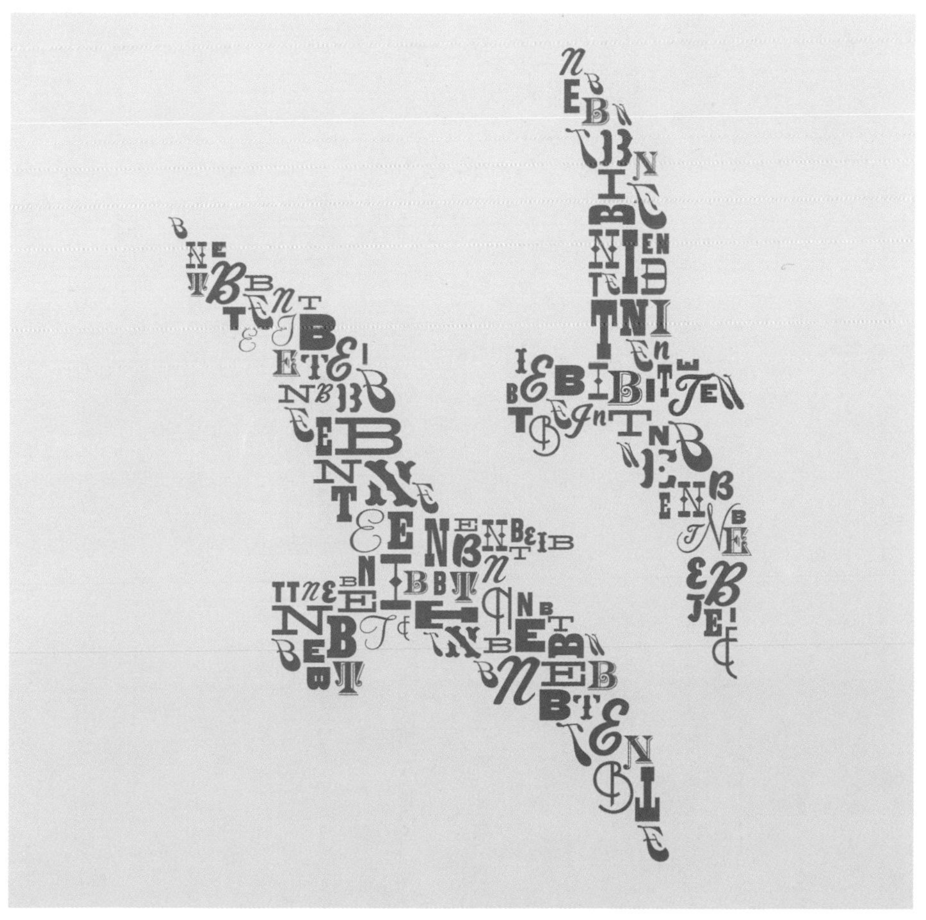

GULLS Letterpress, woodblock typefaces and vernacular retail signage served as the inspiration for this artwork for Sarah Jessica Parker's clothing line at the now-defunct retailer Steve & Barry's.
DESIGN FIRM: Neither Fish Nor Fowl ART DIRECTOR/DESIGNER/ILLUSTRATOR: Jim Datz CLIENT: Steve & Barry's/Bitten Sarah Jessica Parker PRIMARY FONTS: Various wood type

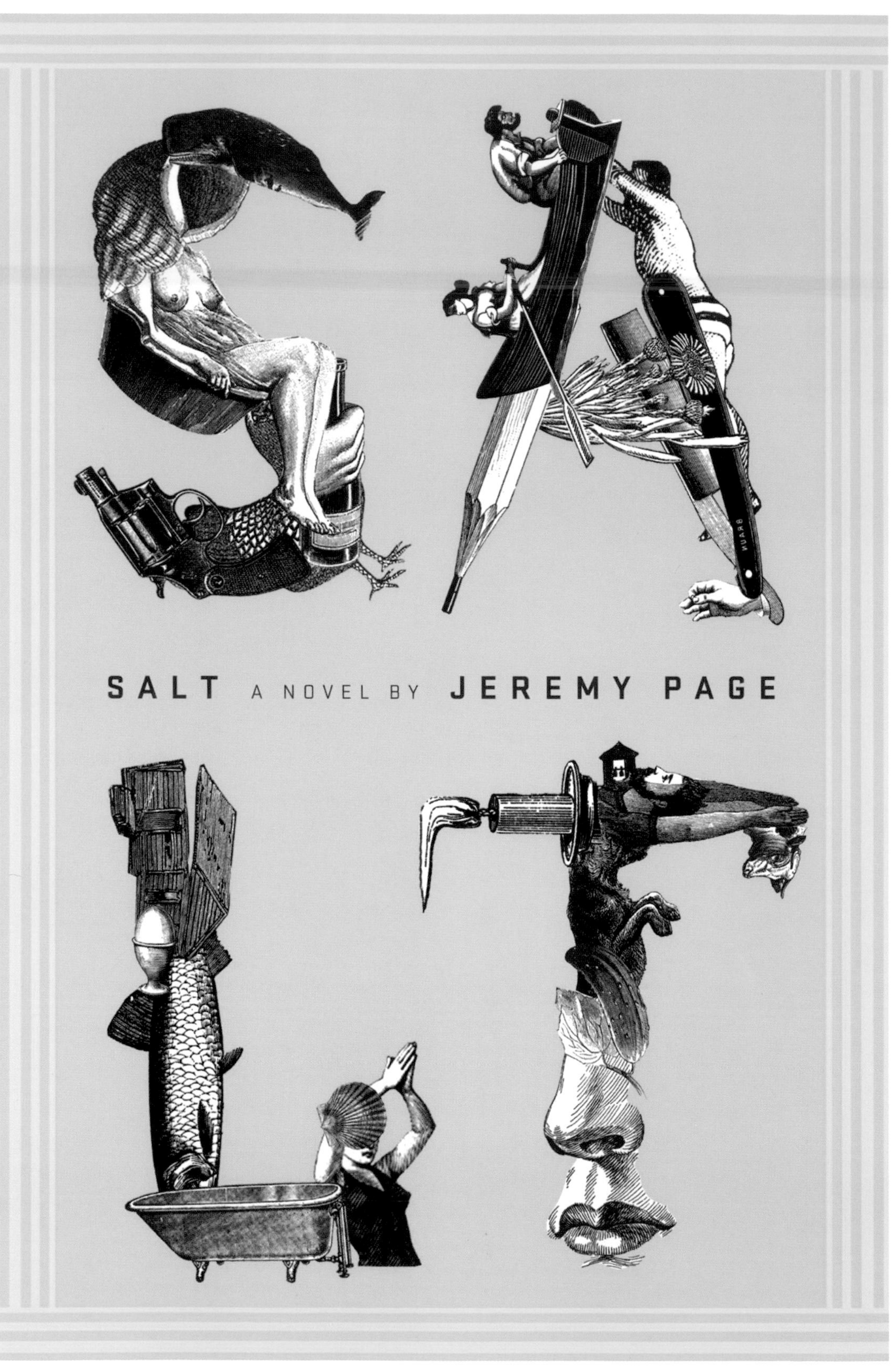

SALT The type design for this book cover was inspired by Roman Cieslewicz's fantastical alphabet, created for the publisher Tchou in 1964, in which fragments of figures and objects were used to create letterforms.
ART DIRECTOR: Paul Buckley
DESIGNER: Jaya Miceli CLIENT: Viking, Penguin Group USA PUBLISHER: Viking PRIMARY FONTS: Custom made, Stratum

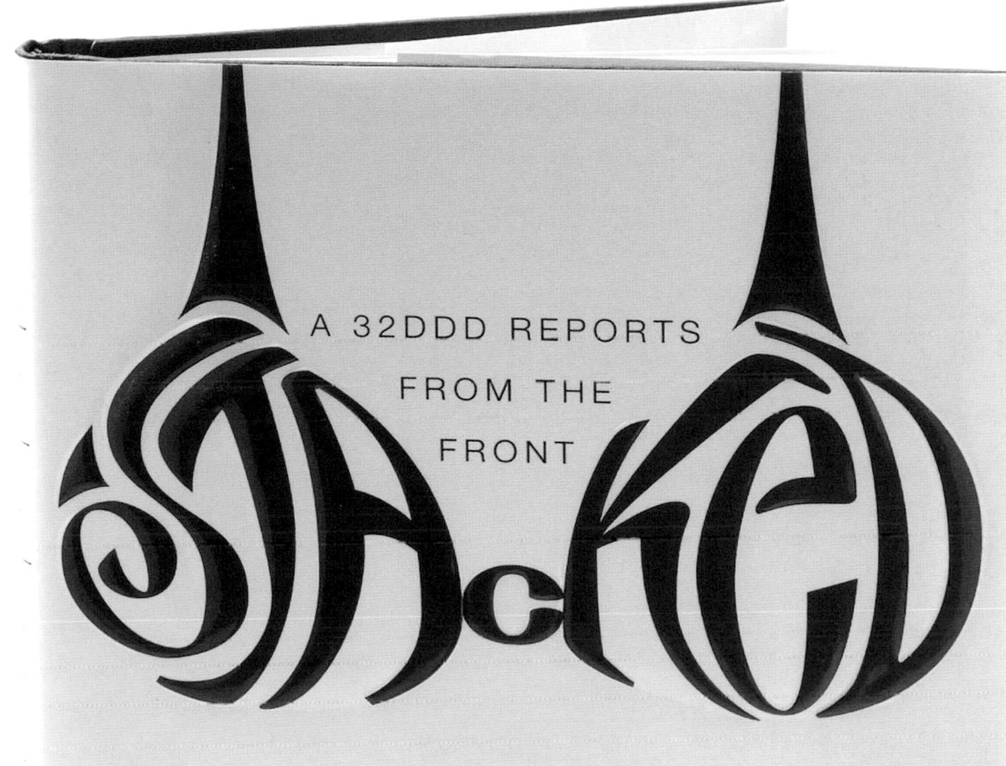

STACKED The hand lettering of 1960s rock posters will never die. Designers such as Roberto de Vicq de Cumptich are continually drawing nourishment from this ad hoc form.
DESIGN FIRM: de Vicq design ART DIRECTOR: Amy King DESIGNER: Roberto de Vicq de Cumptich CLIENT/PUBLISHER: Bloomsbury PRIMARY FONTS: Helvetica Neue, hand lettering

MONUMENTAL

REMEMBER THE FILM POSTERS for Ben Hur *and* The Ten Commandments? *The titles were carved from stone and stood monumentally above the action like mountains overlooking deep valleys. Monumentality is a graphic tool for expressing magnitude: the more monumental, the greater the magnitude of the message. The more ornamental the monument, the greater the effect.*

THE WIRED 40 For this magazine spread, colorful, voluminous forms provide the numerals with a certain gravity that roman letters could not achieve.
ART DIRECTOR/DESIGNER: Maili Holiman ILLUSTRATOR: Satian Pengsathapon CLIENT: *Wired* magazine PUBLISHER: Condé Nast PRIMARY FONT: Custom made

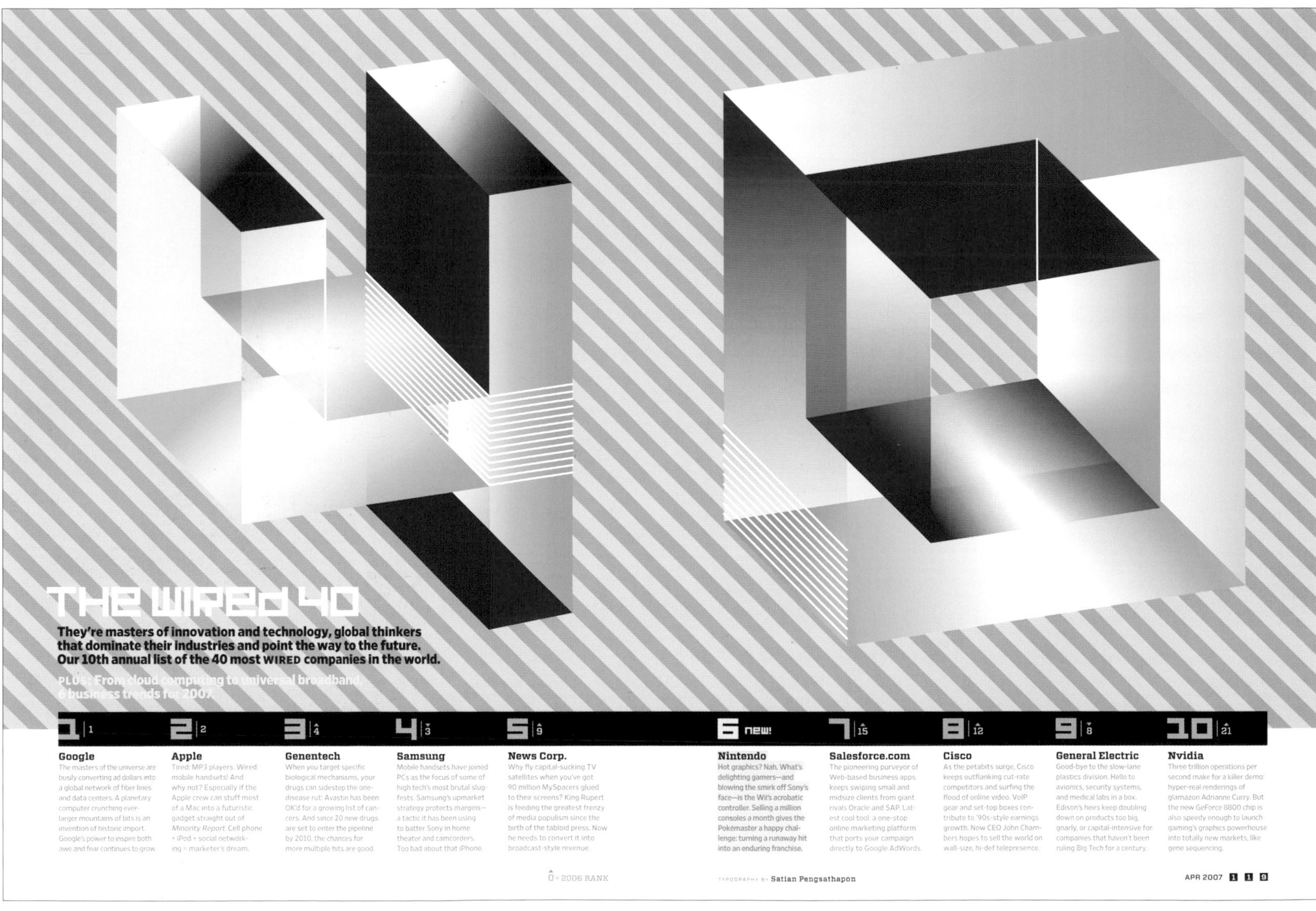

THE WIRED 40

They're masters of innovation and technology, global thinkers that dominate their industries and point the way to the future. Our 10th annual list of the 40 most WIRED companies in the world.

PLUS: From cloud computing to universal broadband, 6 business trends for 2007

1 | 1
Google
The masters of the universe are busily converting ad dollars into a global network of fiber lines and data centers. A planetary computer crunching ever-larger mountains of bits is an invention of historic import. Google's power to inspire both awe and fear continues to grow.

2 | 2
Apple
Tired: MP3 players. Wired: mobile handsets! And why not? Especially if the Apple crew can stuff most of a Mac into a futuristic gadget straight out of *Minority Report*. Cell phone + iPod + social networking = marketer's dream.

3 | ▲4
Genentech
When you target specific biological mechanisms, your drugs can sidestep the one-disease rut: Avastin has been OK'd for a growing list of cancers. And since 20 new drugs are set to enter the pipeline by 2010, the chances for more multiple hits are good.

4 | ▼3
Samsung
Mobile handsets have joined PCs as the focus of some of high tech's most brutal slugfests. Samsung's upmarket strategy protects margins—a tactic it has been using to batter Sony in home theater and camcorders. Too bad about that iPhone.

5 | ▲9
News Corp.
Why fly capital-sucking TV satellites when you've got 90 million MySpacers glued to their screens? King Rupert is feeding the greatest frenzy of media populism since the birth of the tabloid press. Now he needs to convert it into broadcast-style revenue.

6 new!
Nintendo
Hot graphics? Nah. What's delighting gamers—and blowing the smirk off Sony's face—is the Wii's acrobatic controller. Selling a million consoles a month gives the Pokémaster a happy challenge: turning a runaway hit into an enduring franchise.

7 | ▲15
Salesforce.com
The pioneering purveyor of Web-based business apps keeps swiping small and midsize clients from giant rivals Oracle and SAP. Latest cool tool: a one-stop online marketing platform that ports your campaign directly to Google AdWords.

8 | ▲12
Cisco
As the petabits surge, Cisco keeps outflanking cut-rate competitors and surfing the flood of online video. VoIP gear and set-top boxes contribute to '90s-style earnings growth. Now CEO John Chambers hopes to sell the world on wall-size, hi-def telepresence.

9 | ▼8
General Electric
Good-bye to the slow-lane plastics division. Hello to avionics, security systems, and medical labs in a box. Edison's heirs keep doubling down on products too big, gnarly, or capital-intensive for companies that haven't been ruling Big Tech for a century.

10 | ▲21
Nvidia
Three trillion operations per second make for a killer demo: hyper-real renderings of glamazon Adrianne Curry. But the new GeForce 8800 chip is also speedy enough to launch gaming's graphics powerhouse into totally new markets, like gene sequencing.

▲0 = 2006 RANK

TYPOGRAPHY BY Satian Pengsathapon

APR 2007 119

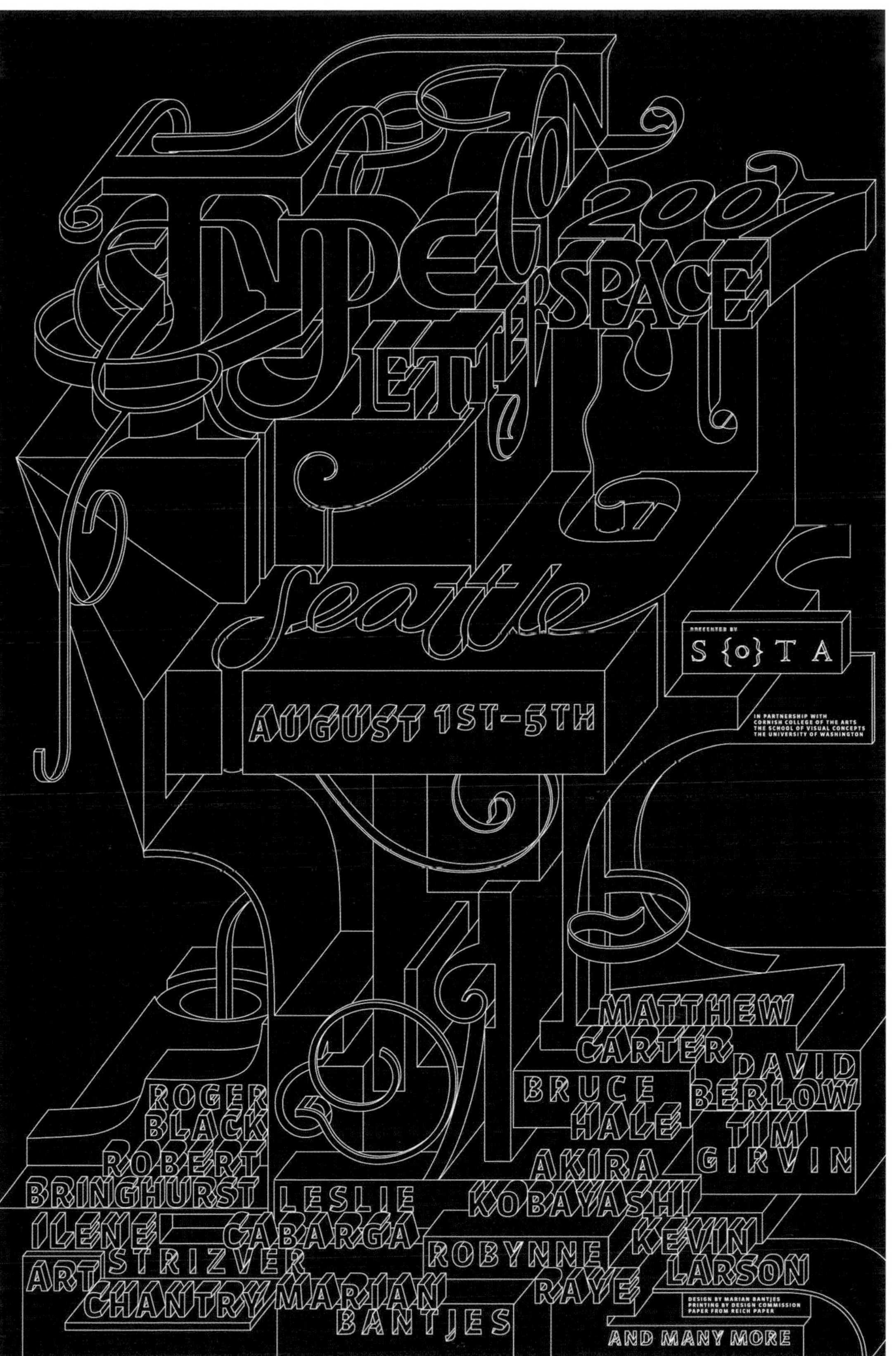

TYPECON 2007: LETTER SPACE

Marian Bantjes created the poster and program for this typography conference, rendering everything in custom-drawn isometric forms, "including a '3-D' extrusion I made of the typeface Sanuk, by Xavier Dupré."

DESIGNER: Marian Bantjes CLIENT: Society of Typographic Afficionados

PRIMARY FONTS: Hand lettering, Sanuk

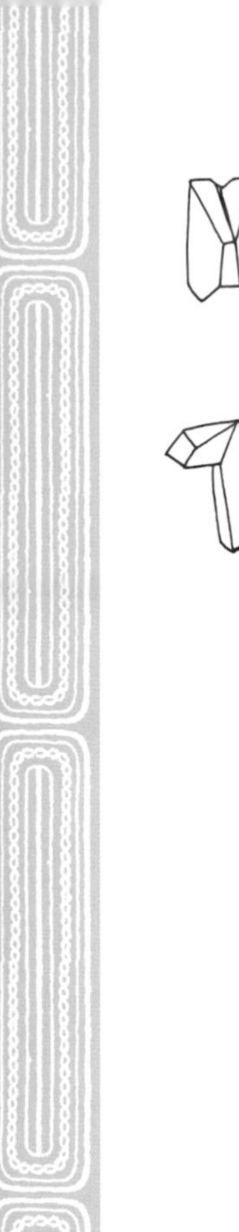

MADINSPAIN PSICOTIPOGRAFICO

Michele Angelo explains: "This poster was made in collaboration with Alex Trochut, who developed the shapes, while I painted the forms in oils, interpreting them with the color and the bubbles." Trochut was influenced, he says, by wood and by the moon. DESIGN FIRM: Superexpresso ART DIRECTORS/DESIGNERS: Michele Angelo, Alex Trochut CLIENT: Madinspain PRIMARY FONT: Oil-painted ITC Serif

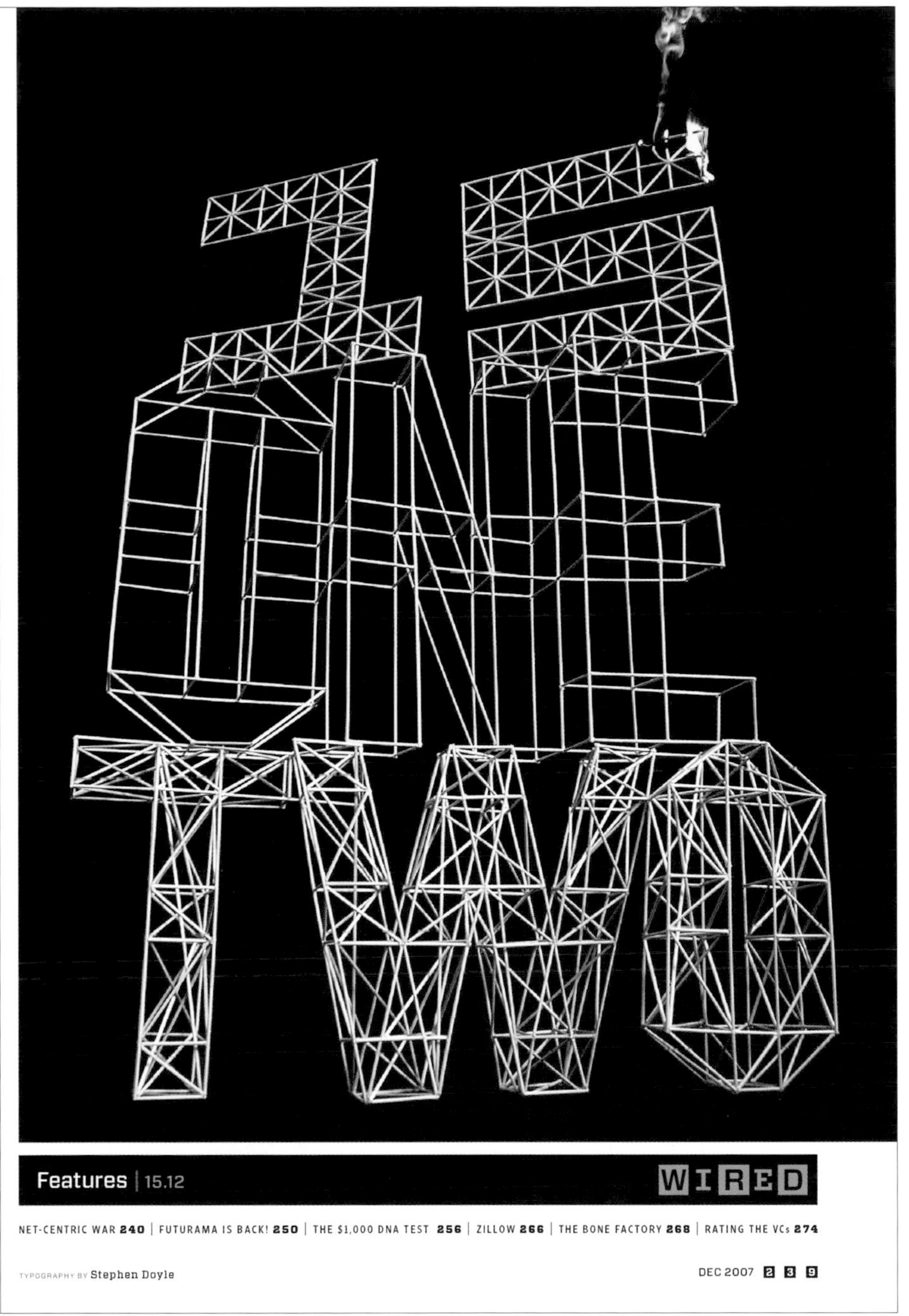

15.12 FEATURES Using architectural letterforms, this *Wired* magazine section opener exudes all the monumentality of a high-rise steel skeleton.
CREATIVE DIRECTOR: Scott Dadich DESIGN DIRECTOR: Wyatt Mitchell DESIGNER: Stephen Doyle CLIENT: *Wired* magazine PUBLISHER: Condé Nast PRIMARY FONT: Custom made

15.06 FEATURES The sci-fi monumentality of this construction, again for a section opener in *Wired* magazine, suggests an edifice of incredible proportions. It derives from the Italian Futurist use of letterforms as architecture.
DESIGN FIRM: MK12 CREATIVE DIRECTOR: Scott Dadich DESIGN DIRECTOR: Maili Holiman DESIGNER: MK12 CLIENT: *Wired* magazine PUBLISHER: Condé Nast PRIMARY FONT: Custom made

RIBBON

LIKE SMOKE, a ribbon is fluid. Unlike smoke, it is more easily manipulated to become a script or other diaphanous letterform. Not surprisingly, in this new ornamental era supple ribbon is used as a way of suggesting beauty, femininity, and eroticism.

SOMETHING IS WRONG This painting was included in an exhibition called "Vapor" (2006, Gallery Engler, Berlin). The text is simple cursive, but the geometric treatment and color palette are somewhat inspired by the graphic design of the 1940s and early 1950s.
DESIGNER/ILLUSTRATOR: Tim Biskup
CLIENT: Self PRIMARY FONT: Hand lettering

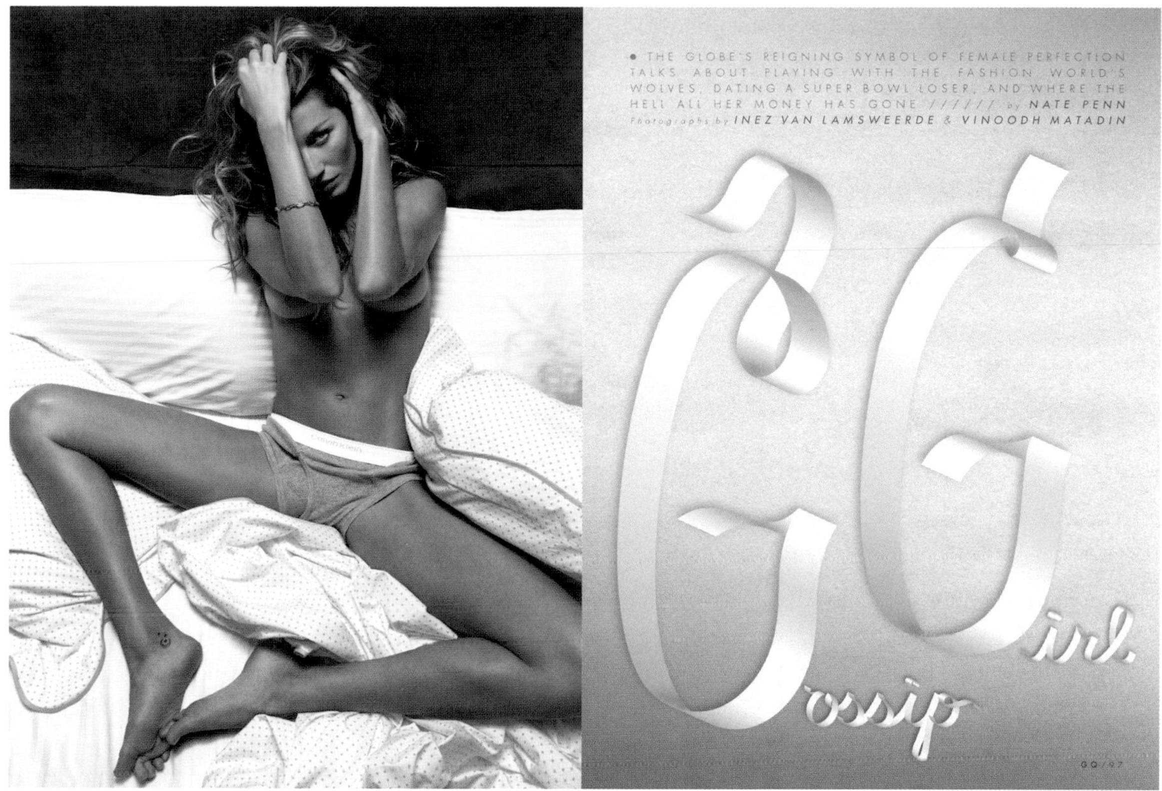

GOSSIP GIRL This magazine type is a clear homage to the painter and printmaker Ed Ruscha's ribbon lettering series.
DESIGN DIRECTOR: Fred Woodward
DESIGNER: Thomas Alberty
PHOTOGRAPHERS: Inez Van Lamsweerde, Vinoodh Matadin
CLIENT: *GQ* magazine PUBLISHER: Condé Nast PRIMARY FONT: Custom made, Futura

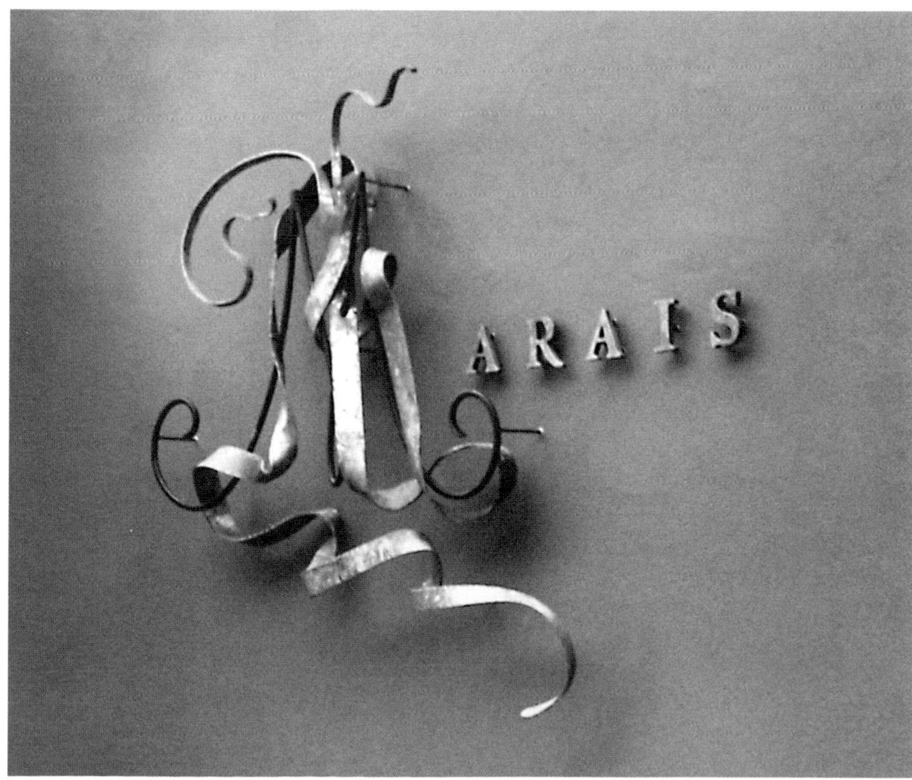

RESTAURANT MARAIS This logo is a three-dimensional iteration of Victorian ornamental initials originally found in a Dover clip art sourcebook.
DESIGN FIRM: Chase Design Group
ART DIRECTOR/DESIGNER: Margo Chase CLIENT: Alan McClellan and Penny DeVries PUBLISHER: Restaurant Marais PRIMARY FONT: Garamond caps

RIBBON

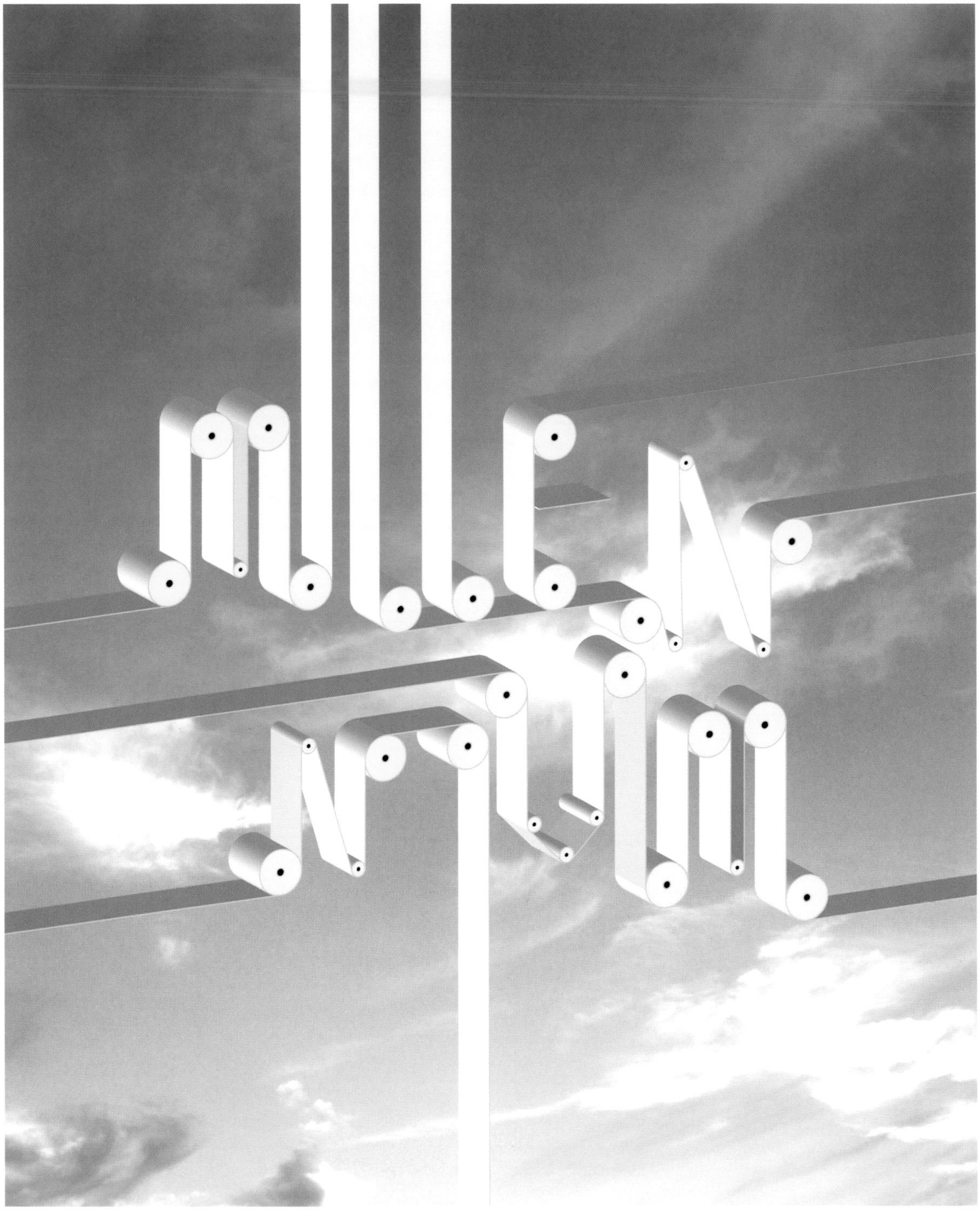

MILLENNIUM This typography was created to accompany an article about Millennium Graphics, a printer in Massachusetts. The article focused on Millennium's use of green printing practices. Adam Larson created a custom type treatment that references the way paper feeds through a web press, set against a blue sky.
DESIGN FIRM: Adam&Co. ART DIRECTOR/DESIGNER/ILLUSTRATOR/PHOTOGRAPHER: Adam Larson CLIENT: AIGA Boston PRIMARY FONT: Custom made

EAST For their annual regional design annual, *Print* magazine commissioned various illustrators to visually interpret the region where they currently practice. The final images were used as section introduction pages in their 2007 annual. This image was created to depict the East. The type was created as part of a surreal scene and intended to be dually abstract and representative.
DESIGN FIRM: Adam&Co. ART DIRECTOR/DESIGNER/ILLUSTRATOR/PHOTOGRAPHER: Adam Larson CLIENT/PUBLISHER: *Print* magazine PRIMARY FONT: Hand lettering

2007 JOURNAL OF AIGA BOSTON For the *2007 Journal of AIGA Boston*, Adam Larson wanted to treat the type in a non-traditional way, given that the primary audience were members of the design community. "I had created an illustration that was very surreal and wanted the type to work but also be challenging at the same time," he says. The result was a hand-drawn treatment that gave dimension to the characters and positioned them in space among the other elements within the illustration.
DESIGN FIRM: Adam&Co. ART DIRECTOR/DESIGNER/ILLUSTRATOR/PHOTOGRAPHER: Adam Larson CLIENT: AIGA Boston PRIMARY FONT: Hand lettering

RIBBON

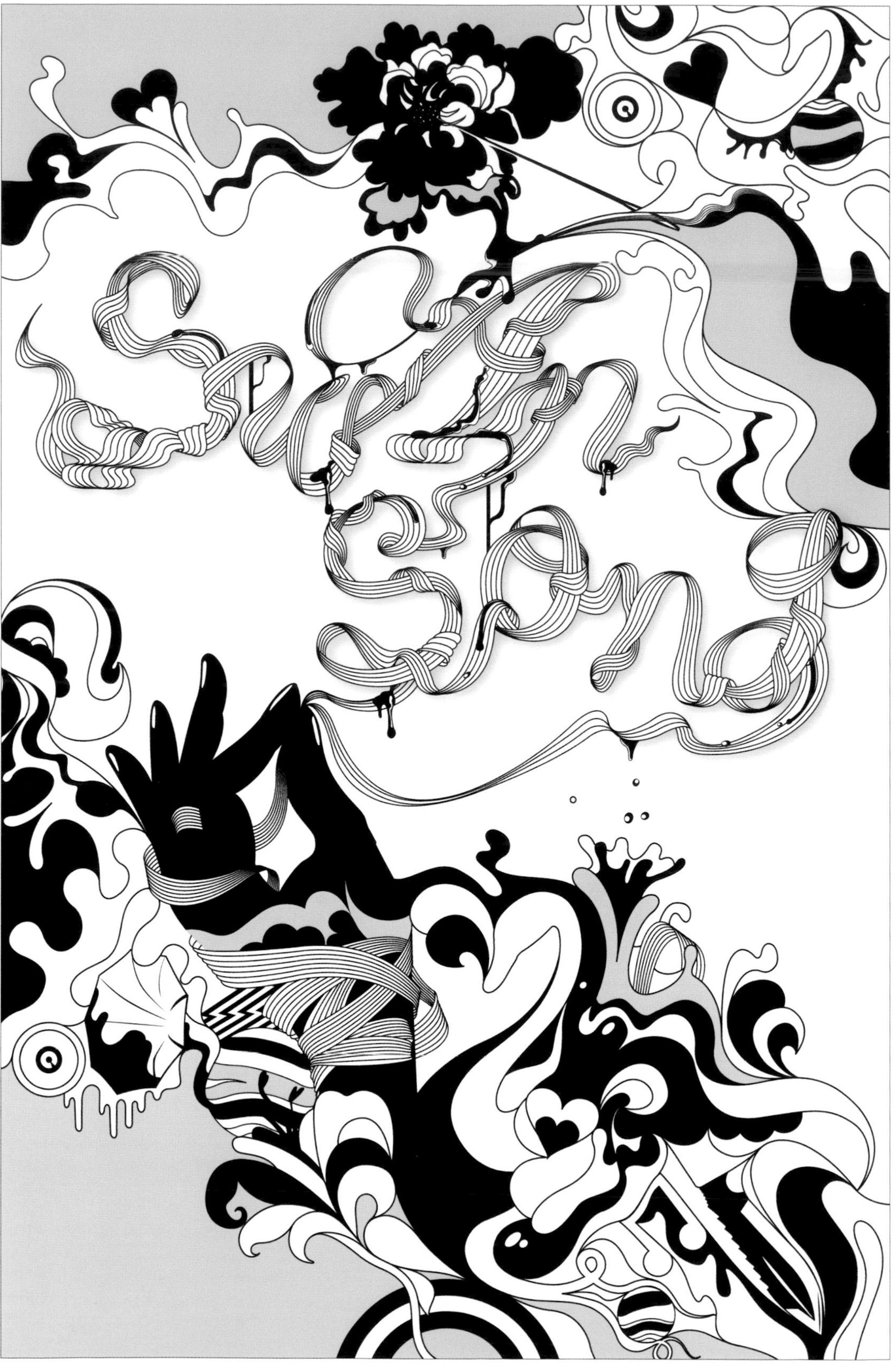

SWANSONG The excessive ornamentation of this self-promotional piece is typical of the free-associative doodling that has become a key feature of contemporary ornamental design. The lettering is based on the font Snell. DESIGN FIRM: Vault 49 DESIGNERS: Jonathan Kenyon, John Glasgow CLIENT/PUBLISHER: Vault 49 PRIMARY FONTS: Hand lettering, based on Snell

THE NEW AFFIRMATIVE ACTION This was for the first annual *New York Times Magazine* "College Issue." The entire issue was inspired by the hand-made quality of zines. "We also felt that it would be appropriate to work with a college in some capacity," says Arem Duplessis. "There was this beautiful magazine entitled *Fishwrap* that was designed by students at Art Center College of Design, California. We contacted Lisa Wagner, a faculty advisor for *Fishwrap* and asked her to put together a dream team of former students who participated in the design. Under the magazine's direction, the 'Fishwrappers' created the titling in the feature well."
ART DIRECTOR: Arem Duplessis DESIGNERS: Arem Duplessis, Jeff Glendenning, Julia Moburg, Nancy Harris Rouemy, Holly Gressley, Hillary Greenbaum LETTERERS: Fishwrappers/ Jacob Magraw-Mickelson CLIENT: *The New York Times Magazine* PUBLISHER: *The New York Times* PRIMARY FONTS: NYT, Cheltenham NYT, Helvetica

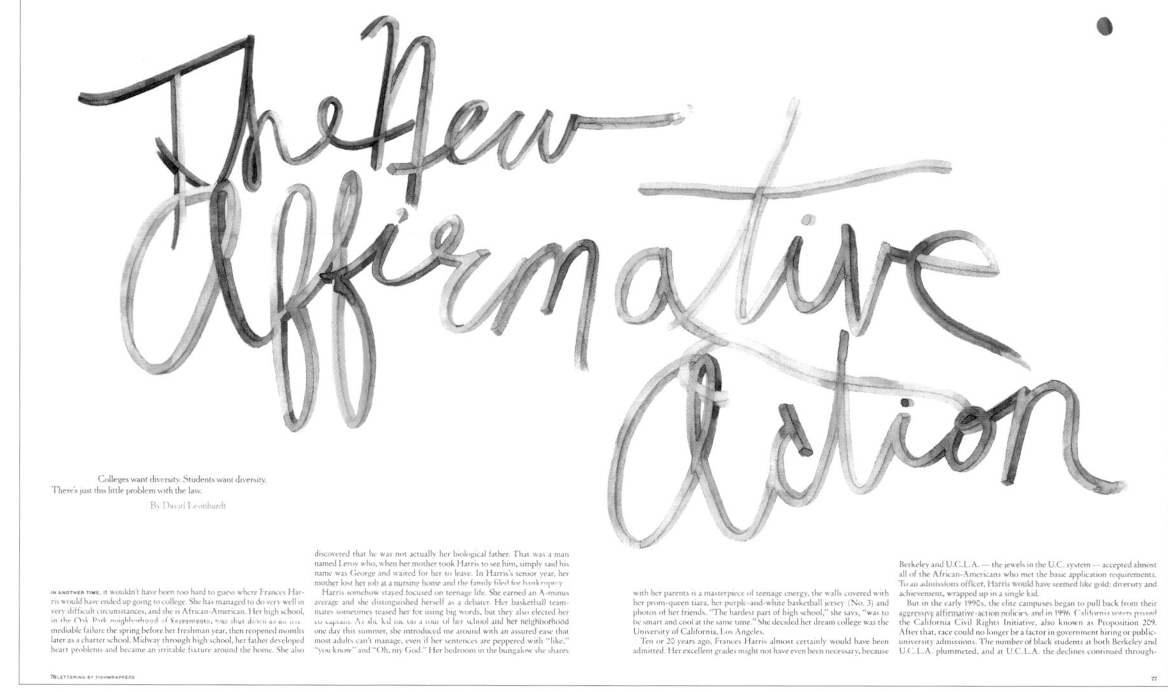

The New Affirmative Action

Colleges want diversity. Students want diversity.
There's just this little problem with the law.

By David Leonhardt

IN ANOTHER TIME, it wouldn't have been too hard to guess where Frances Harris would have ended up going to college. She has managed to do very well in very difficult circumstances, and she is African-American. Her high school, in the Oak Park neighborhood of Sacramento, was shut down as an irremediable failure the spring before her freshman year, then reopened months later as a charter school. Midway through high school, her father developed heart problems and became an irritable fixture around the home. She also discovered that he was not actually her biological father. That was a man named Leroy who, when her mother took Harris to see him, simply said his name was George and waited for her to leave. In Harris's senior year, her mother lost her job at a nursing home and the family filed for bankruptcy.

Harris somehow stayed focused on teenage life. She earned an A-minus average and she distinguished herself as a debater. Her basketball teammates sometimes teased her for using big words, but they also elected her co-captain. As she led me on a tour of her school and her neighborhood one day this summer, she introduced me around with an assured ease that most adults can't manage, even if her sentences are peppered with "like," "you know" and "Oh, my God." Her bedroom in the bungalow she shares with her parents is a masterpiece of teenage energy, the walls covered with her prom-queen tiara, her purple-and-white basketball jersey (No. 3) and photos of her friends. "The hardest part of high school," she says, "was to be smart and cool at the same time." She decided her dream college was the University of California, Los Angeles.

Ten or 20 years ago, Frances Harris almost certainly would have been admitted. Her excellent grades might not have even been necessary, because Berkeley and U.C.L.A. — the jewels in the U.C. system — accepted almost all of the African-Americans who met the basic application requirements. To an admissions officer, Harris would have seemed like gold: diversity and achievement, wrapped up in a single kid.

But in the early 1990s, the elite campuses began to pull back from their aggressive affirmative-action policies, and in 1996 California voters passed the California Civil Rights Initiative, also known as Proposition 209. After that, race could no longer be a factor in government hiring or public-university admissions. The number of black students at both Berkeley and U.C.L.A. plummeted, and at U.C.L.A. the declines continued through-

76 LETTERING BY FISHWRAPPERS

77

LUXURY Yulia Brodskaya wanted to create delicate, organic, "flowy" lettering for this self-promotional piece. "Maybe it is not obvious, but the inspiration here is nature, florals, and so on."
DESIGN FIRM: Yulia Brodskaya ART DIRECTOR/DESIGNER/ ILLUSTRATOR: Yulia Brodskaya CLIENT: Self PRIMARY FONT: Hand lettering

NEW ORNAMENTAL FONTS

FONT: Mommie DESIGNER: Hubert Jocham
FOUNDRY: Hubert Jocham Design + Type

FONT: Carmen Fiesta DESIGNER: Andreu Balius
FOUNDRY: Typerepublic

GOTHIC

FONT: Hel Grotesk Gothiq Black
DESIGNER: Kevin Yuen Kit Lo

VICTORIAN

FONT: Digitized from *Lettera 3* (Haab & Haettenschweiler)

FONT: T Shirt DESIGNER: Mattheu Laroussinie
SCHOOL: École Supérieure d'Art et de Design

HIPSTER

FONT: Penny DESIGNER: Blake E. Marquis
FOUNDRY: You Work for Them

FONT: Version 116 DESIGNER: Jeff Rogers

PSYCHEDELIC

FONT: Typop-up DESIGNER: Lise Bonneau
SCHOOL: École Supérieure d'Art et de Design

HIP-HOP

FONT: Pen DESIGNER: Maksim Loginov, Vladimir Loginov FOUNDRY: Handmade Font

TECH

FONT: Floppy Disk DESIGNER: Arnaud Dupont
SCHOOL: École Supérieure d'Art et de Design

FONT: Scarf DESIGNER: Céline Bouchez
SCHOOL: School of Visual Arts

FURTHER READING

Ackland-Snow, Nicola, et al.
The Art of the Club Flyer (London: Thames & Hudson, 1996).

Adams, Steven
The Arts & Crafts Movement (Secaucus, NJ: Chartwell Books, Inc., 1987).

Ades, Dawn
Photomontage (London: Thames & Hudson, 1986).

American Type Founders Company
Specimen Book and Catalogue 1923 (Jersey City, NJ: American Type Founders Company, 1923).

Annenberg, Maurice
Type Foundries of America and their Catalogs (New Castle, DE: Oak Knoll Press, 1994).

Bierut, Michael, et al., eds.
Looking Closer III: Classic Writings on Graphic Design (New York: Allworth Press, 1999).

Cabarga, Leslie
Progressive German Graphics, 1900–1937 (San Francisco: Chronicle Books, 1994).

Carlyle, Paul and Oring, Guy
Letters and Lettering (New York: McGraw-Hill, 1935).

Chernevich, Elena
Soviet Commercial Design of the Twenties (New York: Abbeville Press, 1987).

Couperie, Pierre, et al.
A History of the Comic Strip (New York: Crown Publishers, Inc., 1968).

Crimliss, Roger and Turner, Alwyn W.
Cult Rock Posters: Ten Years of Classic Posters from the Punk, New Wave and Glam Era (New York: Billboard Books, 2006).

Day, Harold Holland
Modern Brush Lettering (Cincinnati: The Signs of the Times Publishing Co., 1931).

DeNoon, Christopher
Posters of the WPA (Los Angeles: The Wheatley Press, 1987).

Dluhosch, Eric and Svácha, Rotislav, eds.
Karel Teige 1900–1951: L'Enfant Terrible of the Czech Modernist Avant-Garde (Cambridge, Mass: MIT Press, 1999).

Eson, Ron and Rookledge, Sarah
Rookledge's International Directory of Type Designers: A Biographical Handbook (New York: The Sarabande Press, 1994).

Friedman, Mildred
Graphic Design in America: A Visual Language History. Minneapolis: Walker Art Center (New York: Harry N. Abrams, Inc., 1989).

Gandl, Stefan
Neubau Welt (Berlin: Gestalten Verlag: 2005).

Gomez-Palacio, Bryony and Vit, Armin
Women of Design: Influence and Inspiration from the Original Trail-blazers to the New Groundbreakers (Cincinatti: How Books, 2009).

Gress, Edmund G.
Fashions in American Typography 1780–1930 (New York: Harper & Brothers, 1931).

Haab, Armin and Haettenschweiler, Walter
Lettera 2: A Standard Book of Fine Lettering (Teufen AR, Switzerland: Arthur Niggli Ltd, 1961).

Haab, Armin and Haettenschweiler, Walter
Lettera 3: A Standard Book of Fine Lettering (New York: Hastings House Publishers Inc., 1968).

Heller, Steven and Anderson, Gail
New Vintage Type: Classic Fonts for the Digital Age (London: Thames & Hudson, 2007).

Heller, Steven and Ilić, Mirko
Handwritten: Expressive Lettering in the Digital Age (London: Thames & Hudson, 2006).

Heller, Steven and Lasky, Julie
Borrowed Design: Use and Abuse of Historical Form (New York: Van Notrand Reinhold, 1993).

Heller, Steven and Chwast, Seymour
Graphic Style: From Victorian to Digital (New York: Harry N. Abrams, 2001).

Heller, Steven and Fili, Louise
Typology: Type Design from The Victorian Era to The Digital Age (San Francisco: Chronicle Books, 1999).

Hollis, Richard
Graphic Design: A Concise History. (London: Thames & Hudson, 1994).

Horsham, Michael
20s & 30s Style (London: Chartwell Books, Inc., 1989).

Lewis, John
The Twentieth Century Book (London: Studio Vista Limited, 1967).

Lupton, Ellen and Miller, Abbot
Design Writing Research: Writing on Graphic Design (London: Phaidon Press Limited, 1999).

McAlhone, Beryl, et al.
A Smile in the Mind: Witty Thinking in Graphic Design (London: Phaidon Press Ltd, 1998).

Meggs, Philip B.
A History of Graphic Design, First Edition (New York: Van Nostrand Reinhold, 1983).

Meggs, Philip B.
A History of Graphic Design, Second Edition (New York: Van Nostrand Reinhold, 1992).

Meggs, Philip B.
A History of Graphic Design, Third Edition. (New York: John Wiley & Sons, 1998).

Miller, J. Abbot
Dimensional Typography: Case Studies on the Shape of Letters, A Kiosk Report (Princeton: Princeton Architectual Press, 1996).

Müller-Brockmann, Josef
A History of Visual Communications (New York: Visual Communication Books, Hastings House, 1971).

Parry, Linda, ed.
William Morris (New York: Harry N. Abrams, Inc., 1996).

Perry, Michael
Hand Job: A Catalog of Type (New York: Princeton Architectural Press, 2007).

Sagmeister, Stefan
Things I Have Learned in My Life So Far (New York: Harry N. Abrams, Inc., 2008).

Schalansky, Judith
Fraktur Mon Amour (New York: Princeton Architectural Press, 2008).

Svennas, Elsie
A Handbook of Lettering for Stitchers (New York: Van Nostrand Reinhold Company, 1966).

Type Directors Club
Typography 28 (New York: Collins Design, 2008).

Type Directors Club
Typography 29 (New York: Collins Design, 2009).

Wrede, Stuart
The Modern Poster (New York: Little, Brown and Company, 1988).

INDEX OF DESIGNERS AND ILLUSTRATORS

0c/0m/0y/0k 98
www.0c0m0y0k.de

agrayspace 78, 80
www.agrayspace.com

Aeiko 88
www.aeiko.net

Arnold, Dustin E. 33, 150, 162, 163
www.dustinarnold.com

Aufuldish & Warinner 167
www.aufwar.com

Balius, Andreu 39, 146, 165
www.andreubalius.com

Bantjes, Marian 12, 17, 22, 146, 148, 149, 156, 181
www.bantjes.com

Barbanel, Dmitry 67, 73, 75
english.imedia.ru

Beck, Melinda 41
www.melindabeck.com

Bernard, Merci 46, 164
www.mercibernard.fr

Biskup, Tim 42, 43, 184
www.timbiskup.com

Blikdsgn 13, 34, 58, 145
www.blikdsgn.com

Brodskaya, Yulia 50, 88, 189
www.artyulia.com

Buckley, Paul 85, 178
www.penguin.com

Carmichael, Alison 70, 153
www.alisoncarmichael.com

Chase Design Group 15, 16, 185
www.chasedesigngroup.com

Chemnad, Khaleelullah 76, 74
www.worldofcalligraphy.com

Cusack, Margaret 169
www.margaretcusack.com

The Decoder Ring 106, 151
www.thedecoderring.com

De Vicq de Cumptich, Roberto 27, 32, 81, 161, 172, 176, 179
www.devicq.com

Doyle Partners 105, 183
www.doylepartners.com

Duval, Nate 38, 51, 55, 118, 171
www.NateDuval.com

FarmBarn Art Co. 99, 109
www.thefarmbarn.com

Faith Design 7, 10, 13, 47, 128, 156, 182
www.faith.ca

Feerer, Ryan 155
www.ryanfeerer.com

Fella, Ed 126–7, 191
www.edfella.com

Fenwick, Ray 18, 40, 43, 124, 172
www.coandco.ca/ray

Garric, Jérémie 192
www.jeremiegarric.com

Ginger Monkey 154
www.gingermonkeydesign.com

Goldberg, Carin 37, 142
www.caringoldberg.com

GQ magazine 59, 166, 185
www.gq.com

Grandpeople 8, 84, 101, 132
www.grandpeople.org

HandMadeFont 80, 96, 138, 189, 190
www.handmadefont.com

Hannah, Jonny 116, 125
www.heartagency.com

Heckart, Matthew 96
www.mheckart.com

Howe, Daniel C. 64
www.mrl.nyu.edu/~dhowe

Hubert Jocham Design+Type 189
www.hubertjocham.de

Hugo, Mario 103
www.loveworn.com

Hunter, Linzie 41
www.linziehunter.co.uk

Ian Brignell Lettering Design 11, 15, 23, 152
www.ianbrignell.com

Inksurge 79, 86, 91
www.inksurge.com

Jason Rubino Design 143
www.behance.net/JasonRubino

Kaur, Satveer 92
satveerkaur.co.uk

Kay, Justin Thomas 6, 14
www.justinthomaskay.com

Khaki Creative & Design 67, 69
www.khakicreative.com

FONT: Super Veloz Fauno DESIGNERS: Digitized by Andreu Balius and Alex Trochut FOUNDRY: Type Republic

FONT: Stick Together DESIGNER: Tristan Benedict Hall FOUNDRY: You Work for Them

FONT: Ornamental DESIGNER: Tristan Benedict Hall FOUNDRY: You Work for Them

HAIR

FONT: Hair DESIGNER: Maksim Loginov, Vladimir Loginov FOUNDRY: Handmade Font

FONT: Spike Me DESIGNER: Jeff Rogers

LIQUID

FONT: Ketchup DESIGNER: Maksim Loginov, Vladimir Loginov FOUNDRY: Handmade Font

FONT: Phosporous DESIGNER: Mariana Uchoa

FONT: Leaftype DESIGNER: Jeff Rogers

HANDMADE

FONT: Mr. Hyde DESIGNER: Emma Trithart FOUNDRY: You Work for Them

FONT: Fella DESIGNER: Ed Fella

FONT: From *A Handbook of Lettering for Stitchers* (Svennas)

OBJECT AS LETTER

FONT: Isometric Nail DESIGNER: Arnaud Dupont
SCHOOL: École Supérieure d'Art et de Design

FONT: Pastelaria DESIGNER: Eduardo Recife
FOUNDRY: Misprinted Type

CHAOTIC

FONT: Poirographie DESIGNER: Jérémie Garric
SCHOOL: École Supérieure d'Art et de Design

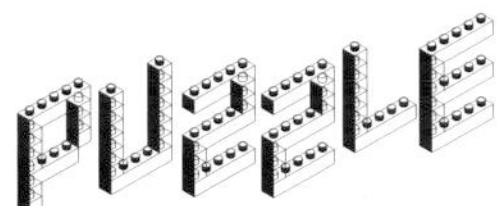

FONT: Lego Font Creator DESIGNER: Blokes
FOUNDRY: Lineto

EMBELLISHED

FONT: Super Veloz DESIGNER: Joan Trochut; digitized by Andreu Balius and Alex Trochut
FOUNDRY: Typerepublic

FONT: Girlyque DESIGNER: Emma Trithart
FOUNDRY: You Work for Them

FONT: Spinster DESIGNER: Tonya Douraghy
SCHOOL: School of Visual Arts

ANTHROPOMORPHIC

FONT: Doggie Type DESIGNER: Dohun Park
SCHOOL: School of Visual Arts

FONT: Polygone DESIGNER: Emily Darnell
FOUNDRY: You Work for Them

RIBBON

FONT: Apple Peel DESIGNER: Adrien Collino
SCHOOL: École Supérieure d'Art et de Design

Koen, Viktor 134, 135
www.viktorkoen.com

Larson, Adam 173, 186, 187
www.adamncompany.com

Leida, Edward 17, 62, 108, 137
www.edwardleidadesign.com

Lester, Seb 133
www.seblester.co.uk

The Letterheads Ltd 37, 49
www.theletterheads.co.nz

Lineto 192
www.lineto.com

Lodma 35
www.lodma.com

Lo, Kevin Yuen Kit 189
www.lokidesign.net

Louise Fili Ltd 28, 33, 159, 160, 168
www.louisefili.com

Maki 24, 29, 117, 118
www.makimaki.nl

Marianek, Joe 36, 46
www.joemarianek.com

Misprinted Type 19
www.misprintedtype.com

Modern Dog Design 52, 55, 121
www.moderndog.com

Morrow McKenzie, Elizabeth 142
www.morrowmckenzie.com

Mr. Keedy 14, 30, 44, 161
www.calarts.edu

Mucca Design 20, 32, 119
www.muccadesign.com

Munk, Kenn 23
www.kennmunk.com

Neither Fish Nor Fowl 177
www.neitherfishnorfowl.com

New York Times Magazine 45, 110, 112, 140, 141, 162, 189
www.nytimes.com/magazine

Nudd, Paul 120
www.paulnudd.com

Onetwentysix 25
www.onetwentysix.com

Ozcan, Serifcan 71
www.obumu.com

Pentagram 122–3, 156
www.pentagram.com

Perry, Mike 113, 121
www.midwestisbest.com

Pettis, Jeremy 174
www.jeremypettis.com

Post Typography 49, 94, 95, 110, 132, 150, 151, 170
www.posttypography.com

Process Type Foundry 65
www.posttypography.com

Qian Qian 9, 66
www.q2design.com

Robu, Andrei 39, 60, 102, 144, 153
www.andreirobu.com

Rogers, Jeff 190, 191
www.frogers.net

Sagmeister, Inc. 82, 104, 114–5, 130, 165
www.sagmeister.com

Seripop 57, 124, 147, 149
www.seripop.com

Shinybinary 90, 159
www.shinybinary.com

Si Scott Studio Ltd 87, 157, 158
www.siscottstudio.com

The Small Stakes 137
www.thesmallstakes.com

Smith, Andy 117, 138
www.asmithillustration.com

Spike Press 48, 139, 177
www.spikepress.com

SpotCo 136
www.spotnyc.com

Spusta, Marq 53
www.marqspusta.com

Staehle, Will 29, 31, 102
www.lonewolfblacksheep.com

Stolze Design 92
www.stoltze.com

Studio Oscar 170
www.studiooscar.com

Sudyka, Diana 85
www.dianasudyka.com

Sudtipos 152
www.sudtipos.com

Sumkin, Fiodor/Opera 21, 56, 68, 77, 84
www.opera78.com

Superexpresso 104, 175, 182
www.superexpresso.com

Tarek Atrissi Design 68, 73, 76
www.atrissi.com

There Is 107, 108
www.thereis.co.uk

Trochut, Alex 6, 45, 61, 100, 131, 182
www.alextrochut.com

Typerepublic 165, 189, 190, 191
www.typerepublic.com

Typodermic Fonts 167
www.typodermic.com

Uchoa, Mariana 190
issuu.com/marianauchoa/docs/uchoa_mariana_portfolio_

Urban Inks 97, 57
www.urbaninks.com

Vault 49 92, 144, 147, 155, 188
www.vault49.com

Visual Arts Press 63, 98
www.schoolofvisualarts.edu

Volinski, Jess 86, 91
www.jessvolinski.com

Ward, Craig 89, 95
www.wordsarepictures.co.uk

Webuyyourkids 26
www.webuyyourkids.com

Williams, Nate 125
www.n8w.com

Winterhouse 25
www.winterhouse.com

Wired magazine 12, 17, 35, 49, 180, 183
www.wired.com

You Work for Them 190, 191
www.youworkforthem.com

Zeloot 16, 54, 103
www.zeloot.nl